RIDE WITH YOUR MIND MASTERCLASS

by the same author

Ride With Your Mind: A Right Brain Approach to Riding

MARY WANLESS

Ride With Your Mind MASTERCLASS

An Illustrated Guide to Right Brain Riding

Photographs by Kit Houghton
Diagrams by Christine Bousfield

The Kingswood Press

First published in Great Britain 1991
by The Kingswood Press
an imprint of Methuen London
Michelin House, 81 Fulham Road, London SW3 6RB

A CIP catalogue record for this book
is available from the British Library
ISBN 0 413 64790 0

Photoset by Rowland Phototypesetting Limited
Bury St Edmunds, Suffolk

Printed in Great Britain
by Clays Limited, St. Ives Plc

To the many people, across the world,
who have welcomed me with open minds and hearts
and shared with me their joy in learning.

And to my teachers and my critics,
who continually demand that I refine my perceptions
and increase my skills.

Contents

List of Diagrams xi
Acknowledgements xiii
Introduction 1

Part One: The Riddle of Riding 9

Thinking, muscle tone and threshold levels – what you have got *v.* what you do with what you have got. The conscious competence model; grooving new co-ordinations. The ability and memory of the right brain; language and experience; the use of images. Cybernetic learning; the visual, auditory and kinaesthetic senses. Neurological wiring and parallel processing. Creating a map of feelages. Muscle pairs; the texture of muscles; slow tension movement. Completing the circuit; transmitting the horse's impulse cleanly. The gaps in the joints. 'Tuning' mind and body.

Part Two: Masterclass 47

Introduction to the Lessons 48

Lesson 1 – **Katie**: An Overview of the Rider/Horse Interaction 51

The balance of the rider's body weight over her feet – the shoulder/hip/heel alignment; the danger of pushing the heels down and bringing the lower leg 'onto the girth'; 'who takes who?'; 'water-skiing', and the need to be causal instead of reactive; the 'pinch' and the 'bearing down'; muscle tone; the correct attitude of hand and arm *v.* pulling; 'push', and the choice to push the pelvis forward towards the hand instead of bringing the hand back towards the pelvis; the effects of the rider on the horse's carriage – the seeking and the cramping reflexes; what changes feel like, and what they look like; feeling and thinking – learning to recognise 'right'.

Lesson 2 – **Gail**: The Leg Aids, Rising Trot and the Transitions 65

Bringing the leg correctly onto the saddle; the dangers of 'driving' with the seat; 'squeeze' and the correct use of the leg; the use of the knee and ankle joints, and the thigh and calf muscles to stabilise the body; the mechanism of rising and sitting; control of tempo and impulsion; staying in place when the horse accelerates or decelerates; stabilising the body in the walk to halt transition.

Lesson 3 – **Jan**: The Positioning of the Body and an Introduction to Asymmetry 78

The correct angle for the pelvis on the saddle; the fork seat and the armchair seat; the importance of having the stirrups the correct length; the flexor

List of Diagrams

Acknowledgements

To the energy source which sustained and inspired me through writing this, thank you.

I would like to thank Clare Bayman, Margaret Burnett, Jan Coath, Sarah Gunn, Carol Jennings, Katie Jones, Val Jurd, Herbert Von Kliffhanger, Janet Parry, Georgina Quincey, Jill Thompson and Gail Wright, who took part in the lessons featured in this book.

I would also like to thank Tricia Gardiner, Julia Gibson, Alexandra Howard, Dane Rawlings, Santiago de la Rocha, Janet Titley and Sorrel Warwick, who took part in interviews for Part Three.

I am indebted to Kit Houghton, who took such good photographs, and to Debbie Cook, whose notes on each lesson were a tremendous help.

I would like to thank the following, who have profoundly influenced my thinking: Richard Bandler, Robert Dilts, David Gordon and John Grinder, my teachers of Neuro-Linguistic Programming; Paul Dennison, my teacher of Educational Kinesiology; and Don McFarland, my teacher of Body Harmony.

I am indebted to the following for permission to use quotations: David Hemery, *The Pursuit of Sporting Excellence* (Willow Books, 1986); Clayne Jensen and Gordon Schultz, *Applied Kinesiology* (McGraw Hill, 1977); Wynn Kapit and Lawrence Elson, *The Anatomy Colouring Book* (Harper and Row, 1977); John Samuel, 'The Man Behind The Champion' (*Guardian*, 23 July 1990).

I would also like to thank my editor, Ann Mansbridge, whose faith in my work has helped enormously, and my partner, Otto Reinschmiedt, who tolerates my exploits with increasing good humour.

When the pupil is ready the teacher will appear.

Old Zen saying

If the pupil has not learnt, then the teacher has not taught.

Anthony Crossley

Introduction

I have been teaching riding now for well over twenty years. In my raw beginnings as a working pupil I had difficulty making a lesson including walk, trot and canter last for an hour; now I can wax lyrical about each of them, and spend whole lessons showing the rider subtleties that I never even dreamt of in those early days! For minute physical changes in her body can make a world of difference to her security and effectiveness, and to the carriage and movement of her horse. My speciality now lies in creating the breakthroughs which demonstrate this – those sudden moments of insight that cause almost instant transformation.

My teaching has been through many stages during these years: I grew confident in the riding school *milieu*, but began to resent having to 'churn it out' to the degree that was required for my employer to be able to earn a living. When I began teaching examination students and competition riders, it all became much more exciting, but I gradually began to lose faith in the dogma I was teaching, and that I myself was being taught. Meeting a continentally trained rider about two years later changed all that, and through him I gained a new understanding of what riding was about. This was inspiring; but unfortunately he seemed unable to pass on many of the secrets of his brilliance to me. I became frustrated by my own lack of progress, especially now that I had begun to measure myself against someone who rode extremely well! My discontent peaked when I became stuck on a plateau from which it seemed that there was no escape. I was also frustrated by my inability as a teacher, and by my pupils' apparent difficulty in learning the simple things that I was now finding easy.

After about two years of work with this extremely good rider, which was one year after I attained my BHSI, I decided to give up riding and teaching completely. I was then a bad case of 'burn out', and I was in the depths of despair. However, after a few months of selling fire extinguishers, I could not resist the temptation to work with horses again, but this time as a side line. Teaching when and how I wanted became much more interesting, especially as my work was now fuelled by the astronomical changes that were happening in my own riding.

In retrospect, I liken the change that occurred to the experience I have often had on losing my keys or my purse. Many a time I have searched the house, running frantically up and down the stairs and looking in the same places over and over again. But when I give up looking, it is not uncommon for me to find that they are somewhere very obvious, and that they have been right under my nose all along. When I gave up the frenzied search that underpinned my riding, I started noticing things that had undoubtedly been going on – under my backside and in my body – all the time, but that somehow, in my desperation, I had missed.

As my skill increased, I felt that I was concurrently beginning to understand *how to learn*, and this automatically began to show me how to teach. My pupils were as fascinated as I was with the discoveries we were making together, and they really helped me to keep faith, and to have the courage to go out on a limb – even when I began leaving behind many of the precepts which they and I had taken for granted. What we were doing was obviously working, but the means whereby we were achieving it were often a real surprise!

During the twelve or so years since this happened, the horses I have ridden have been my primary teachers. Much of my learning has also been by courtesy of my pupils, as well as at the hands of my trainers. All of them have given me very important feedback. After I have brought about the change I am looking for in a pupil, I regularly ask her, 'What have you just done? What was the key to it? What did I say that helped you the most?' Through her responses, I gain a better understanding of how to teach others, and this helps my work to become gradually more streamlined. (The riders who started work with me back then shared my journey with me, and we all went on the scenic route. Now I have the knowledge and skill to take my pupils down the motorway!)

The feedback I have received from my teachers has also been vital: in the early days, when I was unsure of my new discoveries, it was immensely reassuring to have some of the world's most classical riders tell me, 'Yes, that's right, you've got it now.' And when they did not say that, I knew I had to go back to the drawing board. But my teachers have rarely been able to show or explain to me *how* to do something in the way that I can now explain it to others. Perhaps they did me a favour by forcing me to find out for myself – because it is these discoveries, which I had to make from scratch, that are the backbone of my work as it is today.

Since my first book, *Ride With Your Mind* (published as *The Natural Rider* in the United States), was published in 1987, I have had letters and telephone calls from riders all over the world. In effect, many of them have said, 'I felt as if you were writing about me, so much of what you said was a mirror of my own experience. Just working with the book and putting some of your ideas into practice has changed my riding more than lessons have ever done. . . .' I am really thrilled to have made this difference in their lives, and to have given them new hope. On meeting some of these riders in the flesh, I have been tremendously impressed by the work they have done, and by the changes they have obviously made in their riding. (Before the book was published, I never really expected that many people would bother to take the time and trouble to actually *do* all the exercises I gave.) A few, of course, have interpreted my words in ways I did not think were humanly possible, and they needed rearranging yet again when they finally came to have lessons. It has been interesting to experience both the power and the limitations of the written word!

As a result of this response to the book, I have now taught riding, and made new friends, on three continents. Wherever I go, it seems that riders all experience the same problems. Whilst each person and each horse is interestingly different, the same solutions seem to work almost universally. I have tested them again, and again, and again, and I do not think that I shall ever tire of doing so. My test subjects have ranged enormously in age, body shape, experience and natural talent. When I first began to develop my techniques, I did much of my work with people who felt that they had exhausted every other alternative, and who were on the point of giving up. (In those days, I was considered so strange that you had to be really desperate to risk coming to me!) Now, I work with many more riders who are naturally talented, and who are competing at a high level. The difficulties that they have are simply more refined versions of the ones that are experienced by more novice riders, or by people who have their wires well and truly crossed. The basic principles do not change.

I think of myself, like the mythical figure Chiron, as 'a wounded healer' – someone who, through her own wounds and difficulties, has developed the power to heal others. When I see a rider who is having problems, the chances are that I have been where she is now. I can empathise with her experience, and I have a fair idea of how to lead her down from her gum tree, or out of the trap she is in, and back onto the 'straight and narrow' path. In our work together, I bring her as close as I can to the classical ideal – the perfect rider/horse interaction. I believe it is much more difficult for trainers who are themselves naturally talented riders to do this, for they have found the elusive needle in the haystack, and they have no experience of what it is like *not* to have found that needle.

I used to be extremely jealous of these people. (I love the film *Amadeus*, which is a brilliant portrayal of natural talent, mediocrity and the awfulness of not being able to do what you would most love to be able to do.) Now, I am very happy to be me, and to take satisfaction and delight in a learning process that encompasses both my riding and my teaching. I would not like to have to teach or train from the position of one who cannot understand why her pupils cannot understand, and I would also not like to have missed the journey that I have been on over the last twelve years. The skill which I have envied in others, and which I have worked so hard to gain, means a great deal to me. Some good riders take it for granted; I feel enriched by the fact that I do not.

When I dare to profess it, I believe I have solved the riddle which has been facing riders since at least the time of Xenophon twenty-three centuries ago. Generations of riders have asked themselves the question: 'How come he can do it, and I can't? What makes him so much better at riding than me? Why does it work one day and not the next, or on one horse and not on another? How do you get a horse 'onto the bit'? I can now answer these questions with a high degree of accuracy. Fortunately in riding there is always more to be discovered, both in terms of *how you do it* and in terms of *how you talk about how you do it*, so my work can never be complete. But I believe that I have most, if not all, of the essential pieces in the puzzle – and I have a logic that makes sense out of a skill which can seem unbelievably mysterious.

I have now done four more years of research since I finished writing *Ride With Your Mind*, and both books are a presentation of work in progress. Many of my ideas have been extended and developed during that time (my understanding of asymmetries, in particular, has improved), but I still stand by everything I wrote then, and I do not think that future work will bring very much change to the material I am presenting here. Some people, I know, feel that my discoveries are invalid because I have not been demonstrating my competence through riding in competition. In my early twenties I was competition crazy, but since then my life has taken me in directions which have not been conducive to competitive riding. Maybe this will change with time, although it is certainly never likely to be my first priority, either in my life or in my learning (I certainly value the discipline imposed by competitive riding but I cannot get excited by the thought of spending time, energy and money driving horse boxes up and down motorways – even if I had them to spend!).

Instead, I have been riding, learning, thinking and working behind the scenes, often with very limited resources. Einstein was once heard to muse to a friend that he was doing 'thought experiments', contemplating the effects of placing clocks in various parts of the universe long before he could afford to buy a carriage clock for his own home. In a sense, I have been in the same situation, although my 'thought experiments' have always been based on my experiences riding and my attempts to teach others what I have just learnt to do. In time, I am most likely to be acknowledged through my pupils' successes, for the youngsters I am currently teaching will mature into exceptionally capable performers.

I have sometimes heard people comment: 'Oh yes, Mary Wanless. What she's done is to analyse riding.' In a sense that is true, but it did not happen in the way that many of these people assume it did. I did not just sit down and analyse it through logic. (I find this idea somewhat insulting!) My actual experiences on the horse are always my starting point, especially when I am struggling with some new co-ordination, and in that frustrating stage where I continually 'get it' and then 'lose it' again. I remember a time when I was training intensively in Portugal, and driving myself nuts with my inability consistently to position the horse precisely enough in the lateral movements. I could not fathom out what I was doing when I did get it right that made the difference, and in desperation one day I lay down on my bed to use mental rehearsal. In my mind, I practised riding the movements, recreating the feelings that I had in my body and the horse when everything went well, and then contrasting them with times when it did not. (Many people use mental rehearsal to prepare for a jumping round, or a dressage test, but very few use it to help them in their learning. When I use it this way, I find that it is valuable to make these comparisons, although people more commonly just use it to practise their own personal bests.) After about three-quarters of an hour – much longer than I would normally spend – the answer came to me in a flash, somewhat reminiscent of Archimedes and his 'Eureka!' In that moment, I identified 'the difference that made the difference', and when I leapt out of bed to tell the friend I was with, we both looked at each other in amazement, asking, 'Why didn't we think of this before, it's so obvious . . . ?'. (It is more to the point, perhaps, to ask why *nobody else* ever thought of it before!)

The answer, when it becomes clear, is always devastatingly obvious, both to me and to other people. Now I routinely explain the lateral movements to riders in that way: it makes immediate sense to them, and it helps them enormously. It has its own logic, but I did not arrive at it through logic. Mental rehearsal is the vital ingredient, just as it has been for scientists throughout the centuries, who arrived at their discoveries in a very different way from the children who learn about them in school. (Einstein was never considered a very good pupil; in fact, he was renowned for day-dreaming in class. Unbeknown to his teachers, he was dreaming up the theory of relativity!) If I have a talent, it is the ability to make left-brain sense out of my right-brain experience. This is so tricky that I can understand why it has eluded us all for so long. The skill, the knowledge and the motivation are not easily come by.

I used to insist that all of this work had nothing to do with my degree subject, which was Physics. Now I am more willing to admit the connection. When I make adjustments to a rider's seat, much of what I do is simple mechanics, and I can justify it in those terms. (I have to say, though, that mechanics was never my strong point! I was much more interested in esoteric subjects like quantum mechanics and cosmology, which taught me to delight in abstract ideas and paradox.) So I did not start from the laws of mechanics and then apply them to riding: instead, I started from riding and gradually began to realise how all the images and corrections which worked well were an expression of the laws of mechanics.

In this book, I talk briefly about many ideas which are explained in much more depth in *Ride With Your Mind*. You will get an outline of them here, but I encourage you to find out more about the detail of them there. In particular, I wrote more about the physical, mental and emotional factors affecting the ways in which people learn, and also about the use of mental rehearsal. I wrote much more about the experiences of riders at different levels, and about rider/horse interaction. I also suggested physical exercises which can have a tremendous effect on your riding. In the first section of this book, where I have also written about learning, I have attempted to express my ideas in different language, using different models from those which I used in *Ride With Your Mind*. I think you will find that there is very little repetition. Learning about learning has become a major interest of mine (and this part of the book may well be of interest to non-riders); but if I cannot persuade you to become fascinated by it too, go straight on to the second section of the book. Some of the ideas will not then be as meaningful to you – so perhaps you will become motivated in retrospect!

Some time ago, somebody who did not ride asked me at a party what I did for a living. I always find this difficult to explain, and I play with the roles of rider, teacher, trainer, sports psychologist, writer and researcher. As I was struggling for words to convey to him the essence of my work, he said, 'Oh! So you mean that you're a remedial riding teacher!' Although I did not find his description particularly flattering – and I had never thought of myself in this way – I realised that actually he was right. I believe that there are very few riders who do not need to do this remedial work: probably 5 per cent of riders (at the most) use their body correctly, and have an intuitive understanding of its influence over the horse. We call them 'talented' – they already know the secrets that I teach to others, but they vary enormously in how much they know about what they know! In interviewing some of the successful, talented riders who have contributed to the last section of this book, I found very few surprises, but a lot of fascinating and delightful stories which validated my own ideas. It was interesting for me to discover that their success was often based not on the *absence* of problems but on their ability to find *very creative solutions* to the problems that we all encounter.

My primary aim is to help people to cross the great divide which separates the average from the talented rider. Even good riders have some grey areas where their technique is not all it could be, and they benefit from using the principles I advocate to clarify these and to refine their perceptions even more. But I can show the components of skilful riding to anyone who wants to learn them, so that they too can piece them together and begin to look like talented riders. Once they have made that transition, I work with them much more in the role of a conventional trainer, commenting on difficulties which they now know *how* to correct. I get enormous pleasure from seeing the riders I work with performing well, but I get even more pleasure when they can produce these results consistently, and then generate the next step for themselves. The bottom line lies in *learning how to learn*. This is extremely valuable, because it generalises into other contexts: my writing, for instance, has developed quite painlessly because I knew *how* to learn *how* to do it.

Although I use very strange words, and some unusual concepts to describe it (like 'pinching' and 'bearing down'), I believe that I am teaching riding in its most classical form. I am very grateful that I met Dan Aharoni, Erik Herbermann and finally Egon von Neindorff at the time when I did. I have also been profoundly influenced by working with Desi Lorent and Nuno Oliveira. Several other top-class competitive riders in England, France and Germany have also helped me; but it is the philosophical stance of these other classically based riders which underpins my work. There have been many occasions when I could happily have throttled them, but I am profoundly grateful for their insistence that I learnt to work the horse correctly instead of just trying to force its nose into place. My riding still bears some of the scars of my misspent youth, and, like everybody else, I have my blind spots. But my learning takes me closer and closer to becoming the immaculate rider I would love to be, and my commitment is to a classically based philosophy, understanding and skill. I believe that this is within the grasp of practically everyone, and that good riding need no longer seem so mysterious. It has finally yielded its secrets to us, and all that is required is an open mind, a willingness to leave behind the familiar and comfortable, and the humility to let the horse help us discover *what actually works*.

PART ONE

The Riddle of Riding

A good rider has a thinking mind,
fine emotions and a sensitive hand.

Tu Yu, 72 BC

It is the commonest of mistakes to consider
that the limit of our power of perception
is also the limit of all there is to perceive.

C. W. Leadbeater

The Riddle of Riding

When I was about six years old, long before I began to ride, my best friend of the time decided that she would like to teach me to swim. There was one condition to her offer, which was that I had to promise to do exactly what she told me. With the utmost faith, and in a state of complete naivety, I promised. So she showed me how to do a breast-stroke leg-kick and the corresponding arm movements, and we talked our respective parents into taking us to the local swimming-pool. On the great day itself, I have no recollection of their presence. All I know is that I practised my arm movements whilst standing on the bottom, and then practised my leg-kick whilst holding onto the bar. 'Now,' said my friend, 'you have to take your feet off the bottom, let go of the bar, and do them both at once.' I really do not remember whether I chickened out there and then, or whether I made some kind of attempt which sent me spluttering towards the bottom. What I *do* have, is a clear memory of my friend's voice as she wailed, 'But you promised! You promised you'd do exactly what I told you!'

This incident has always stuck in my mind, perhaps because it was, in a sense, prophetic. At that time I had no idea that my future was to revolve around riding, and finding teaching methods which worked for people who were, like myself, not 'naturals'. Although I loved ponies, and I dreamt of becoming a riding teacher, it seemed that there was very little chance of taking even the first tentative steps and getting myself near (or preferably on) a pony. I also had no idea that my eventual success in this would lead to some very frustrating experiences. These left me with extremely mixed feelings about riding lessons, and as they culminated, I began to feel that I had been backed into a corner from which there was no escape – I did not want to give up but I could not see a way forward. Although none of my riding teachers ever yelled at me, 'But you promised!', the implication was often there (along with the implication that I *ought* to be able to do it). I felt guilty and inadequate when I found myself unable to do what they seemed to find so simple – although one has to realise that if all pupils could immediately do exactly what their teachers told them, I and many others would be out of a job! (This really is a possibility in the work I do now, as riders become independent of me far faster than they do through any other teaching method I know.) For my own self-esteem, I felt that I either had to give up or solve the riddle of riding, and lay its 'mysteries' out on the table for all to see. I finally came out of my corner by transforming my learning into a quest, seeking to break the skill of riding down into learnable pieces, the 'bite-size chunks' that I, and later my pupils, really *could* promise to do, and then gradually piece together into the finished skill.

As well as learning a great deal about horses and riding, I have also learnt a fair bit on the way about people, and especially about how different we all are. I was talking about this recently with a friend who is a highly respected instructor, and I was focussing particularly on the different ways in which people think. I told her of an exercise I often use to illustrate my point in my dismounted teaching. (I hold workshops in which I teach riders about learning, concentration, body awareness, etc., *away from* the horse, where they are much easier to learn.) In this particular exercise, I give exactly the same stimulus to a group of people, by repeatedly saying just one word to them. My favourite is 'strawberries'. After I have said it several times over a period of about a minute, I ask everyone what went on inside their heads. Some people tell me that they created a picture in their mind's eye of the strawberry patch in their auntie's garden, or of a field of strawberries, and that they imagined picking them. Others created a picture of one luscious strawberry, which grew bigger and bigger every time I spoke. Others imagined eating a plateful, complete with the sensations of taste and smell. Some had a voice inside their head which commented on what I was doing, and asked, 'What the heck is going on here?' The possibilities are infinite, and the ramifications of these differences are huge. My friend was very surprised to realise how unique each person's experience was. 'Oh,' she said, 'I thought everyone thought the same as I did.'

Her response may seem to you to be slightly naive, but I can assure you that this is a mistake that we all continually make. Riding teachers make it every time they assume that their pupil will react to a situation or a command (for instance, 'hold him together') in just the same way that they would. But this is far from true, and there are, for example, many, many ways of attempting to 'hold a horse together'. The picture in the pupil's mind's eye, the voice inside her head and the sensations within her body may well be dramatically different from those of the teacher. ('Help!' says the pupil to herself, as her body turns to jelly and she imagines the horse accelerating fast. 'You dare!' says the teacher to herself – and the horse – as she feels her seat firm up and imagines his carriage and rhythm becoming more stable.) Each person will 'hold the horse together' with a different attitude, and this in turn creates a completely different use of her body: so of course it is no surprise to find that the pupil's aid will almost certainly not have the same good effect as the trainer's would have if *she* did it. But on many occasions the teacher is unaware of this. 'Do that again,' she says . . . and somehow she manages to be almost equally surprised when it *still* does not work!

The ways in which people interpret the input they are given are as unique and multifaceted as each individual. We dwell on the characteristics of different breeds of horse – how to ride and train a thoroughbred as opposed to a warmblood, for example, or how to choose a horse which is suitable for a certain discipline – but we never think of the human population quite in the same way, even though our world is peopled by folk who are as different from each other as are these different horses. I myself (although of dubious ancestry) am something of a thoroughbred in build and temperament. I am small, slight, highly strung and emotional. I am very sensitive to being shouted at and to atmospheres. I get upset when I do not know what I am supposed to do, or how I am supposed to do it, and I am very dependent on an internal sense of 'rightness'. When I do not have this, I tend to panic. There are many people who gallop across the English hunting field with very little concern for whether they can stop or steer. I am not one of them. For whilst they are perfectly happy, my sense of 'not rightness' becomes triggered to an uncomfortable degree. For years, this sensitivity has worked against me, and thwarted my progress in riding – as well as in life in general. It has taken me a long, long time to learn how to use it so that it can work *for* me. Undoubtedly, it has played an important part in motivating me to find ways of organising my body, and the horse, that felt 'right'. Today, with my sense of 'rightness' satisfied most of the time, I regard my sensitivity as one of my greatest assets.

If I had had a warmblood temperament, however, it would have been significantly easier for me to learn to ride. If I had been more easy-going, less fearful, more stable, I would have taken it all in my stride. There are significant physical differences that go with these emotional differences, and make riding difficult for people who are, like me, rather ethereal. Most, if not all, of the good riders I know are much more 'solid' physically than I am. This difference refers more to muscle tone than to size, and also to the way one senses one's body. (When muscles are well toned they feel quite firm. This sign of healthy functioning lies between the extremes of excessive relaxation and high tension.) Strange as it may sound, I have often found it difficult to have a clear sense of my physical boundaries, and to distinguish my body from the air around me. I have tried to explain this to my partner – who used to be an unusually good footballer – but he looks at me in a perplexed state of non-comprehension. His body is so obviously different from the air around him, and its edges are so distinct, that he is at a loss to know what I mean. If he decided to work on his riding, he could easily be very good. The quality of his physical presence makes him a natural athlete in a way that I have never been: his sense of 'solidness' and his high muscle tone give him an enviable baseline from which to develop his skill.

One of my psychology teachers states that if you could step into the mind, the body and the emotions of the person sitting next to you, you would have an experience which would make the effects of hallucinogenic, mind-altering drugs seem trivial. This is a far cry from our normal assumptions that really, people are all the same! We may share the same configurations of muscles, and the same basic neurology, but the ways in which we develop and use them are markedly different. My teacher refers to some aspects of these physical and emotional differences as 'threshold patterns', and he illustrates the idea by talking about his two children, who are markedly different in this respect. His son is very sensitive. If you raise your voice to him, or even threaten mild punishment, he quakes slightly and immediately promises to shape up. Like me, he has an active sense of 'not rightness' which is easily triggered. But his sister is not so sensitive, and she does not respond to such subtlety. In fact, my friend has resorted to putting her across his knee and spanking her hard. Eventually she sighs, looks around with a rather bored expression, and says, 'Have you finished yet?'

I have met horses who regarded all my attempts to send them forward with equal disdain, and at times they have left me wondering if they even noticed what was going on! They were not nappy, and in other ways they were not particularly difficult – they just had high threshold levels. (It is as if one has to scale a high brick wall, or turn up the volume, in order to get through to them.) Sometimes, more sensitive horses need only one little touch to trigger their sense of 'not rightness', and send them into the middle of next week: their threshold levels are so low that they can easily feel as if their senses are bombarded. They cannot order and understand all the information which seems to come at them so quickly – and as a result, they easily become overwhelmed or frightened. Of course, they require a very different kind of riding.

Just think of the implications of realising that people, too, have thresholds which vary as much as those of our horses, so that what is a whisper to one person is a shout to another. I immediately find myself asking, 'If we are all this different, how can we possibly all learn to perform the same skill with equal finesse?' Most people would use the information I have given to argue that inevitably we cannot, but I take the stance that we *can*. In a way, this is a philosophical position rather than a practical one, and I know that I, for one, have neither the desire nor the temperament to take part in top-class competition. (I keep open the possibility, however, that I might one day surprise myself!) But at the very least, each individual has his own 'gold medal level'. This idea always reminds me of the story of the Japanese Master Suzuki, who taught the violin to young children. When he took on a spastic child as a pupil everyone thought he was crazy. To begin with, each time he put the bow in the child's hand, his fingers automatically opened and it flew across the room. In time, the child held the bow, and in even more time he played the violin. If Suzuki had said, 'This child will never be able to do it,' the child would never have been able to do it. It was only his willingness to act *as if it might be possible* that created the possibility. Where many people would unknowingly have closed a door to this child, Suzuki opened it.

It is interesting to make a comparison with horses: not all of them have the temperament and physique to win at a high level, but stories of some of the great rider/horse combinations show that not all top-class horses are as straightforward as one might be tempted to believe. A few make it to the top despite their riders, but many are only there because their riders were able to work so well with their impetuousness, or their nervousness, or their sluggishness. There are many others who did *not* make it simply because their riders could not bring out the best in them. But each horse, like each person, has his own potential and his own personal best – be it his best jump or his best movement. If we could capture this much more of the time, we, and our horses, would all be performing at much higher levels than we are.

The issue at stake here is not what we have got (as so many people think), but what we *do* with what we have got: this, I believe, is the primary factor which separates the average from the talented performer. What counts is *not* the facets we all envy so much – a naturally good body shape or good balance – but the ways in which we *apply* ourselves. When we approach learning in this way, it becomes much more challenging. It is somewhat awesome to realise that our sole task is to uncover our potential, and that it is simply lying hidden, waiting to be found. It is the gift that we are given when we learn how to use our minds and our bodies in the right way. This knowledge forces us to take far more personal responsibility – we no longer have reason to regard ourselves as inherently lacking what it takes; instead, we act from the philosophical stance that 'the oak already exists within the acorn'. This pushes us actively to seek out the next steps in our learning, regardless of our present level. It becomes much harder to make excuses, to justify our inability, or to resign ourselves and our horses to the scrap heap.

Learning to ride poses some very challenging issues for us as people: we have to learn how to adjust our threshold levels, balancing the ways in which we take in and give out information. We have to process enormous amount of input, which comes at us on many different levels simultaneously. We must learn to recognise the difference between stillness and passivity, between realistic demands and impatience. We must also distinguish between the facets that *we* must take responsibility for, and those that we must delegate to the horse. One of my teachers used to talk in very poignant terms about what it takes to become a good rider: 'You have to have authority, and you have to have sensitivity. The problem is that the people who are naturally authoritative are not often sensitive, and those who are naturally sensitive do not usually have authority. It is so rare, and so difficult, to have both at once.' Although he did not realise it, he was talking about the implications of high and low threshold levels, and alluding to the very different ways in which each of us has to develop if we are to become good riders. To me, this is the ultimate challenge of learning to ride, and also of training a horse. Very few people, and very few horses, are such 'naturals' that they do not have to transform themselves in these ways. Almost all of us do, and compared with this, learning the necessary co-ordinations of riding is the thin end of the wedge.

When sports psychologists talk about learning new skills, they often use the 'conscious competence' model. Many riders come to a new teacher or trainer in the state where they are 'unconscious of their incompetence', i.e. they do not know what they do not know. This is the time when ignorance is bliss! Perhaps the pupil has yet to become a 'serious' rider, so she rides with a naivety that she will probably envy when she starts to realise the existence of riding's finer points, and then to grapple with them. Or she may have had lessons previously, but still be unaware of some of the basic patterns inherent in her bodily use – as well as the effects that these are having on her horse. I have had some exceptionally good trainers expose patterns to me after *twenty years* of ignorance, and I am extremely grateful for the subtlety of the 'eye' which allows them to see so much. It can be an uncomfortable experience suddenly to become 'conscious of your incompetence', but this is the starting point for all future change: for until you know what you are doing wrong, how can you hope to correct it?

It is unfortunate, however, that there are so many riders in the world who have reached the stage of 'conscious incompetence' and then got stuck there. At the beginning of a first lesson with me, new pupils are often keen to say something like, 'Well, I have all these problems. I collapse to the left, and my left leg is weaker than my right. I can't keep my hands still, and I get very tense through the arms and shoulders. It's hard for me to do sitting trot because my back is too hollow, and when I go into canter. . . .' Sometimes the list seems endless, and sometimes there are one or two that have stuck in the minds of both rider and teacher, and have effectively become labels ('Annette is stiff and has a head nod') which are very difficult to move beyond. When I was in this position many years ago, I found it devastating. While I was desperately trying to make my problems go away – or even, at times, to pretend that they were not there – I, and also my teachers, failed to realise that the primary stumbling block was that I was *not conscious enough* of my incompetence.

Moshe Feldenkrais, the originator of the Feldenkrais system of body work, used to say that, 'When you know what you're doing, you can do what you want,' and in riding, I have found this to be absolutely true. So – as you will see in the 'Masterclass' section – I like to 'unpack' the problem for the person, so that she discovers exactly what is going on. When you find out *how* you are crooked, or *how* you are stiff, it is relatively easy to do the opposite, and to straighten or soften your body. With enough information, the state of 'conscious incompetence' leads directly into 'conscious competence'. This is where the hard work of learning takes place, for it requires tremendous dedication and concentration to stop oneself acting on 'automatic pilot', and to substitute new co-ordinations for old. Sometimes at this stage in learning people baulk and say, 'But it feels like starting all over again,' or 'Do I really have to think this hard about everything?' and I try to assure them that whilst their progress might at this time seem painfully slow, they are not just treading water in the way they were previously. They are, in fact, on the fastest route to change.

Patting your head and rubbing your stomach at the same time is a simple example of learning a new co-ordination – and it is also a demonstration of the confusion that this can create! Riding, of course, is infinitely more complex – but so is driving a car, and the vast majority of people can learn to do that successfully. Changing gear was overwhelming for me at first, and I struggled to take my right foot off the accelerator, put my left foot on the clutch, move the gear lever, keep holding the steering wheel, look where I was going, keep control of the revs and time it all precisely. Now I do it with consummate ease, and where it used to feel like having to think about ten things at once, there is now only one – one action which I can do any time, anywhere, without having to think about it. This is the stage of 'unconscious competence'. The pattern is wired into my neurology so that the same impulses pass from my brain to my muscles in exactly the same way, which gets reinforced with every repetition. When new co-ordinations become 'grooved' like this in the nervous system, it is rather as if someone has made a pathway through long grass. The more that path is used, the easier it is to keep using it, and the more effortful it becomes to carve out another.

To illustrate this to yourself, stop reading now and fold your arms. Then unfold your arms, and fold them the other way round. Could you do it? Was it difficult? When I do this exercise with people in dismounted workshops, there are always a few who end up with their arms folded in exactly the same way as before! Somehow they failed to interrupt their 'automatic pilot' response to folding their arms, and their neurology took them for a ride. Others stop in mid-fold and start to look extremely bewildered as they try to fathom out which way is which. Having eventually succeeded, practically everyone finds that the sensation of having their arms folded in this new way is uncomfortable – and some complain bitterly. It is just the same in riding. Making changes in even simple co-ordinations often involves a sense of disorientation, and the result – when one finally succeeds in making the change – is not always comfortable.

When one has achieved the state of 'unconscious competence', it is very tempting to leave well alone, and not to tamper with a pattern which seems to work reasonably well. I shall probably continue to change gear in exactly the same way, unless I go on an advanced driving course and submit my driving to the scrutiny of someone who will start the cycle all over again, make me 'conscious of my incompetence', take apart my familiar patterns and encourage me to rebuild them in a more efficient way. We often hear in the media about well-known tennis players who are taking apart their serve, or about golfers who are taking apart their swing – and these are people who take part in top-class international competition! The cycle is not meant to end at 'unconscious competence'; very often, however, a rider passes through it only once, creating the patterns that she then uses for the rest of her life. But, in quality learning, it begins all over again, taking the student up to a new level each and every time that she goes through the cycle again.

For some reason, riders seem to be extremely slow to realise that it is the structure of their *neurological* patterning which determines how they use their bodies. Our muscles function like robots, who cannot think for themselves and have no choice but to do what they are told. It is the brain which does the telling, communicating via the tentacles of the nervous system, which reach out to every part of the body. With each repetition of a particular action, the neurological pathways which are *already* in use are deepened, and this means that practice makes perfect not what you *think* you are practising, or what you *ought to be* practising, but what you are *actually* practising. It is extremely unfortunate that our sport has an ethos which makes it so tempting for riders to continue riding round and round, ingraining the same patterns even more deeply (this continues well beyond the stage when they become known as 'bad habits'!), but somehow believing that they and their horse are bound to get better if they keep going for long enough.

The second problem is that very few people are willing to take a risk which involves *unlearning* when there is no guarantee that what they *relearn* will eventually work better for them. There is no problem when someone is already at their wits' end, feeling stumped by the puzzles posed by riding and the idiosyncracies of their particular body. They have nothing to lose. But the competitive rider whose bodily use is good enough to win sometimes, but not good enough to do consistent, classical work, often has a difficult time trying to stomach my insistence that the only way to become really good is through 'rewiring' her neurology. I often explain to her that it is like the situation that arises when you are knitting a jumper, and you suddenly realise that you made a mistake a few rows back. Will you ignore it and keep on knitting, or will you unpick your stitches, go back and correct it? The further back the mistake was, the more you have to undo (and in riding, you cannot ask your mother to redo it for you!). To get a rider's commitment to this process, I often ask her if she is content simply to win at the level she is at now, or whether she would prefer to put in the background work which will eventually enable her to win at a higher level.

Two of my heroes are golfer Nick Faldo and his tutor David Leadbetter. Faldo has worked relentlessly to find a swing which would withstand the rigours of the toughest competition: he was not afraid to 'undo his knitting', and he has reaped the rewards with a most impressive series of victories. Leadbetter plays the role for him that I play for many riders. In an article in the *Guardian* on 23 July 1990, John Samuel writes about Leadbetter: 'He was never, he says, cut out to be a touring professional. As an analyst for top players' swing styles and rhythms he is now unsurpassed.' When they began working together, Leadbetter worked out why it was that Faldo ballooned some shots and was inconsistent in certain conditions. He changed some elements of Faldo's stance and his swing. 'What I offer Faldo now,' he says, 'are little triggers. More width. Stand a little taller. More coil . . . Each day it may be a different trigger . . . No one is more aware of the sensations of the golf swing than Nick . . . Faldo feels the parts of his body very acutely. He's not out there on the course thinking about nothing but striking the ball. He is feeling for the right swing sensations all the time. You see him at it before every shot . . . He won't set up until he is totally happy with his swing impression.'

Most riders have extremely low expectations of their trainers, who rarely intervene enough to make changes at this level. But perhaps many riders do not want to be helped in such profound, far-reaching ways: it amazes me that people are content to be told,

'Ride half-pass across the diagonal, and make sure the horse stays bent.' This is logically equivalent to telling a golfer to 'Hit the ball down the fairway and make sure it goes straight.' Would golfers at any level pay to be told this? They *expect* to have to think about their swing; but riders expect only to think about their half-pass – the equivalent of thinking about 'striking the ball', which Faldo apparently does *not* do. He knows the importance of his 'swing impression'.

A renowned continental dressage competitor and trainer recently came to this country for the first time and taught some of our better riders. Many were offended at her insistence that they pay attention to their bodily alignment, making basic corrections here instead of simply riding the advanced movements. Rarely do riders show the kind of commitment and humility that is demonstrated by Faldo – and this is particularly true at the higher levels. Not everyone needs to do remedial work; but in those that do, I often see a kind of arrogance which suggests that they – unlike other committed athletes – are above such things. Beneath their arrogance, I suspect, lies fear: fear of taking a risk, fear of the unknown, fear of being seen to take a different path, and fear of acknowledging their imperfections to themselves and others. Like every golfer and every tennis player, the rider alone must make her choice: does she continue as she is, or does she 'undo her knitting'? I totally respect the decision of people who find that they would rather not bother.

In terms of the way in which the brain operates, there is very little difference between being unconscious of your competence and being unconscious of your incompetence. The external results, of course, can be worlds apart, because the richness, subtlety and effectiveness of the neurological patterns used are so different. But in each case the rider simply uses the patterns she has available to her, with no conscious knowledge of what she does, and without becoming embroiled in the rather messy process of turning conscious incompetence into conscious competence. The transition from one level of functioning to the next is not always smooth: a friend of mine who teaches similar techniques to business managers often tells them, 'If you want to make an omelette, you have to break the eggs'; to go forwards, you may appear to go backwards, but what a difference this can make!

This is why Zen philosophy states that the beginner and the Master are so very close together, whilst the student who has committed herself to the learning process is in a different position entirely. She can only learn and change by making the unconscious conscious, and with every little breakthrough – the sudden realisation that 'I just pulled my stomach in again', or 'That's why I can't sit. I'm curling my toes up!', she gains the ability not only to ride, but also to talk clearly about how she does it. This gives her what I call 'whole-brain knowing'. I have found this to be a tremendous gift, which more than compensates me for the rather long-winded learning process I have been through. This is largely bypassed by the talented rider, the fortunate 5 per cent (if that) who naturally stumble across 'unconscious competence' and ride well from the beginning. They never have to 'undo their knitting' and repair the damage of their inefficient co-ordinations. When 'unconscious competence' is all you have ever known, it is very difficult to appreciate the experiences and the pitfalls of being a less talented rider. It is also extremely difficult to give accurate descriptions of how you do what you do.

The Master, and to a more limited extent the beginner, have only unconscious knowing. This is directly analogous to the right-brain knowing I talked about in *Ride With Your Mind*, where I described the learning process by discussing the roles and functions of the left- and right-brain hemispheres. Conscious knowing is the same as left-brain knowing, and it implies that one knows something through language. You utilised your left-brain hemisphere to memorise all those dates you needed to learn for your history examinations – and which you then promptly forgot! Right-brain knowing is much more pervasive and enduring: it includes the ability to recognise faces, music, tastes and feelings within the body – whether you are learning to turn a backward somersault, ride a bicycle or ride a horse. This knowledge, by its very nature, is not so easily put into words.

The unconscious mind (or right brain) has a filing system which stores visual information as images, and kinaesthetic, or bodily, information as 'feelages'; so, without recourse to language, it can flip through its files in any situation, and find out if the face, or the feel, matches up to anything it has previously experienced. It also has a tremendously sophisticated library of tastes, smells and sounds. The right brain can distinguish and store about three hundred thousand different voice tones and over two million shades of colour. This includes, for example, many, many more shades of blue than you could ever possibly put names to. It recognises the faces of people you have not met for years (regardless of the fact that your left brain probably long ago forgot the people's names). Its ability with 'feelages' is equally astounding: a participant in one of my workshops told me about the time when she picked up her clarinet for the first time in over ten years, and began to play. She embarked on a rather complicated classical piece; to her amazement, she discovered that her fingers 'knew where to go'.

I once witnessed an extremely interesting example of the right brain's ability when I was teaching a woman in her early thirties who had recently returned to riding. This was the first lesson she had had in a very long time and, as her horse began to work extremely well, she stopped, turned into the centre of the school, and looked at me with an expression which I knew meant something important. 'I've felt this before,' she told me. 'When was that?' I asked. 'When I was a child . . .' Then, the whole story came out: as a child she had ridden and evented a good deal but had had very little tuition. Then, in her mid-teens, she was 'talent-spotted' as a possible candidate for international competition. She was sent away on training courses, and was rather overawed by the whole procedure. However, she tried her hardest to do what she was told . . . and as a result she lost access to her natural ability, as well as the feelings she had previously been creating. She soon gave up riding, only to return to it a short time before I taught her. Her brain had remembered the feeling of correct work for nearly *fifteen years* – and her recognition of it was almost instantaneous! In contrast, most people bemoan the difficulties they have in learning to recognise and create the correct feels: the difference is *not* that my pupil was blessed with the right equipment and that they were not. She was one of the few who instinctively knew *how* to use her body and brain – but her natural ways of doing this were tampered with when she began to have lessons. The real problem is that the most sophisticated technology in the world – the brain – does not come with a user's manual. (Instead, many of us seem to operate as if we have been handed a loser's manual!)

The way that the two brain hemispheres specialise in processing information has far-reaching consequences: one of them is the difficulty which most riders have in communicating the 'how' of riding. It is not easy to describe the feeling of a correct half-pass. (Similarly, I am sure that you can recognise the taste of strawberry jam, but have you ever tried to describe it to anyone?) When the teacher creates good learning experiences, she manoeuvres the pupil into the right feeling, and then says, effectively, 'There you are, that's it! *This* is strawberry jam.' The only way that you can learn to recognise it, after all, is by getting a taste. But very often, the teacher's and pupil's work produces *raspberry* jam instead – so the trainer takes the easy way out, gives up on the spoken word and rides the horse herself! This can be helpful if the pupil can then get on and maintain the same feel – but this too may not succeed. In our culture, we automatically suppose that the best riders must be the best teachers – and they inevitably have the most kudos. But their conscious knowledge of what they do can be limited. A friend of mine approached one of our leading dressage riders and asked her: 'How do you bring your horses onto the bit? How do you sit . . . ? And what do you . . . ?' Her reply went something like: 'I don't blooming well know, do I?', and I have to say that I have a great deal of respect for her honesty. Many others would have invented some cock-and-bull explanation bearing very little relation to what they *actually* do.

Interestingly, dressage riders are the most guilty of this – and they have been doing it for generations. It is as if the left hand (or brain) does not know what the right hand (or brain) is doing; but this does not stop the left brain from theorising, and inventing explanations! Show jumpers, however, are more inclined to say, 'Well, you kick it in the ribs and keep hold of the front!', with less desire to theorise and little awareness of the subtle moment-by-moment corrections which their right brain is making behind the scenes. A friend of mine who is an extremely skilled show jumper recently went on a course with one of our top international competitors and trainers. She found the exercises that he set extremely challenging and helpful, but whenever she queried how she could improve her horse's jump, he said, 'You'll just have to work harder.'

'Yes,' she would say, 'but do I need more impulsion, more lightness in the forehand, or a better rhythm?'

'Just work harder,' was the inevitable reply!

(My friend was not even asking *how* to create the impulsion, lightness, etc.: she is skilled enough to know that already, which under the circumstances was probably just as well!)

Sometimes, teachers are reluctant to speak at all. I heard a story recently about another well-known show jumper who had been asked to teach abroad. My friend, who had known him for a long time, knew that talking about riding was not his forte: conversations about horses rarely went beyond, 'He's a good one,' or, 'I don't like that one.'

So he asked, 'What are you going to say to them?'

The answer: 'As little as possible!'

The success of a teacher in any skill is dependent on the size of the pieces into which she can break down that skill, making it accessible to learners at different levels. I think of these pieces as 'bite-size chunks' – they make the skill digestible. The inability to do this causes problems in many different contexts. Thus concert pianists and university professors do not make good teachers for children and beginners. Many good riders who become teachers have the same limitations, and riding is an exceptionally difficult skill to break down into chunks which are learnable yet make a significant difference. I recently heard of one European dressage trainer who obviously did not do this very successfully. In his work with riders at international level, he was soon reduced to yelling: 'Ride better!'

I often imagine how the great Masters set about writing their books: I think of them riding their horse one day and asking themselves, 'How am I doing this circle?' So they scan through their body and notice that their inside leg is on the girth, their outside leg is behind the girth, their outside hand supports the bend with a clear contact and their inside hand opens a little and stays light. So they go away and write all of this down. But what they have failed to realise is that their legs are only in this position because they are *fixed onto their pelvis*. Their pelvis is angled on a diagonal with their inside hip in advance, and it has a certain special relationship with the horse's long back muscles. All of this is very subtle, but it is the key to all the rest: it is as if the pelvis were a stone thrown into a pond. The stone is difficult to detect, but as the ripples spread outwards through the body they become larger and more obvious. Because of this, most riders find that what happens in the extremities of the body is far more obvious and easy to talk about than what happens in its centre. This has had a huge influence on the way that our theories have developed, and on the ways in which riding has always been taught.

It has also caused me immense grief in my own learning, and has nearly brought me to blows with some of my teachers. I remember one in particular, who – and I give him credit for this – understood much more about how riding works than most teachers. He really did try to make his commands very simple and accessible: the problem was that he was effectively saying, 'Do X' (with 'X' usually relating to the hand or the leg), knowing that for him, X worked perfectly. What he did *not* realise, however, was that he was also doing A, B, C, D, E, etc. All of these underpinned X, which was effectively like the icing on the cake. Once I had discovered for myself about A, B, C, D, E, etc., I had some magical experiences with him; but until that time my apparent stupidity often left me feeling an uncomfortable mixture of rage and humiliation. Since the extremities of the body are dependent on the centre, it is *absolutely impossible* for the student to reproduce the way that the Master uses the hand and the leg unless she *already* has her pelvis correctly in place. My teacher was unable to identify and communicate the key pieces which underpinned his skill. The effects of this were devastating; but he was totally oblivious to them. He could not perceive the problem through the eyes of the student, and, as a result, he was unable to understand why I (or anyone else) could not understand. When teachers reach this point, it is usually the beginning of the end of their ability to teach.

Unlike that teacher, the vast majority of our young instructors are rich in left-brain, conscious knowing – the analytical, intellectual knowledge that they glean from teachers and books, and low in right-brain, unconscious knowing. This means that they can talk very eloquently about riding, but do not have a rich store of right-brain 'feelages' which enables them to practise what they preach. (Teachers like my friend above, however, have the opposite problem, in that they do not preach what they practise!) Hearing my teacher's words of wisdom, or reading the classic books on riding, rarely helped me one jot when it came to the nitty gritty of sitting to the trot, and the fact that it has obviously not helped these teachers either does not seem to deter them from continuing to tell others what they themselves were told! We are in the desperate situation where one group of riders (the great Masters and the competition trainers) can do and not talk, whilst the other group (the younger teachers in riding schools) can talk but not do. Unless the pupil is one of the talented 5 per cent who is able to work it out for herself, this is a no-win situation in which it is impossible for her to progress! We are drastically in need of people, like myself, who have been through such a profound learning process that they can both ride *and* talk about riding in a way that enables them to transfer their skill to their pupils.

I really believe that the traditional sayings in riding – sit up straight, stretch your legs down, push your heels down, spread your seat out over the saddle, relax, push the horse forward, etc., are not good descriptions of what talented riders actually do. I was misled by them for many, many years, and I am continually meeting other riders who, to my eye, are doing totally the wrong thing, but who justify their riding style in these terms. As Gregory Bateson, anthropologist and one of the most original thinkers of the twentieth century, once said, 'Language is a very useful servant, but an extremely poor master,' particularly when – as in riding – there is such a big gap between the *experience* and *the words which are used to describe that experience*. I often wish that I could go back through time, and talk with the riders who originally coined these phrases. Then, at least, I could mitigate the effects of the ways that they have been reinterpreted and changed as they have been handed down through the generations. (I think of this as being rather similar to the children's game of 'Chinese whispers'.) But goodness knows what replies I would get if I could go up to them and ask, 'What exactly did you mean by that?'

For instance, take the phrase 'push the horse forward'. Much to my amazement, everybody acts, and continues to act, as if they know what that means: but, other than myself, I have never met a teacher who delineated exactly what the rider should push with and how she should push with it. Is she supposed to push in a forward direction or downwards? Is she supposed to do it through moving in the saddle or through sitting more still? The ideas of 'use your back' and 'use your seat' are even more questionable, and even simple phrases like 'sit in the deepest part of the saddle' are surprisingly vague. The distance from my pubic bone to my coccyx is sixteen centimetres. Which bit of that sixteen centimetres is supposed to be in the deepest part? Does it change with circumstance, or does it always stay the same?

You might think that I am being pedantic, but I am convinced that this rather fuzzy use of language is responsible for many of the problems which we experience in our attempts to teach and learn. If our survival as a species depended on our being able to communicate the subtleties of riding to each other, we would have found much more precise ways to do it – just like the Eskimos, who in their language have over seventy words for snow. They do not, however, have different eyes and different neurology from everyone else, and with the correct teaching, we could all train our senses to make the same distinctions as they make. We could also learn the words with which to talk about them. In riding, we simply have not bothered. We have a very skimpy vocabulary, and our stock phrases – for instance 'on the bit' – are like umbrella terms which are open to a variety of different interpretations. (They also often cover a multitude of sins!) If the Eskimos were as imprecise as us, they would build igloos out of the wrong snow and walk in the wrong places . . . with disastrous consequences.

I came across a phrase new to me recently in Franz Mairinger's book, *Horses Are Made to be Horses*. In it, he tells of his experience one day when he was training at the Spanish Riding School and they were riding the stallions outside after a long winter indoors. Not surprisingly, the atmosphere was electric, and when a train passed by on the nearby railway line, Mairinger was run away with. The next day his teacher (whom I believe was Colonel Podhajsky), rode the horse to show him how to do it, and, of course, he sat there and did a beautiful piaffe as the train roared by. He told Mairinger that all he had done was to 'let his weight down through the horse'. Unfortunately, Mairinger does not tell us how he interpreted Podhajsky's words, and whether he was able to go out the next day and reproduce his actions. When I read this, I recognised the feeling that Podhajsky must have meant – although I suspect I might talk more about a sense of suction between me and the horse, and of the horse coming *up* underneath me. I would use different language because I know how 90 per cent of the riding population would respond if told to 'let their weight down'. They would push down into the saddle and press their body downwards as if they wanted to squash the horse. This was definitely not what Podhajsky meant to suggest. Unfortunately, he did not realise that his words could be open to any other interpretation than the one *he* would apply to them. One of my pupils illustrated this beautifully by giving me a poster which reads, 'I know that you believe you understand what you think I said, but I'm not sure you realise that what you heard was not what I meant!'

Over the last twelve years or so, I have been through an interesting cycle in my learning. To begin with, I found myself gradually abandoning the tenets I had grown up with. The first to go was 'sit up straight and push your heels down'. At first I was shocked by what I was doing, but my progress, and the progress of my pupils, was undeniable – even to unbiased and extremely knowledgeable eyes. Over time, I became braver in my own use of language, but I was still curious to know how these expressions could ever have been coined. Then, as I improved more, I found that I began having experiences which got me thinking, 'Wow!' Yes, I *could* describe this by saying that I am sitting up straight and pushing my heels down!': but what I was doing was hugely different from my original attempts to interpret these words. I would rarely, if ever, say them to a rider, because there is a 90 per cent certainty that she would translate them into action in much the same way that I used to. The vast majority of riders are making exactly the same mistakes, and making them because they all interpret these phrases in similar ways. To their originator, they were equivalent to a certain neurological pattern. To the present-day pupil, however, they are equivalent to a different pattern entirely.

Naturally talented teachers get around this problem by communicating through the use of images. This is nothing new: what is new is our realisation that far from being simply amusing and eccentric, images actually enable both sides of the brain to receive the message of the communicator, with much less slippage with regard to its meaning. For example, I might say to you, 'If you were standing on a diving board, about to do a backward dive, you would have to balance very carefully. You would put the balls of your feet on the edge of the board, with your heels possibly lowered a little and your knees slightly bent. Then you would take your time in that position before you propelled yourself up and over backwards. As a rider, your balance over the stirrup must be exactly the same as the diver's balance on the board.' You would know exactly how to respond to this, and if I asked you as you were riding round, 'Are you still on the diving board, or have you dived off backwards?' you would have no difficulty in answering my question. I have given you words, which satisfy the left brain's need for language, and I have created an image, or a feelage, which satisfies the right brain's need to think not through words but through the senses. 'A picture is worth a thousand words', and my communication is far more explicit than it would be if I told you to 'push your heels down', 'place your foot correctly in the stirrup' or 'keep your body in balance above your feet'. Alternatively, I could show off my knowledge to you and blind you with science, by talking about different muscle groups, their functions and the ways you needed to use them. But this, too, would leave you none the wiser once it came to the stage of translating my words into action.

There are many images which I have found to work almost universally for everyone. Others are more idiosyncratic, and the best images of all are made up by the pupil herself. One of my favourite examples of this happened on a day when I was teaching in the pouring rain, huddled into my waterproofs and watching my pupil sploshing through the puddles in the arena. Suddenly her horse started to work really well, a broad grin spread all over her face, and she yelled, 'I feel like a meringue!' At the time I was mystified, but given the conditions we were working in, it did not seem appropriate to stop her and ask her what she meant. So I stood there, and every time she seemed to be losing the good work, I brought her back into the state of 'conscious competence' by telling her to, 'Keep feeling like a meringue!' At the end of the lesson, as we both dried out in the tack room, she was thrilled with the work she had done. With an almost dreamlike expression on her face, she looked at me and said, 'I used to feel like suet pudding . . .'

Our communication in that instance might have sounded very strange to a passerby, but it was actually extremely precise. In my pupil's mind the words, 'like a meringue', were linked with a certain specific right-brain feelage, and a certain neurological pattern. Whenever she or I used those words, she made a left brain–right brain link-up which stimulated precisely that pattern and no other. There was none of the vagueness which surrounds all these phrases which sound so sensible but mean so little. I spend my life talking to people about diving boards, balloons, mantraps, iron bars, and other bizarre-sounding phenomena. They all originated for me as right-brain 'feelages' which I translated into left-brain language, and I offer them to my pupil's left brain for her to translate into right-brain action. In cases like the above, we work the other way round, from my pupil's right brain to her left brain, to my left brain, and finally to my right brain, as I identify with the feeling she is talking about. This kind of accuracy in communication is extremely rare. I find it a very gratifying experience to know that I am speaking exactly the same language as another human being.

The human brain is unsurpassed as a learning mechanism, but it can only operate effectively when it knows its goal, and when it receives clear feedback from the body and the environment. When these conditions are met, it operates as a cybernetic mechanism. A good example of this is a self-guided torpedo, which has a metal detector in its tip so that it can home in on the ship at which it has been aimed. It also has a rudder and a propulsion system. So when it realises that it is off-course, the rudder acts and automatically corrects it. If it then gets feedback that it has over-corrected, the rudder makes another correction to bring it back onto course, and through a series of ever-decreasing adjustments it gropes its way towards the goal.

The body naturally likes to work in this way: as an example, stand on one foot and feel the minute adjustments that your body automatically makes to keep you in balance. This is cybernetics in action, and with practice, of course, the wobbles become even smaller as your body realises more quickly when it is off course and responds to a much more refined feedback loop. One tremendously important point about the torpedo is that, in effect, it remembers its successes and forgets its mistakes: when it gets feedback that it needs to change course, it simply changes course – without berating itself or getting upset. When it gets feedback that it is already on the right track, it keeps doing what it is already doing – without becoming full of self-congratulation. This optimises its performance and parallels the ways that human beings can also optimise theirs.

However, there are several traps into which we all very easily fall. The first lies in knowing the goal. My experiences in teaching (even when working with quite advanced riders) suggest that most people are very woolly in their conception of what is 'right'. Many are kidding themselves when they assume that they can recognise the correct feeling, whilst others admit that when they ride, it is as if they are stumbling along in a fog, not at all sure about what they are supposed to be doing and where they are supposed to be heading. Many are shocked when I manoeuvre them into what is for them – at this stage in their learning – the best goal. Here again, we meet the problem of explaining the taste of strawberry jam: verbal descriptions of the goal are of little use unless they are based on images which help the rider to 'think through her senses' and rearrange her body in the best possible way. The first task is to give the pupil a taste of strawberry jam; the second is to deal with her shock ('You mean it's *supposed* to feel like this? You must be kidding!') and entice her to keep the feeling for long enough to begin to realise its advantages.

The next problem lies in making sure that the rider is getting the feedback which tells her how clearly she is recreating this goal. Riders usually miss this for two reasons. Firstly, they are often paying attention in the wrong sensory system. We have our visual, auditory and kinaesthetic senses (as well as taste and smell), but the brain can only 'tune in' to one of these at a time – rather like a television or radio set. So if you ride around and talk to yourself, you do not perceive the feedback that you are continually receiving through your kinaesthetic sense. Similarly, if you use your focussed rather than your peripheral vision, the act of staring also cuts off your ability to feel. (When using focussed vision, one tends to focus on a particular area, and to see little of the world around it. In using peripheral vision, one focusses on nothing in particular: it is like letting the world come into one's eyes, and it is easy to see through at least 180 degrees. Experiment with the two until you can clearly perceive the difference.)

There is much less mystique to feel than most people think there is: it is mainly a question of tuning your brain into the right 'programme', and this is a skill which can be developed through practice. However, there is one more major stumbling block: when the rider *does* pay attention in her kinaesthetic system, her attention is very easily drawn to her hand, the rein contact and the horse's head position. She is sidetracked away from the feeling sensations which really matter – the ones that happen beneath her backside.

When the right conditions are met, however, learning becomes automatic and inevitable, just as it is for very young children who master the skills of crawling, walking and talking with no instruction at all. In fact, it is the instruction which seems to create the problems, since it violates the brain's natural learning process and *stops* it from perceiving both the goal and the feedback which helps it to stay on course. (This is the point where the user's manual usually becomes a loser's manual!) To illustrate this, I often do an exercise in workshops where I ask for two volunteers. One of them has to lie down on the floor on her back and the other has to instruct her in how to get up. I tell the one on the floor that she is to follow her instructions to the letter and do no more, and no less, than she is told. No one has yet succeeded in getting up! Usually, the poor person finds herself stranded, pushing for all she is worth on her hands, but not achieving anything because she has been given no instruction about how to use her abdominal muscles. Very often her tutor starts to get frustrated with her, and keeps repeating herself in the hope that her message will get through. To make it even clearer why we are doing this exercise, I often add a commentary which draws the same conclusion as most riding teachers who are unable to communicate effectively with their pupils: 'It's a pity about Jane, isn't it? After all, she comes every week for her lesson and she does try really hard. But she just doesn't seem to have what it takes . . .'

When I have been the tutor in this exercise, I *have* succeeded in getting people up off the floor, but only by lying down, getting up with them, and giving them a commentary as I go along. This enables me to give them feedback in much smaller chunks, which guides them much more precisely through the movements they need to make. It also gives them a series of much smaller goals, which are achieved more easily by choosing the simplest way to get up – rolling onto one's side rather than pushing straight up. Most of the tutors happily launch themselves into giving instructions without realising what a difficult position they are putting themselves in; but by the end of the exercise, it is usually the tutor who feels that *she* has had the hardest time. Then, when she has failed in her aim, she suffers the further embarrassment of seeing the person on the floor get up in her own way – which of course, she can do with consummate ease.

Another exercise, often used in management training, illustrates these principles very well. Somebody is sent out of the room, and the rest of the group decides on an arbitrary goal for him – perhaps sitting in a certain chair or picking up a cup. When they bring him back into the room, they do not tell him what the goal is but they hit him lightly with a rolled-up newspaper every time he gets it wrong, in the hope that their deterrent will eventually help him to get it right! They then play the game again with a different goal, but this time they blow a whistle every time he shows a sign of getting it right. (This is rather like the child's game of 'hunt the thimble'.) Inevitably, the second method is always faster, as well as being much more pleasant for the person involved. In business, where time is money, this is important; but how often do we treat our pupils and our children in this way? In one experiment young children were hooked up to a microphone which recorded their oral interactions at home and school. Over 80 per cent of the communication they received was of the nature of, 'Don't do that,' 'You're not to . . . ,' etc. Very little information was given to them about what they *were* allowed to do or about how they could do it. This is tantamount to instructing someone who is dialling a telephone number, and saying, 'That's the wrong number. No, it's still wrong. That one's wrong too . . . ,' and giving them no information about the *right* number. I find it devastating to realise how much we frustrate our children and put them in an impossible situation. This inhibits their natural spontaneity as well as their ability to learn in the way that nature intended them to. Equally awful is the comparable way in which we so often treat our horses during the process that we call 'training'.

Young children develop 'unconscious competence' simply through their play, which is based on imitation and experimentation. When your six-month-old baby starts to drop things on the floor (over and over again), and your two-year-old starts to paint the dog red, it is difficult to believe that a very sophisticated learning process is taking place. But through these activities, she is homing in on goals and refining her feedback systems, giving her an appreciation of movement and space which you could not teach her through words. The problem within our adult learning is to instill the same curiosity and the same desire to experiment. Nine times out of ten, our experiences in school knock this out of us, and we expect to learn by sitting still: we wait for instruction instead of actively experimenting and gathering feedback.

The more rigid we become, the more we develop the tendency to *keep doing the same things over and over again* (kicking the horse even harder, or shouting louder at our pupils), even in the face of overwhelming evidence that what we are doing is not working. We bash our heads harder and harder against the same brick wall, not realising that usually the wall is of our own making. When we find ourselves *trying hard*, it is usually because we are using one set of muscles which are attempting to do the job and another set which oppose the first and make success impossible. This is like treading on the brake and the accelerator at the same time and it is a very frustrating, exhausting procedure, particularly when it becomes habitual. Each person has a choice: to allow her neurology to follow its old, familiar, inefficient tramlines or to start exploring herself and the environment in a way that literally develops and enriches the neurological patterning in the body, just as it does in the learning of the young child.

The sophistication and extent of our neurological 'wiring', and its capacity for learning, are astronomical. In the human central nervous system, which controls our voluntary muscles, there are one hundred billion neurons, which are its basic building blocks. This is about equivalent to the number of stars in our galaxy. Each neuron is made up of a central cell and tentacles of various lengths which connect it to other neurons. In the brain, each neuron makes connections to at least one thousand others, and in the deeper parts of the brain to up to one hundred thousand others. This gives a total of one hundred trillion synapses – the minute gaps between neurons. There are subtle chemical differences between the neurons which allow them to recognise each other, so that the chemical neuro-transmitters, or 'runners', which convey a message from one neuron to another do not get confused, and our messages do not get jumbled. The messages travel at about 225 miles per hour, which means that they take one-fiftieth of a second to get from your brain to your big toe! The density of the nervous system is such that if you were able to get into a bath which dissolved every other part of your body, you would come out having lost your hair and your skin, and you would look a rather strange colour, but you would still be able to wear your clothes, and would still be recognisable as you.

By the time a child is born, almost all the neurons are already formed. This means that the foetus in the womb must form 250,000 neurons per minute! Seventy per cent of the 'wires' are also in place at birth, which means that the foetus must form 175 million per minute, or 3 million per second. The remaining 30 per cent of these connections forms after birth, and half of these are made in the first five years of life. This means that your toddler, as she explores her world, and learns by imitating you, is forming 4.5 million 'wires' per minute!

The memory capacity of this system is almost infinite, and there is much evidence to suggest that the brain does in fact store memories of everything that ever happens to us, different areas of it holding information in different ways. The visual and auditory cortexes are particularly interesting: they develop in conjunction with, and in response to, the environment. If new-born kittens have their eyes taped shut until the visual cortex has developed fully, they never learn to see. If they are placed in environments where they can see only horizontal lines, they later cannot see vertical lines. The parts of the visual cortex which should detect 'verticalness' do not develop, and the kittens will literally walk into chair legs. This would be true of humans too, as has been shown when surgeons have attempted to restore the sight of people who have been blind from birth. When human babies have been brought up by wolves, they have learnt to understand and reproduce wolf language, but when they have later been introduced into human society, they have never become able to understand and reproduce our language. These parts of the brain have a 'use it or lose it' quality. The wiring which is not used during the critical growing time is effectively lost, and it is not possible to 'programme' it later. The brain functions as if it were a pocket calculator which was never wired to add.

The wiring in the cerebral cortex, which includes the right and left hemispheres, develops rather differently. It grows with your toddler regardless of circumstance, but it may not become *actualised*. The nervous system has a built-in redundancy, so that within the brain itself we use one part in ten, and within the rest of the body, one part in three. So, when you want to learn to tap dance, or play music, or ride a horse, you can activate some of the wiring which has hitherto lain dormant and waiting to be 'programmed'. (In this sense, the cerebral cortex is like a computer, which can be programmed at any time given the right software. This is not possible with a pocket calculator, which, like the visual and auditory cortexes, is complete in itself.) When your young child explores the world, or when you teach her a skill, she is literally growing the wires to store what she is learning. But if the adult was deprived of particular experiences as a youngster, she cannot now grow the wires but has to call upon her spare wiring.

In discussing the functioning of the cerebral cortex, the American researcher Paul Goodwin has coined the term 'actualised neural network density'. This describes the amount of our neurological potential which we have actually brought into use, and this varies tremendously between individuals. Think of the difference between a public transport system which operates a great many buses on a small number of routes, and a system where they can travel more widely: many more routeways are 'actualised'. This enriches our options – but fortunately, unused paths are always left open for future use. We would be infinitely less capable of learning if all of the brain had the 'use it or lose it' quality which makes vision and hearing such precious gifts.

There are enormous benefits to be gained by thinking of riding as a neurological puzzle. Its common ground with other such puzzles concerns the sheer amount of information which has to be processed: in effect, one is training oneself to cope with overload and disorientation. As an example of this, think of the experience that you may have had in driving somebody else's car: when you mean to operate the indicators, you find that you have switched on the headlights (and then, you have to regain your equilibrium and find the indicators in time for the corner – which is now approaching fast!). Many amateur riders have a similar problem when they ride somebody else's horse. To the professional rider or driver, however, the ability to adapt quickly to a different equine or mechanical partner is one of the most fascinating and exciting aspects of her skill.

But even without this added complication, the rider needs access to a fair few of her neural networks: she has to think about her body and its various parts, the horse and his movement patterns, where she is, where she is going, what is about to go wrong, how to correct it, etc. (And at the same time, she is supposed to look up, smile and make it all look easy!) Inevitably, the beginner riding a horse for the first time experiences the greatest sense of overload and disorientation; but this does not go away – not, at least, if the rider continues to challenge and develop her habitual ways of using her body, cycling again and again through the stages to 'unconscious competence'. Even after twenty years, I still find that I cannot keep track of all the things that are vying for my attention, though fortunately, they are much more sophisticated than they were a few years ago. On the more simplistic end of the scale, I often hear riders complain that, 'I can think about myself or the horse, but not about both at once!', or, 'I can think about my left side or about my right side, but not about both at once.' One of the primary limitations in both learning and performing concerns the ability to think on many different levels simultaneously.

One of my psychology teachers is extremely enthusiastic about this same ability, which he calls 'parallel processing'. Because this is such an important part of many skills, including riding, he uses specific exercises to teach it. Among these is one where you look at a cross on the wall. Firstly you have to say 'right', and *afterwards* move your eyes to the right. (This in itself is difficult.) Then you do the same to the left, then up, then down. Whilst you do this, a partner gives you simple mathematical puzzles to solve, and you have to say the answer without disturbing your rhythm. He may give you this input by telling you, or by showing you the sum on a piece of paper, or by tapping the numbers onto your body – utilising each of your main senses. He may also distract you by touching you, talking to you or showing you other things. The brain is presented with a problem which, by virtue of being so multi-faceted, is surprisingly similar to riding. (Do not be put off by the mathematics. The sums involved are of the 'two plus two' variety!)

Knowing my fascination with such puzzles, friends and pupils often tell me interesting stories about experiences of overload and disorientation. One involved a man who owned a small JCB digger. He reckoned that he could operate it so precisely that he could pick up an egg placed on a shelf. (In operating any machinery, or in riding a horse, you effectively extend your sense of your body boundaries outward to include the machine or the animal. This allows you to know exactly how small a space you can drive your car through, and the same should apply if you were piloting a jumbo jet!) However, one day he borrowed a larger digger to do a specific job, and found to his horror that the hand which operated his machine on the left–right axis was now responsible for the up –down axis and *vice versa*! I do not envy him the experience of relearning, but I gather that he did succeed. A teacher of mine who was once a pilot told me of his experience when he was the first person to fly a plane after it had been serviced, during which the controls had been connected the wrong way round. When he moved the joystick in a way which should have taken it up, it dived, and when he wanted to lose height, he gained it. He thought that to attempt to land the plane using the normal procedures would confuse him to a dangerous extent, so he brought it down by intermittently switching off the engines – and he lived to tell the tale. A friend of his did not, however, when he flew a plane in which 'left' had been connected as 'right', and 'right' had been connected as 'left'. On a more everyday and light-hearted note, one pupil of mine has a clock in her kitchen on which 'one' is to the left of 'twelve', so that the hands go round counter clockwise. Telling the time then requires an interesting double-take!

All of these people coped more or less well in situations where their environment changed in unexpected ways. This happens to riders time and time again – for example when they discover that the way in which one turns a horse is almost completely *opposite* to the way one turns one's own body. Then, as they begin to tackle this, they discover the additional complications of their own asymmetry. As they unravel these, they inevitably tend to focus on the side of the body that seems to present the problem. They then work extremely hard, only to find (when they eventually succeed) that their neglected side comes to the fore, making them asymmetrical in the other direction! Since the right-brain hemisphere controls the left side of the body, and the left-brain hemisphere controls the right side of the body, the person who complains that she can only focus on one side of the body at a time is effectively saying, 'I can use my left brain, or my right brain, but not both brains together,' and this is the nub of her problem.

This difficulty goes right back to the developmental stage of crawling. Problems arise when a child does not crawl, or crawls homolaterally, i.e. by moving its limbs in the way that a horse walks, instead of cross-crawling, and moving its limbs in the way that a horse trots. In cross-crawling, both sides of the body are moved simultaneously, so that both brain hemispheres are activated at once, and the corpus callosum which connects the two is strengthened. In a homolateral crawl, the brain works in a 'one side on, one side off' way, and it tends to continue to do this throughout life. This makes it difficult to *think and move both at the same time*, and it causes reduced hand/eye co-ordination and the tendency to confuse letters like 'b' and 'd', which are mirror images of each other. Dyslexia and many other learning difficulties have their origins here, and the new discipline of Educational Kinesiology has devised exercises based on cross-crawling, which can dramatically improve the ability to read and co-ordinate in both children and adults. This affects everything from school work to riding, and a remarkable number of people are involved: confusions over left and right, and a reduced ability to think and move simultaneously have profound effects, but these can go almost unnoticed. In a repatterning exercise which I recently did with a group of pupils, I was able to predict almost exactly which of them were affected. Fortunately, improvements can be achieved in a very short space of time, since the brain will naturally choose the most effective option it knows.*

The Feldenkrais system of body work also has an important contribution to make.† It shows each individual how to refine and broaden her movement patterns, mirroring the ways in which babies and young children first learn to use their bodies. In 'Awareness Through Movement' classes, students are led through very slow sequences of gentle, non-habitual movements – so non-habitual that they seem unbelievably strange. In the nicest possible

* Consultants in Educational Kinesiology work with children and adults who have dyslexia and other learning or co-ordination difficulties. For a list of practitioners, write to: Body Balance, 12 Golders Rise, London NW4 2HR.

† For a list of Feldenkrais Teachers, contact The Feldenkrais Guild UK, P.O. Box 370, London N10 3XA.

way, these force the nervous system to abandon its old tramlines and to make new connections, utilising neurological pathways which have never been actualised. This can make a staggering difference to one's posture, movement and overall sense of one's body; but at times the new experience is extremely disorientating. Training both brain and body in these contexts takes much of the burden of learning to ride *off* the horse (who often suffers unnecessarily in the process), and puts it where it belongs, firmly in the hands of the rider – where it can yield benefits that far outweigh just the ability to ride.

I spend a great deal of my time encouraging riders who are learning to take on the attitude of an experimenter, or an adventurer who is exploring new territory. As soon as we leave play school, our culture demands that we 'do it right' in the shortest possible time; as a result, we forget about the natural learning process of the young child, whose brilliance is our birthright. Whilst children experiment and find new ways to do things, adults have a horrible tendency to keep bashing their heads against the same old brick wall. (God forbid that we should ever experiment on our horses; but to torture them by repeating the same mistakes over and over again is apparently quite acceptable!) As a friend of mine loves to say, 'If you always do what you always did, you'll always get what you always got.' But how slow we are to realise this. Whenever riders complain to me that they have reached a plateau in their learning, I know that this is their situation. Their first step is to stop waiting for instructions, to start gathering feedback, and to discover *what is actually happening*.

I cannot think of this without remembering the story I once heard about a man who had a recurring dream in which he repeatedly found himself in front of a wall with a small door in it. Struggle as he might, he could not push the door open, and it seemed that there was no other way round, over or through the wall. Eventually his frustration reached such a pitch that he went to see a specialist in dream interpretation whose background was not dissimilar to my own. The man was asked to see the door in his mind's eye in order to find out if there was anything about it that he had not previously noticed. After a while he began to chuckle; he realised that in his struggle he had somehow failed to see a small notice which read, 'Please pull'!

When riders complain that they are on a plateau I sometimes offer them this analogy: it is as if they know they want to get to Paris – some mythical place in which their body is perfectly aligned and the horse responds to their aids in exactly the way that the textbooks say he should. In their riding, they try harder and harder to get to Paris, blaming their difficulties on the horse or their bad co-ordination. But in reality all their efforts are doomed, and they are practising neurological patterns that they know will fail them. Like the man in the story above, they are missing the obvious – and the truth is that they cannot even begin their journey until they take time to look more closely at their starting point. (We have come back full circle to the idea of becoming conscious of one's incompetence.) For to get to Paris, you have to travel in completely different directions depending on whether you start from London, Berlin or Stockholm.

The ability to discover where you already are has extremely profound implications, and there are two immediate benefits. The first is that you shift your perspective from *how it ought to be*, to *how it is*. This means that you start to notice things you have never noticed before, and it is this which gives you the 'Aha!' experience, the breakthrough in which the right brain reveals its secrets to the left. ('That's the problem! My left seat bone is always slightly behind my right!') With a deeply entrenched pattern, one has to have this knowledge before any change is possible. Then, it becomes relatively easy to actualise some new wiring, and to do the opposite. Secondly, instead of waiting for your teacher to tell you exactly what you should be doing, you bring the ball into your own court. Like the young child, who provides such an exemplary example of learning, you become self-reliant and self-motivated.

Along with this comes a certain quality of paying attention, which is very different from the trying we tend to indulge in. Again, young children and animals provide us with the best models; look at a cat stalking a bird when you want to see concentration in action. Talented riders all share the secret of how and where to focus their attention, but this eludes many others. It is obvious that tennis players need to watch the ball, but what is the equivalent of this in riding? When I ask riders this question, some tell me that they watch the horse's head to make sure it is in the correct position. Others realise that they have to 'watch' with their feel sense, and they tell me that they pay attention to their horse's hind legs: but when I ask them how they feel the hind legs, they make it sound like some sort of magical mumbo-jumbo. I suspect that they do not actually know!

I believe that the rider (like Nick Faldo) has to pay attention to her own body alignment, particularly to the *interface* through which she makes contact with the horse. A small, rather hard-to-decipher movement in his back muscles becomes a very large movement by the time it has connected through to the hind foot; but it can only be felt and influenced through its subtle origins in the horse's back. Horses react to the rider's seat in one of two ways, which takes them into either the 'spiral of increasing ease' or 'the spiral of increasing tension'. Either the horse takes his back, his sides and his mouth *away* from contact with the rider's seat, leg and hand, or he seeks contact with them. When he takes them away, his movement becomes much more difficult to sit on – making it harder for the rider, who in turn tends to bump more, thereby making it harder for the horse. The spiral can wind itself tighter and tighter until the rider begins to influence the cause, changing her interaction with the horse's back so that he *seeks* contact with her seat, hand and leg. This changes his carriage and movement, making it easier for her to sit better, which in turn makes it easier for the horse to move better: they both move into 'the spiral of increasing ease'. The visible changes created extend right out to the extremities of the horse's body, but they begin in the centre, with the rider's way of sitting. Anyone who says, 'I can think about myself, or about the horse, but not about both at once,' has fundamentally missed the point. When she pays attention to the interface through which she contacts the horse's back, she learns exactly how her body is influencing him, and this will produce a dramatic increase in her skill.

The rider/horse interaction is such an intricate mechanism, however, that this is not easy to learn. Even when we know where to 'look' for feedback, we often blink and miss the most important points: for example, the way in which the rider's seat interacts with the horse's back is complicated by her asymmetry. Practically everyone has one thigh which rests more snugly on the saddle than the other, and one seat bone and one stirrup which they weight more heavily than the other. Almost always, the horse consistently carries his rib cage to one side, and falls more heavily on one shoulder than he does on the other – and all of these are linked together in an interesting chain of cause and effect. But 95 per cent of riders are gaily oblivious of all of this: usually they are just vaguely aware that the rein contact is stronger in one hand than it is in the other. But the same people could almost certainly give a detailed explanation of how the rider *ought* to be positioned on a circle, and how the horse *ought* to respond. The problem is that they have never explored the territory which lies between what ought to be (their left-brain knowledge) and what is (their right-brain knowledge). Here lie the secrets of riding – the feels and skills which they are lacking.

Learning is primarily a process of *noticing*, in which one becomes aware of increasingly subtle sensations – the 'news of difference' which the nervous system naturally screens out when a rider's threshold levels are too high. High threshold levels are dangerous: as an example, consider the following. If you put a frog into a pail of water, and begin to heat that water very slowly, the frog could jump out at any time. But he chooses not to. In fact, he will stay in there until he boils alive, because the gradual change in temperature is too subtle for his nervous system to register. (Perhaps this has been happening to us, too, as our planet bears the effects of increasing pollution and global warming.) The challenge that faces us as riders is to learn to perceive such tiny increments of change that we are never left powerless by the horse's evasions. A good rider's strength lies not so much in sheer muscle power, but in the ability to deal with what is *about to happen* before it even manifests itself. Prevention is always much better than cure.

When the rider's threshold levels are lower, the correct information may reach the brain, but so do other irrelevancies, creating such a confusing jumble that the rider is easily overwhelmed. In our attempts to make this information make sense, and to understand cause and effect, we often make important mistakes. This happens in many other contexts too (and if it did not, our experience of life would be very different!). A friend recently told me about a classic mistake of his. He cycles every day from his home in Islington to his office in Baker Street. On the way home this is up-hill, and he found that he was becoming increasingly short of breath. He soon became worried about the state of his heart, and just before he was due to see the doctor, his teenage son volunteered to check his bicycle for him. It turned out that one of the brake pads was rubbing against the wheel, and that this was the cause of the strain he was feeling. He had got the right feedback, but had attributed it to the wrong cause!

When the rider can pay attention selectively, and can make sense out of the information she receives, she begins to understand it in terms of cause and effect. She then knows – on the most fundamental level – how her interaction with the horse works: she does X because she wants to create Y, which she knows will put herself and her horse more securely into 'the spiral of increasing ease'. It is as if she creates an internal 'map' of feelages which enables her to know where she is, where she is going, how to get there, etc. Many riders are attempting to work from maps which are incomplete, and at times extremely inaccurate – it is all too easy, for instance, to misdiagnose an asymmetry, or to blame the horse for a problem which really belongs with oneself. An accurate, detailed map takes time to create, and it usually takes the help of a teacher who has travelled the same territory and who can introduce the rider to the important landmarks and the hidden paths.

As I have been learning over the last twelve years, I have discovered a tremendous amount about the body and how it works, and this has caused me to develop some ideas which are contrary to most of the riding texts. They are, however, backed up by research which has been done in other areas, since I have learnt a great deal from Alexander and Feldenkrais teachers, from physiotherapists and from Touch for Health practitioners. Touch for Health began to interest me when I read about its approach to muscle tension, which mirrored the ideas I was using. Whilst most body therapies work with the muscles which are tight or in spasm, and therefore causing pain, George Goodheart, a chiropractor, realised in the early 1960s that it might be more productive to work with the opposite muscle of the pair which was invariably weak and flaccid. To visualise how they work together, think of a swing door which is held in place by two springs. When there is equal tension in both springs, the system is in balance; but if one spring is lengthened and weak, the other must contract to take up the slack, with the result that the door does not close properly (see Diagram 1). Oiling this spring and lengthening it out can make no permanent difference, because it must always contract and knot up again to take up the slack. To make lasting change, the weaker spring must be strengthened or replaced.

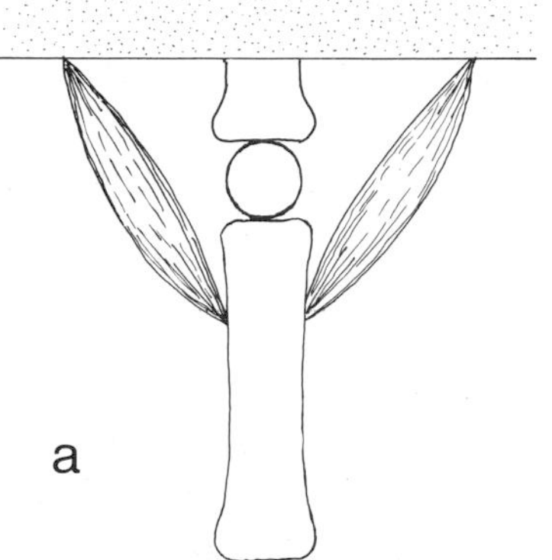

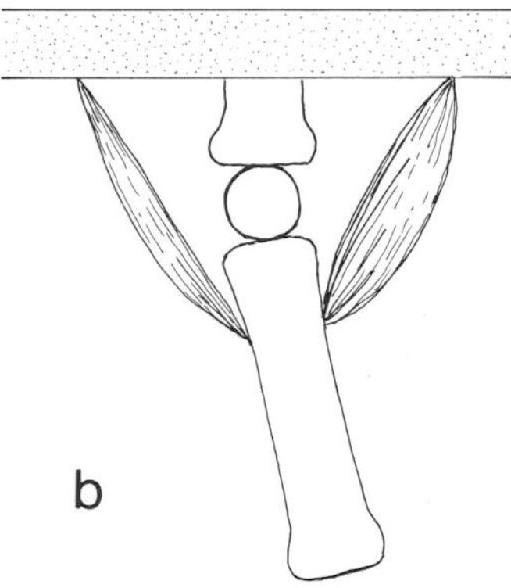

Diagram 1. It is helpful to think of opposing pairs of muscles as being like the springs on a swing door. In (a) they are both in balance, but in (b) one is weak, which forces the other to tighten in compensation. The shortened muscle will only lengthen when its partner is strengthened.

In my teaching, I aim to increase the tone in the rider's weaker muscles, knowing that as this happens the tighter ones will let go, bringing the whole body into balance. To open the angle at the hip joint, for instance (so that the rider's knee does not creep up), I may well need to persuade the muscles at the back of the thigh to shorten. Almost every other riding teacher I know would use the opposite approach; but I have rarely seen this work. It is important to work with the muscles in a certain order: I very rarely begin work with a rider's hands and shoulders, even though the tightness there may well seem to be an obvious starting point. Usually, these stiffnesses are only symptoms: the cause lies in the *flaccidity* of the muscles nearer to the centre of the body, particularly around the pelvis and thighs. Only when these are strengthened and working at higher tone will the peripheral muscles release. It is as if the body, in its own instinctive wisdom, knows that it has a job to do – and when the central muscles are unavailable, it substitutes any other muscles which are – usually in the arms and shoulders. I know people who have spent twenty years trying to get rid of the tension in their shoulders, but their attempts were inevitably doomed. It is a good general rule to think of the difficulties which appear in the extremities of the body – including the lower legs and feet – as having their origins nearer the centre. When someone's bodily use is inefficient, it is as if their muscle system is tied in a knot: one cannot release it simply by grabbing the nearest free end and pulling. Instead, one has to work one's way into the knot, find its centre and unravel it from there.

Another important factor concerns the *texture* of the muscles. One of my old teachers used to say that the rider should look like a hunk of raw meat or putty that had been thrown onto the saddle. He did indeed look like that, but as I felt myself wobble and bump my way around the riding arena, I knew that I did not! For years I tried to solve the problem by relaxing more, but it never worked, until I eventually realised that the answer lay in *more* muscle tone rather than less. Think of it this way: if I were to punch a feather pillow, how would it respond? How would a piece of putty respond, or a sand bag? How would a sponge respond? The cushion would deform. The putty and the sand bag would change little if at all (but I might hurt my fist!). The sponge would contract inwards and then bounce out again to its original shape. I am sorry to have to report that in most women, the muscles of the buttock – particularly in the underneath layer of flesh between the seat bones and the saddle – act like sponges, and this is why we all bounce about so much.* This 'squishiness' is different from bumping; it is more a case of 'wibble wobble, wibble wobble, jelly on the plate' than of the whole pelvis leaving the saddle *en bloc*. When this *does* happen it is usually because the pelvis is angled wrongly, tipped so that the pubic bone is lowered and the coccyx lifted. Then, it offers much less shock absorption than it does when tipped the other way (see Lesson 3). What we think of as 'bouncing' is more often squishiness than bumping, and this diagnosis is important, because the two problems have rather different solutions.

So why is it that we have all spent our lives attempting to relax more? I think it is because the most talented riders – who write the books and form our dogma – always have the naturally high muscle tone which enables them to sit like putty: this inherent strength is an important factor in their talent. Very often these talented riders are men, who have on average about 35 per cent higher muscle tone than women. (To convince yourself, touch a man's and a woman's body, particularly in the region of the pelvis and the thigh, and feel the difference.) They might well tell you, 'I feel perfectly relaxed,' but let us suppose that this natural level of muscle tone was a zero on their scale. What they do not realise is that on the scale for the average unfit woman, this might well be

* I am grateful to the biophysicist Averil Cox, who first put forward this idea.

a forty, since her zero, which represents her natural level of muscle tone, would occur at about minus forty on our rider's scale! To make her body work in the same way that his does, she will definitely not feel relaxed; but he is completely unaware that this fundamental difference exists.

Another factor at work here is an interesting optical illusion which exists within the body itself. One of the best illustrations I ever had of this happened one day when I was working with a woman who had requested some help with her sitting trot. About six of her friends were watching the lesson, seated at a distance where they could see but not hear. As my pupil began to 'bear down' (see Lesson 1), and to get more holding in the central muscles of her body, her sitting changed dramatically and she began to take on the quality of putty. 'This is amazing,' she said to me, 'I've never sat like this before in my life! But it's such hard work. I never realised that I had to do this with my muscles. This is so difficult . . . can I rest now?' Exhausted, she walked her horse over to her friends. In unison, they all said, 'We've never seen you looking so relaxed!'

In our riding ethos, we assume that a still rider is a relaxed rider, and a rider who wobbles or bumps is a tense rider. But it is really not this simple, and we could more correctly say that a rider who is too *relaxed* in the central muscles of the body is the one who bounces. We have to stabilise our bodies by keeping our muscles appropriately tight, just like the springs on the swing door. In learning about this I have referred a great deal to the textbook *Applied Kinesiology* by Clayne R. Jensen and Gordon W. Schultz. In the section on 'Kinds of muscle action', they discuss slow-tension movements: 'When speed and force are not of prime importance, and great steadiness and accuracy are needed, slow-tension movements are used. Examples are threading a needle, slow and graceful movements in modern dance and ballet, and slow, steady, and precise gymnastic movements. In these kinds of movements the forces applied by the opposite muscle groups are almost equal to each other. If the opposite forces were equal, the body part would be stabilised and steady. As the force of one muscle group overcomes that of the opposite group, slow, steady movement occurs. The fact that all opposing muscle groups apply almost equal tension causes the body part to be highly stable and subject to quick adjustment in direction and rate of movement. One's ability to keep the forces of opposing muscles equal is the limiting factor in steadiness, and the effort greatly taxes one's muscular endurance.'

This sounds to me like a very good description of riding – and most of the people who come on my courses become painfully aware of the need for muscular endurance! (Massaging your thighs after riding and before going to bed can considerably reduce the stiffness you feel next day.) To understand more clearly how this works, think of the body like a system of elastic bands: one represents the torso from the hip upwards, another the thigh and another the calf. Imagine that there is a small gap between one elastic band and the next, and that the end points – at the ankle and the neck – act as if they are fixed. Without this, they literally wave about – as do many rider's heads and lower legs. If the elastic bands are under stretch, they will barely vibrate in response to any impulse: however, if they are *not* under stretch, they move much more, creating the lack of body control that plagues most riders. Furthermore the *bones* are jiggled about, instead of being held securely within the stabilising framework of highly toned muscles. The 'give' that is needed to go with the horse's movement lies in the *joints*, not in the muscles. If the muscles act like floppy elastic bands, the extraneous vibrations in them interfere with the rider's perception of the horse's movement, and they drown it out. The rider cannot perceive the horse clearly, and neither can the horse perceive the rider clearly: *the rider/horse interaction takes on a very different form from that presupposed by the great Masters when they taught and wrote their books.*

This analogy is extremely useful, but it is important to remember that although elastic bands come under tension by *increasing* the distance between their two ends, muscles come under tension by *decreasing* the distance: in relaxation, the muscles are at their maximum length, and from this they can only contract. They cannot be stretched, as many people believe. For example, think of the biceps muscle (made famous by Popeye), which runs along the inside of your upper arm and bends your elbow. If you put your arm straight out in front of you, the muscle is at its resting length, and it contracts as you bend your elbow to bring your hand up in front of your face. (You can use your other hand to feel the bulk of the muscle increase.) This is an *isotonic* use of the muscle, in which the muscle fibres contract to move the bones. However, you can also contract your muscles and put them under increasing tension without actually moving the bones they attach to; this is known as an *isometric* contraction of the muscle, and it is the basis of slow tension movement.

To make the analogy one stage more real, think of the torso as four elastic bands – one for the front, one for the back and one for each side. The muscles of the thigh could similarly be thought of as four elastic bands, and the muscles of the calf as two, representing the muscles at the front and the back of it. The tension in all of these muscles has to be balanced like the springs of the swing door, which hold the swing door in just the right position. Where there is imbalance, the body will come too far forward or back – or it could lean over to the side. When there is an imbalance in the tension of the thigh muscles, the thigh could be pulled up too much, down too much, or into or away from the saddle too much.

These problems do more than take the rider away from the classical seat: they stop her from 'completing the circuit'. This idea comes from the Canadian trainer Erik Herbermann, whose book *The Dressage Formula* offers some wonderful insights about riding. The impulse from the horse's hind leg travels up through the hock and stifle, to the point of the buttock and the croup. It then passes along the horse's back to the wither, and up the neck to the poll and jaw. It passes through the bit to the rein and the rider's arm, then through her back to the horse's back, allowing the cycle to begin again (see Diagram 2). It is reinforced by the use of her leg, which feeds more energy into the circuit, as do the muscles of the horse's quarters. The circuit can get blocked in many places, both by the rider and by the horse, typically at the horse's loin area, the base of his neck, the fourth vertebra, the poll and jaw, and in the rider's hand, elbow, shoulder, back and pelvis. Most teachers

Diagram 2. The complete circuit: the impulse from the horse's hind legs is transmitted through the horse's and the rider's bodies, without being blocked or dissipated.

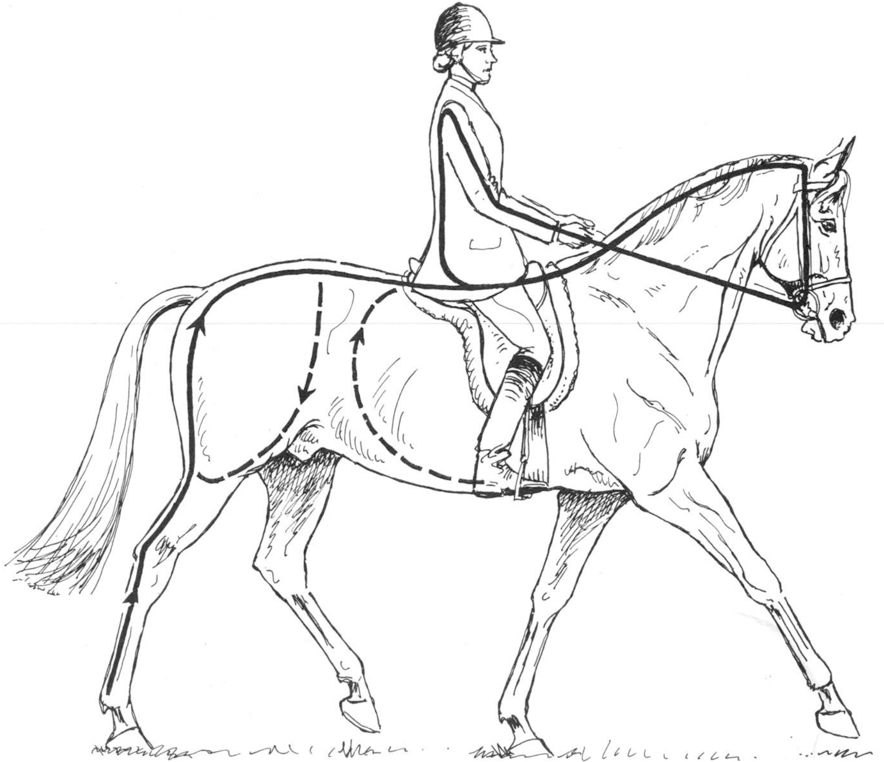

would tell you that the blocks are the most significant problem; but the impulse can also become drained and disorganised. I think that many people underestimate the effects of this, as well as the effects of the body's compensations – for it will instinctively create a dam in one area as it attempts to make up for a leak in another. The human nervous system has a similar circuit, and in his writings about it, Moshe Feldenkrais identifies several problems – namely diffusion, damping, deviation, loss of impetus and break in continuity. All of these are relevant to the rider/horse circuit; muscles which act like wavy elastic bands cannot transmit the impulse without altering it, and jiggling bones add yet more interference. The continual disturbance of the horse's gait leaves most riders unable to transmit the impulse cleanly.

Left to themselves, about 5 per cent of people develop the stillness and accuracy which enables them to do this. At the same time, they transform their body into a stable framework which *stabilises the horse's carriage, whilst letting the impulse flow through.* This skill is the ability to balance the tension in each muscle group, pitting the muscles against each other in order to gain stability, and to transmit the impulse without altering it in any way. In addition to this, the skilful rider can deliberately *upset the balance* of her muscular system – just enough to create small, precise movements in the joints. By producing no more, and no less, than is required, she enables the movement of her body to become an exact mould for the movement of the horse. But she has to go one stage further, so that she can *lead* the dance instead of following it. This enables her to reinforce and redirect the impulse. This type of muscular use is not a part of our everyday movement vocabulary, and the body does not expect to have to work like this; but if you are one of the 95 per cent who wobble, bump and break the circuit, be heartened. With a little guidance you can learn to transmit the impulse instead.

Whilst highly toned muscles stabilise the system, the gaps within the joints provide the softness, fluidity and shock absorption which have been wrongly attributed to relaxed muscles. The gap between the neck and the head is necessary to stabilise this end of the system; if the head is rammed into the neck there is tremendous compression which often causes pain in the neck and back. Although using awareness and imagery can work wonders, freeing this is the specialist work of Alexander teachers and other body workers. Creating a gap at the ankle joint has the effect of fixing this end of the system, stilling the lower leg and offering fine control. Most riders, however, deliberately do the opposite – ramming their calf bones into their ankle bones in an attempt to get their heels down. They too often create compression and pain. The gaps at the knee and the hip are equally important, giving independence to each body part, and enabling the whole of the rider's leg to mould around the horse.

The rider's muscles work best when the tone in them is naturally high and in balance, and when they have a long resting length. It also helps to have ligaments which do not bind the joints too tightly, restricting the little gaps. But when the ligaments and muscles have become *permanently* shortened through a rather stooped posture, or through wearing high heels, they cannot work so effectively. Riders who cannot squat with their heels on the ground always have more difficulty in their riding than people who can – this is a sign that they have lost much of their childhood flexibility. However, it is still possible to overcome this and to ride well; but it requires dedicated practice (and possibly some exercises done away from the horse) to regain at least some of the freedom that has been lost.

There is one other little-known and extremely important elastic-band system within the body. This involves the muscles lying deep within the abdominal cavity, forming strong columns which lie on each side of the vertebrae, which at this level project a long way forward into the abdomen. The columns, or psoas muscles, join with the iliacus muscles which cover the insides of the pelvis, lying underneath the bones that you feel when you put your hands on your hips (see Diagram 19, page 181). Together, these muscles pass down towards the seat bones to form the central core around which the rest of the body is organised. With the seat bones, they are the nub of the rider's contact with the horse's back, the fundamental organising principle of her sitting. When this is correct, the rest of the body tends to come into balance around it. Even as I sit on my stool and work at my computer, I find that thinking of these makes me want to sit much straighter and more symmetrically. Everything else – including will-power – fails abysmally!

I encourage riders to think of their body–mind system like a musical instrument: before they can learn to play music with it, they must firstly learn how to tune it. But most riders want to play complicated music without ever having done this, and as a result there is always discord. Like the strings of a violin, the muscles of the body can be too tight or too loose, and different muscle groups might well need different adjustments. The mind too can be *under-focussed*, where it perceives a large amount of information as a blur, or it can be in the state of *overfocus* which comes from trying too hard. Very, very few people have naturally the right 'tuning' in either body or mind, and developing this is the primary challenge facing us as riders. Finding it makes riding – and learning to ride – very much easier than most people believe it is. For some, it makes the apparently impossible become possible; for others, it adds ease, grace and an intuitive understanding of how to approach each horse's problems. It also opens the door to many other skills, and if you let it, it has the potential to change the quality of your life. I invite you to follow the riders in these pages as they learn how to fine-tune themselves; some of their problems will be similar to yours, others will be very different. I also invite you to take on the same challenge of this 'tuning' for yourself.

PART TWO

Masterclass

As all limitations share a common process,
removing one is much like removing any other.
It's only a matter of focus, intention and the proper
application of appropriate physics.

Don McFarland

Introduction to the Lessons

The photographs for this section were taken on two occasions: Gail, Val, Margaret and Sarah rode on a two-day clinic at Decoy Pond Stables, Beaulieu Road, Hampshire, on a seeringly hot day in July 1990. The photographs were taken on the first day of the course, since the first lessons were likely to produce the most significant visible changes in both horse and rider. All the other riders were taking part in a four-day course held at my home base, West Wilts Equestrian Centre, Holt, Trowbridge, Wiltshire. This was held in August 1990. Again, the photographs were taken on the first day. I am very grateful to all of these people for their willingness to be photographed, and to let me write about them. I am well aware that this is extremely exposing, and I appreciate their selflessness and courage in becoming 'guinea pigs' so that others can learn. At times I have written humorously about their difficulties: I often encourage my pupils to laugh at themselves and their problems, and I abhor the way that riding so often becomes 'serious'. I am sure that you, the reader, will recognise yourself in some of these people, and will relate easily to their problems. (If you do, there is a good chance that you, like they, will be able to find the solutions.) I hope that you too will be able to laugh at yourself – with kindness, and with a tolerant appreciation of the struggle which most of us go through in learning to ride. I hope that you will also be able to empathise with the riders who are not so like you – perhaps the more novice ones, the more sceptical ones, those who are more entrenched in their difficulties, or even the more accomplished ones: if you are tempted to judge them – or to judge yourself in comparison with them – ask yourself, 'Is a rosebud worse than a rose?' Understandably, some of the riders have wished to protect their identity, and they have chosen to take assumed names.

Rarely in a riding text does one see photographs which illustrate the contrast between a rider who begins a lesson with a certain set of problems, and discovers the solutions to some of those problems as the lesson progresses. It is much more usual to see exemplary riders demonstrating the classical ideal. However, you have probably seen many photographs of this type before, and I suspect that they did more for your knowledge of how things *ought* to be than they did for your practical skill. Since the brain can only learn by making comparisons, I am hoping that these illustrations will prove more useful, and will relate more directly to your own riding experience.

Introduction to the Lessons

These lessons illustrate how the underlying principles involved in riding remain the same for each individual horse and rider, whilst, paradoxically, each partnership is unique. For me, this brings endless fascination into teaching. At times I have tackled the same difficulty in two very different ways, each with a different level of complexity. This, of course, is what happens in learning, as one cycles through the same territory again and again. Some of the explanations given here are quite intricate and complicated. If you skip over the words as you read, you will gain very little from them. Instead, you have actively to engage your brain: imagine what it might be like to be the rider I am talking about. Do mental rehearsals of being that rider, and making the changes she is making. Discover how your own body is different or similar from hers. Take time to make the mental images or feelages that my words evoke for you, and to play with different possibilities. Then, take your discoveries with you when you ride (but remember that any significant change in your posture will always feel very much bigger than it looks). Your horse will tolerate your experiments much better than you might imagine: in fact, you could change his life in ways that he will appreciate forever.

This section of the book unfolds rather like a 'who dunnit' murder story. Riding itself is rather like this, since when you know the answer it is always so simple and obvious, but until you find it, everything seems so elusive and complicated. If I told you 'who dunnit' straight away, there would be no story, and if I gave you all the major clues at the beginning it would not be half so exciting. This is impossible anyway, as you cannot get the whole picture in one riding lesson – whether you experience it on a horse or through these pages.

I have given you information in an order whose logic might not be immediately apparent. The first lesson is intended as an overview of the rider/horse interaction. Subsequent lessons discuss this in more detail, and each one covers several different aspects, showing how more novice and more experienced riders solve the same basic problems, each at the appropriate level. Some important concepts which I usually teach very early on (correct breathing, for instance), have been left until later because they do not make interesting pictures. It was more important for me to start by giving you the basic information which did.

I have often felt that my own teachers have tried to tell me 'who dunnit' or 'how to do it' in a few simple statements which meant nothing to me. At the time I thought I was stupid: I now realise that they had drawn the wrong conclusions – their reasoning was flawed, and they had not unearthed some of the vital clues. In murder stories, and in learning, one usually only discovers 'who dunnit' by following red herrings and eliminating the suspects.

Through this process, one gains a tremendously rich understanding of the complexities of the situation, which are often not appreciated by the person who already knows the murderer's identity. (In fact, this is usually the downfall of the murderer himself!) I want you to understand these complexities in riding; knowing them will help you to appreciate the origins of your own and other people's problems. Since the brain learns by contrast, I have deliberately given you plenty of information which illustrates the differences between different riders, between right and wrong, and between different versions of wrong. Only with this information can you begin to appreciate what riding is really about. You will understand the misunderstandings, and understand how the solutions to the problems are simple demonstrations of the laws of physics. This knowledge can make much of your previous struggle seem like an unnecessary waste of time, which in many ways it was. I hope you will not feel badly about this, and blame yourself or your teachers. I firmly believe that people always do the best they can with the resources they have available.

With the extra knowledge you will gain from this book, you will not attempt, as most people do, to 'jump the gun' and offer instant accusations or solutions. In themselves, these often sound very reasonable, but only a full understanding of the facts shows them to be inappropriate or inaccurate. I myself have gained this understanding over twenty-four years of riding, including twelve years of committed research. With the benefit of my experience, you can gain it much, much faster, and it will offer you insights which have the power to transform your riding.

Lesson 1

Katie: An Overview of the Rider/Horse Interaction

As Katie came into the arena and began to work in, I was surprised to hear her story: George, her horse, is a nine-year-old threequarter-bred gelding, whom she has owned since he was four. She bought him from one of our well-known dressage riders and trainers, so of course when she first set eyes on him he was working in a way which was very impressive, especially for such a young horse. Katie has gained enough dressage points with him to be out of Novice classes, and she has competed in Elementary and Medium tests. She works with a trainer near her home who has herself been taught by a rider who learnt at the Spanish Riding School in Vienna. It was obvious from looking at Katie that she had not been subjected to what I think of as the (all too common) push-pull school of competition riding. This crudely suggests that you dominate a horse by pushing at the back end and pulling at the front end, using hand, leg and an iron will to bring him into shape.

1. This shows Katie warming up. As you look at it, ask yourself, 'If I could remove this horse by magic from underneath the rider so that she dropped down onto the riding arena, how would she land on it?', and, 'What would happen to this rider if I cut the reins?'

Katie was obviously a rider who thought and cared a good deal about her work and her horse, but given the passivity and lack of muscle tone which I saw in her body, I was surprised to discover that she had been competing at such a high level. She said of herself that she had very little feel, and as the course went on, she admitted that she had found it extremely disappointing to discover that the horse who had once looked so promising and easy was in fact quite difficult for her to ride. She feels responsible for the fact that he has never consistently lived up to his true potential ('I suppose I've ruined him really'). There are tantalising moments, however: whenever she goes away on holiday, she leaves George with her trainer and by the time she returns, his carriage and movement are totally different. However, the inevitable happens, and over the next one or two weeks their work gradually deteriorates back into the state which is their mutual norm. Katie feels that her own lack of ability is responsible for this. Her experience is made all the more painful by the fact that she has a very sharp intellect and a clear theoretical understanding of the principles that underlie what *ought* to be happening.

When I first look at a rider, I ask myself several questions, which you can ask yourself too as you look at Figure 1. The first is: 'If I could remove this horse by magic from underneath the rider so that she dropped down onto the riding arena, how would she land on it?' The second is, 'What would happen to this rider if I cut the reins?' This photograph was taken as Katie was warming up, before I had intervened in any way, and it is typical of her overall balance. In answer to the first question, my senses tell me that she would land on her bottom, *and not on her feet*. You will see this over and over again with the riders who appear in these pages (Figures 13, 22 and 43 pages 66, 79 and 21) and also as you look around you at your riding colleagues. It is more than likely to be your own starting point as well. With Katie, though, the answer to the second question reveals how she is compensating for her lack of stability; for if we cut the reins, I think she might topple over backwards.

Not all riders attempt to solve the problems presented by their instability in the way that Katie has done – and it is probably better for their horses if they can find a way which does not involve the reins, even though it may require a strange set of balances and counter-balances within the body itself. The fundamental problem is that if the rider does not have her centre of gravity (slightly below the navel, and about half-way between the back and the front of the body) directly above her base of support, she cannot take responsibility for her own body weight. The fact that she would land on the arena on her backside and not on her feet is a demonstration of this. So, in effect, she hands over this responsibility to the horse: she becomes a much greater burden to him, and this inevitably hampers his carriage and movement. (It is bad enough carrying a rucksack on your back anyway, but have you ever tried to carry one that has been very badly packed? Having the bulk of the weight away from your spine, too low down or off to one side forces you to make compensations which can become back-breaking by the end of the day.) Only when the rider's body weight is directly above her base of support is she truly in balance, and this is what balance means: the ability to stay in this alignment on the horse and to make all the minute adjustments which are necessary when positioning onto a circle, changing the bend or riding the lateral movements – regardless of the pace you are in and regardless of any antics which the horse might get up to underneath you! This is no mean skill, but it is absolutely vital – a fundamental principle on which there can be no compromise.

However, Katie has an apparently very good reason for arranging her body in the way she has done: like every other rider, one of the first things that she ever learnt about riding was that she should push her heels down. As a result of this, she has pushed them down and forward, out of the correct shoulder/hip/heel vertical line which she herself believes to be the correct body alignment in walk, sitting trot and canter. The conflict, however, was not obvious to her until we began work in this session. For her and many others it is heightened by the fact that she has also been told that she must have her lower leg lying 'on the girth': but how can the rider have her body aligned with a vertical shoulder, hip and heel, *and* have her lower leg 'on the girth' at the same time? The two are mutually exclusive.

Whenever I begin work with a rider who is new to my ideas, we almost always have to talk through this dilemma, which I believe to be a good example of the inaccuracies and contradictions inherent in our riding dogma. The solution to the dilemma has become obvious to me in practice because the effects which I feel in myself and see in others when they bring their heel back under their hip are so profound: being able to take responsibility for one's own body weight has extremely far-reaching results. It is also helpful to look at the pictures of exemplary riders in some of the older riding texts, as well as in more modern ones. Think particularly of photographs you have seen of riders at the Spanish Riding School. They show this shoulder/hip/heel line beautifully, and if we could take their horses out from underneath them by magic, they would undoubtedly land on the riding arena on their feet, all in a neat little row! Each rider has his heels down, but they are distinctly *down and back*, rather than *down and forward* (see Figure 2). This is initially beyond the ability of the average rider (who has to begin by having the sole of her foot horizontal), and it is extremely difficult to maintain through the rigours of riding the various paces, etc.; but to substitute down and forward for down and back is a grave mistake which – because of its devastating effect on the rider's balance – creates many more problems than it cures. Perhaps the expression 'on the girth' originally referred to jumping position, where the foot is much nearer to the girth, with the heel down and forward. But very few teachers have clearly delineated the difference between the correct lower leg position for jumping and that for flatwork, which has certainly added to the confusion. I am not sure that 'on the girth' should not be taken with a certain amount of poetic licence, since it is in reality an impossibility, and the primary use of the expression is to make a distinction between the position of each leg when riding on a circle, where the outer one lies further back 'behind the girth'.

2. Riders from the Spanish Riding School demonstrate exemplary balance: their heels are down and back, instead of down and forward, and if their horses were removed from underneath them, they would all land on the riding arena on their feet. (*Bob Langrish*)

This theme is so important that we will come back to it with several of the other riders, but as I watched Katie working in there was another question in my mind, which this time I addressed directly to her. So I warned her that this might sound slightly strange, and then asked, 'Are you taking him, or is he taking you?' She immediately understood what I meant and told me that he was taking her. I often make my meaning clearer by offering the following analogies: when you ride a bicycle you push the pedals round, providing the power which drives it forward. But when you come to a steep downward slope, you might find that the bicycle speeds away from underneath you so that you cannot pedal fast enough to keep up. Then the bicycle takes you. I have had a similar sensation when working an electric sewing machine: if I suddenly press too hard on the foot pedal, it runs away with me so fast that I cannot feed the material through quickly enough. This is not dissimilar to the feeling you get when the horse takes you.

In essence, Katie's body position gave the horse responsibility for her weight, putting him in the position where he was taking her. Thus it rendered her reactive rather than causal. This means that with her body in this aligment, she inevitably becomes the *victim* of his chosen carriage rather than the cause of it. In fact, she has ended up in a posture which one of my old teachers used to call 'water-skiing'. George, in his way of taking her and becoming heavy in her hand, has fulfilled his part of the equation and become the motor boat – an essential part of every water-skier's equipment! He is so kind-hearted and calm that there is no danger involved in this – but with other horses there often is. Some people demonstrate this pattern by being run away with in walk, others in trot, and some at a flat-out gallop: the worst victims are ardent 'water-skiers', riding horses who are uptight and sensitive enough to become ardent motor boats (Margaret, whom you will meet in Lesson 7, had been terrified by precisely this). But on a more subtle level, Katie found herself powerless to influence her horse in the ways that she wanted – and she has experienced the inevitable frustrations. Gaining the influence she wanted to have requires a fundamental change in balance, which Katie initially found quite difficult physically, and rather a shock to both her physical and mental perceptions of 'right'.

I began my work by realigning Katie's body (see Figures 15 and 16 in Lesson 2 with Gail, where I talk about this in detail), and putting her stirrups up one hole, so that the angles in her hip and knee would be more acute. This usually makes it easier for the rider to make the change I want in the positioning of her lower leg. (There is more about this later too.) I then showed her what I believe to be the two most important elements in a good rider's bodily use: the 'pinch' and the 'bearing down' feeling. Figures 3 to 6 illustrate the pinch in my body. I usually explain it to riders by finding the bony projection at the top of each thigh and pressing into it. This is known as the greater trochanter of the femur, and it lies just on the outside of the thigh as it comes to the pelvis. To persuade the rider to take on the pinch feeling, I usually say,

3 and 4. Figure 3 shows the pinch feeling from the side, in contrast to Figure 4, which shows a natural standing posture with the knees slightly bent, as if on a horse. My finger-tips are resting on the greater trochanter of the femur: notice how the pelvis has come forward in Figure 3, making creases in the seat of my breeches and changing the angle of the thigh so that it is almost vertical.

'Imagine that there is a bolt passing through you just here, and that somebody is tightening up the nut which draws the two sides of you in closer together.' (Find the greater trochanter on yourself now, and imagine this as you make the movements of Figures 3 to 6 in front of a mirror.)

In Figure 7 I have my hands on Katie in a different way, which also encourages correct use of the muscles which lie underneath my hands, bringing them in towards the line where her thigh joins her pelvis. This was a surprise to her ('But I'm tightening my buttock muscles, surely this can't be right?'), and I assured her that the muscles involved in this are different from those you use if you simply tighten the buttocks. This does not involve the sensation of the bolt which is being tightened up, and does not involve

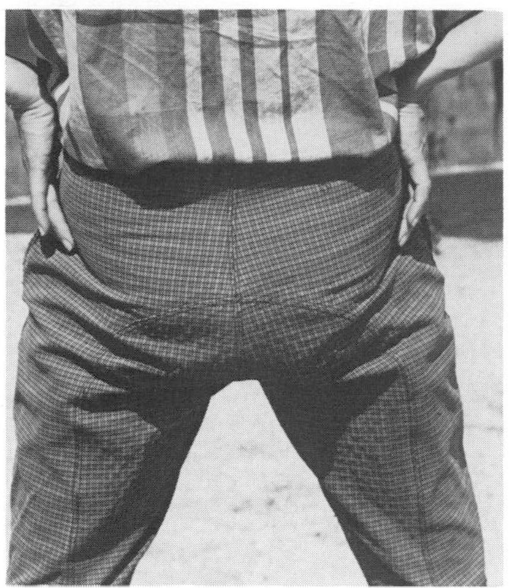

5 and 6. The pinch feeling in Figure 5 contrasts with the natural standing posture in Figure 6. Notice how the buttocks are drawn forward and in, making creases in my breeches. This muscular holding changes the texture of the buttock muscles, making them less spongy and more like putty. To demonstrate this to yourself, use your hands to give an impulse to your backside, and find out how it responds in each case. This difference will be much greater for women than it is for men, who naturally have about 35 per cent higher muscle tone.

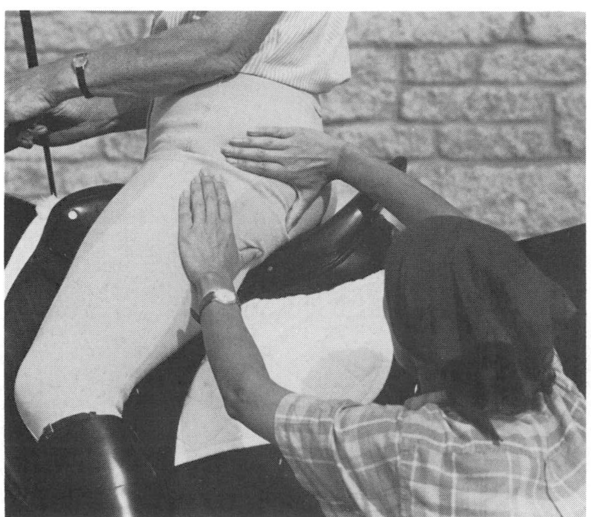

7. When the rider makes the pinch feeling, the line between the thigh and the backside becomes much more clearly defined, and you often see more creases appear in the rider's breeches. The muscles which lie underneath my hands feel as if they move in towards this line. You may understand the pinch feeling better if you get a friend to touch you like this, applying a gentle pressure towards the line.

the muscles of the outer thigh. (This is a mistake which people sometimes make: be sure that you can differentiate between the two when you practise the pinch feeling standing up.) I explained to Katie that we were simply changing the angle of her pelvis and increasing the tone in her muscles to bring it up to the level that a talented rider would have naturally. However, this idea did not sit comfortably with her, and her fears about being 'stiff' or 'tight' persisted for at least the next two days. She expressed these through many 'Yes, but . . . ,'s and I found it difficult to persuade her to put aside the responses of her intellect and try my suggestions anyway. Gradually she did, however, and she began to realise that there was a big payoff for this extra effort, which did indeed render her much more causal. But before this happened she wrote me some notes – which I asked each of the riders to do – in which she explained her predicament: 'This new seat is so completely different from what I've been taught before that I experienced conflict in mind and body during that first lesson.'

I then showed her the bearing down, and asked her to put her own hand on the front of her body just below her sternum. I said: 'Please forgive my bluntness, but I would like you to imagine that you were sitting on a toilet and that you wanted to pass your daily motion. What happens then to the muscle underneath your hand?' Katie felt, as most people do, that the muscle beneath her hand pressed outward, against her hand. Try this for yourself, and if it does not come naturally to you to firm up the muscles and press them outwards, practise until it does. In Figure 8, I have my hand against her body to feel the strength of this push. (I learn a good deal by feeling people's bodies like this and discovering how different each one is in its proportions and development. It is helpful to have a direct assessment of how strong or weak a rider's muscles

8. My hands are resting just below Katie's sternum, and also on her back at the same level. I am making sure that she does not hollow her back as she pushes out against my hand, and also that she does not round her back and push outwards at the back instead of the front. The back and the front of the body should remain as two parallel, vertical lines, with the muscles below the sternum pushing out against my hand at the front, and the long back muscles each side of the spine pushing out against my hand at the back. Both sets of muscles become more clearly defined: this is an example of isometric muscle use which stabilises the body.

9. Bearing down at the level of the top of the bottom segment of the rectus abdominus muscle, between the pubic bone and the navel: the push out of the muscles here is extremely important.

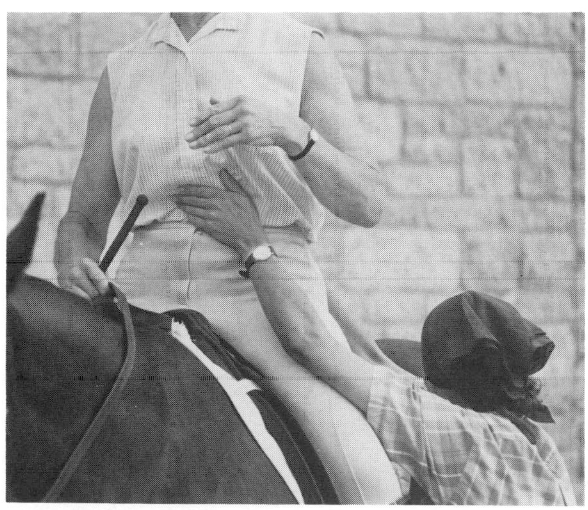

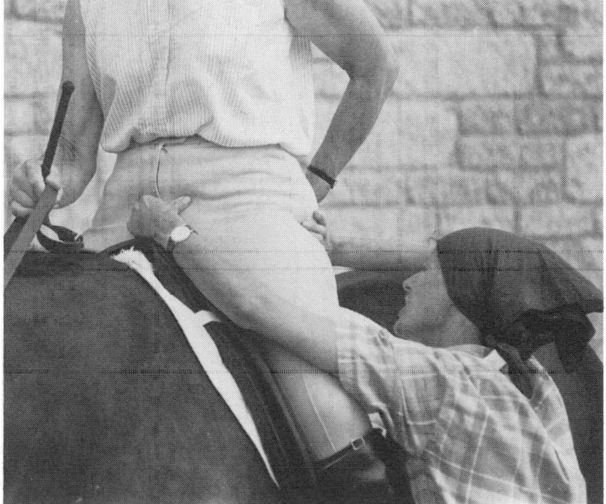

are, and how easy or difficult it will be for her to make the changes I am asking for. I also often ask the rider to feel the equivalent muscle on my body, so that she gets a comparison against which to gauge her own strength.)

In Figure 9 I have my hand against Katie's body much lower down, about half-way between her pubic bone and her navel – just below the level at which you might well have a small roll of fat. (Anatomically, this is the top of the bottom segment of the rectus abdominus muscle.) I also made her push out against my hand just here, since this is perhaps the most important element of the bearing down. Many women have likened it to having a baby (which is where the expression came from); but it is important to realise that it is just as much a push *forwards* as it is a push *down*.

As you attempt this now, sitting in your chair and reading this book, I imagine that your reaction might well be one of shock. This is a far cry from sitting relaxed in the way you probably thought you ought to, especially when it is done alongside the pinch feeling! It feels less horrific when it is actually done in movement, although a lot of people find it very difficult initially to pinch, bear down and breathe all at the same time. Usually they find that when they pinch, they automatically begin to pull the stomach in, and this in turn affects their breathing. I can assure you that there is no such thing as a good rider who does not pinch and bear down – even though she probably does not realise that she is doing it, and she certainly could not tell you about it. Interestingly, some of the best riders in the world are men who have a sizable gut, which they could not pull in even if they wanted to! If you are a woman who has spent her life pulling in her stomach, this is your opportunity to feel that you no longer have to. I hope you will not find the idea so appalling that you resist making the change which will probably have a more profound effect on your riding than anything else you will ever learn.

I then sent Katie out onto the track to walk her horse and to pinch, bear down, breathe (more of that in Lesson 7 with Margaret), and align her body all at the same time. Even this basic beginning is a difficult exercise in parallel processing which requires considerable brain power. Katie found the shoulder/hip/heel alignment so difficult that I had to walk along with her for a while, holding her thigh and foot in place so that they could not revert to their old familiar, more forward position. After a while they stayed there when I let go, but it was apparent to me that she would not sustain the change unless I also intervened to stop her using the rein as a counter-balance. Even though this was no longer necessary, it persisted as a habitual response in her body, which was so used to 'water-skiing'. It undermined our rebalancing, causing her to fall – hand and body backwards, leg forwards – into her old position.

Figure 10 shows me with my hand on Katie's hand, and also on the rein closer to the bit ring, so that I could assess how strong her hold on the rein was. As I had thought, there was a continual tension in the muscles in her lower arm, meaning that she was continually pulling against the horse – who was also, not surprisingly, continually pulling against her. One of Katie's early statements to me was about how heavy he tended to become in her hand, but I do not think she was fully aware of the part that she was playing in this, for (as I used to hate being told by my riding teachers) 'It takes two to pull,' and if the rider acts like a water-skier, she unwittingly forces the horse to pull her along.

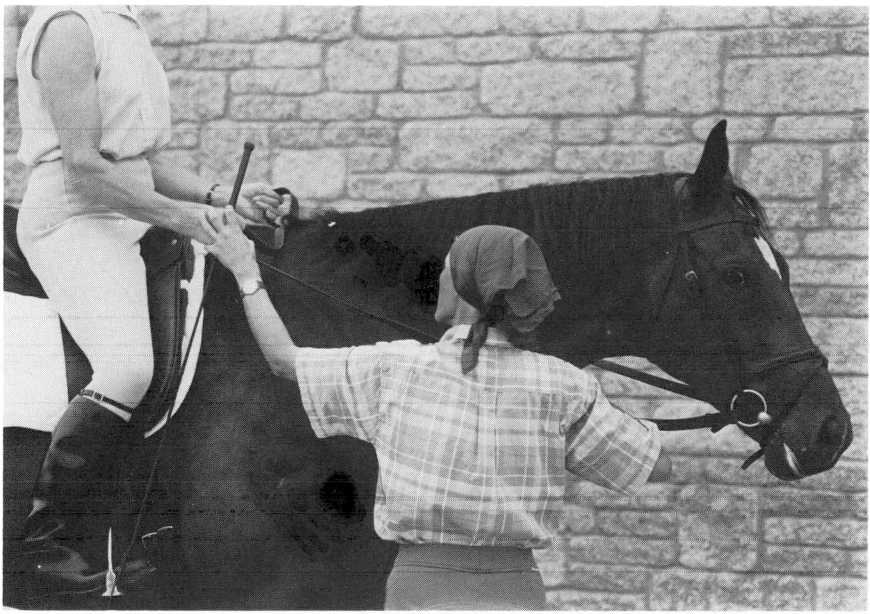

10. Putting my hands here enables me to assess the tension in Katie's lower arm, and to show her what it feels like to resist passively by closing her fingers without tightening her arm muscles and drawing her hand backwards. She also becomes able to assess the correct length for the reins, and to give the hand forward when the horse needs more rein.

Many years ago, I used to find that however much I tried not to pull, it seemed impossible to stop myself; but when I discovered about bearing down I had an instant solution to my problem. Releasing the pull back in my stomach allowed me to release the pull back in my hand; in some way that I still do not completely understand, they are inextricably connected. So I asked Katie actively to bear down, and then made sure that she was willing to give the hand forward should I (the horse) ask for more rein. I also wanted her to understand how to resist passively if necessary, holding her hand in place without any muscle pull in her arms. Whenever you feel your arm muscles tighten, it is a sure sign that something has already gone wrong with your pelvic positioning, and that you have already become reactive. The hand is always simply put in place, with no backward muscle pull, and then the contact is created by having the reins just the right length. If you feel that you have to draw your hand backwards to make a contact, your reins are too long.

With her body now rearranged, Katie produced the walk in Figure 11. She certainly would not fall backwards if we cut the

11. Katie is very nearly in balance over her feet, which still need to come slightly further back to give her a genuine shoulder/hip/heel vertical line. However, freed from the tension in her lower arm, she is no longer counter-balancing on the rein. To assess how she is doing, ask yourself the questions you asked in Figure 1.

reins, and with any luck she would land on the riding arena on her feet should we whisk her horse out from underneath her. Without even focussing on it, or 'asking' for it (a term of which I am highly

12. Some nice trot work, which (as far as we can see from this angle) shows Katie in balance above her feet. Her horse has responded by offering a very nice carriage in the seeking reflexes.

suspicious), she has produced a tremendous change in her horse. His new carriage has naturally come about as a response to the change in *her* carriage – they have both 'completed the circuit'.

Figure 12 shows very similar work in trot, with George beginning to reach beautifully down into the rein, showing a posture in which his back is seeking contact with her seat, his sides are seeking contact with her leg, and his mouth is seeking contact with the rein. I call these 'the seeking reflexes'; they underpin all correct work and lead both horse and rider into the spiral of increasing ease. They are the direct opposite of 'the cramping reflexes', in which the horse takes his back, his sides, and often his mouth, *away* from contact with the rider's seat, leg and hand – a response which is likely to take both of them further into 'the spiral of increasing tension'.

I believe that the rider essentially has two choices: either she advances her stomach towards her hand – the push forward of the bearing down – or she draws her hand back towards her stomach. She may know that she should not pull back, she may try her heart out not to, and she might shed tears of grief about it, but the mechanics of her situation demand that she has to pull back. If the stomach is retracting backwards, the whole pelvis is drawn backwards, so even though the horse may be going forwards, the rider is not! At sitting trot this effect is particularly devastating: if you have ever had lessons on the lunge, I am sure that you found it relatively easy to sit well as long as you could hold onto the front of the saddle. But what happened when you let go? Ninety per cent of riders begin to bump, and they gradually bump their way towards the back of the saddle – almost as if the horse moved forward underneath them but they stayed in the same place, going up and down instead! It would be ridiculous to think of somebody whose bumping carried them *forward* in the saddle: the direction is always backwards.

I conclude from this that a force is required to hold the rider's backside towards the front of the saddle as the horse moves forward underneath her. When holding the saddle, this force is provided by the arm, but all too often in normal riding, people unknowingly provide it – as Katie did – through supporting themselves on the rein. To sit really well and to become causal, however, the rider has to provide the equivalent force as a push from the back towards the front *within the body itself* – and the bearing down provides this, supported by some other important elements which I shall explain in later lessons (especially Lesson 8). I am convinced that whoever first said that the rider should 'push' was actually talking about bearing down. Contrary to popular opinion, the correct 'push' is not a push down into the horse's back, or a shoving of the seat backwards and forwards in the saddle. It is a 'push' within the body itself.

In *Ride With Your Mind* I wrote at length about the effect which a reactive rider has on the horse as he retracts his body into 'the cramping reflexes'. His carriage, and the mechanism of his movement, are totally different from that shown by the horse who *seeks* this contact with the rider's backside, leg and hand – drawing his body up and stretching his top-line into the correct form (there is more detail on this in Lessons 7 and 8 with Margaret and Carol). The difference between Figures 1 and 12 illustrates this very well, as do the photographs in many of the other lessons (see Figures 13 and 21, 22 and 27, 29 and 35, 37 and 38, 42 and 45, 53 and 55). Some people would look at Figure 1 and say: 'This is not a dressage horse,' whilst they would look at Figure 12 and say: 'Aha! now *this* is a dressage horse!' The point I wish to make, however, is that they are both the same horse, ridden by the same rider, using a totally different technique in each case: furthermore, this transformation was made within one forty-five-minute lesson.

In developing my ideas over the last twelve years, I have worked with riders and horses of all descriptions, and, in the early days in particular, many of them did not look like very promising candidates for reform! But having seen so many ugly ducklings turn themselves into swans, I have total faith that this transformation is possible for every rider and for every horse (barring physical injury), regardless of make and shape. Whilst it is very nice to work with riders who have beautiful horses with superb conformation and powerful movement, this is not necessary for learning, or for enjoying the feeling of a horse working well. Each horse has his own personal best, in which he utilises the mechanism of correct movement regardless of his make and shape. When this happens, he will literally change shape so that he both looks and feels like 'a dressage horse' – whether he be an eventer, a cob or some kind of badly-put-together mongrel. When you develop the skill to draw this out of him, you will probably find that you are in for the most delightful surprise . . . particularly if you own the mongrel, or are consistently let down by your dressage performance, or if, like Katie, you bemoan the disappearance of a beauty which you have only occasionally glimpsed.

Only about three days after this first lesson did Katie begin really to register the delightful surprise which was already rightfully hers. On this first day she admitted with some bewilderment that she did, much to her surprise, feel better balanced in rising trot. But still she could not get her brain to accept that these changes, which felt so very strange, could perhaps be justified: the hardest thing for her was to keep her lower leg in place, and I kept reminding her to think of bringing her knee down and her heel back, so that she kept feeling as if her heel was coming *back and up* instead of forward and down. You can see from the photographs that her heel was still on or below the level of her toe, but to her feel sense it seemed as if it was up, and that she was balancing on tiptoe. Her body was responding as bodies always do, registering the *difference* between this and her old way, and not giving her an absolute measurement. It took a session with my video camera to convince her of this effect, which also floors many other riders. I often tell people that their feel sense will register a change as being at least ten times greater than it looks – and very often they respond by saying, 'It's not times ten, it's at least times fifty!' (Think of the sensation you get when you lose a filling, or develop an ulcer in your mouth. Your tongue – which is particularly rich in nerve endings – convinces you that there is some enormous blemish. But when you look in the mirror you realise how tiny it really is!) One of the major reasons why so many riders remain stuck on a plateau is because the change they need to make feels *times fifty* greater than they expect it to be – and the accompanying sense of disorientation is so profound that, of course, they never make it. This could well be one of the limiting factors on the progress which *you* make in working with this book.

Katie found it helpful to think of making these corrections in a certain order: firstly she had to make the pinch, then check the alignment of her lower leg, then check that she could lighten her hand. She did not include the bearing down in her list, but this is a statement about how difficult she found it to focus on everything, rather than a statement about its relative importance. (In fact, it probably says more about how particularly alien and difficult this feeling was in her body.) Because I knew that her brain was already in overload, I let this be during our first lesson. The corrections gave her some discomfort in her right hip, which she felt was just some unused muscles registering unfamiliarity – what I call 'good pain', rather than 'bad pain' which is potentially damaging. Over the next three days we were able to begin working on her asymmetry: she had less difficulty accepting my input here, perhaps because she already knew from her trainer at home that her right hip was out of place, and she was pleased to discover that she now had something more that she could do about it. We did a little sitting trot in which she was less successful: she admitted that in her usual seat she felt that she was 'floating above the horse's back', and the first step of making more contact with it and feeling its movement was not a pleasant one for her! She did not go through the next barrier of pushing forward enough to mould onto the movement of the trot and become causal on top of it, so I suspect that she will probably revert to her old way now that she is back at home. However, if she can take what she has learnt about the pinch and the bearing down into sitting trot, this will undoubtedly have a great effect.

On the fourth and last day of the course, Katie told me that the two things she felt she had gained most were the realisation that she had to concentrate 100 per cent of the time instead of just before she rode a movement. She also gained the ability to start making many more discriminations for herself. Previously, she had been dependent on her trainer to tell her that the horse was not bent correctly or that she was out of balance or sitting crooked. Given how unaware Katie was of her body and its interaction with the horse, it is not surprising that she had been so in need of feedback from an outside observer – and I have to say that if I, personally, had so little sense of what I and the horse were doing, I would dread the thought of having to ride the movements of a Medium test! Katie, perhaps, had never realised how different her experience could have been: although she knew that something was missing, she was in the paralysing situation where she did not know what it was that she did not know.

Some riders find it much more difficult than others to accept new ideas, and this was certainly not easy for Katie. She told me that she felt the need to question everything in order to make sure that she really understood. Like most riders, she had been taught many different things in her day and, understandably, she had gradually become more sceptical. When I am training teachers, I often make an analogy between people's receptivity and the game 'post box', in which young children have to fit coloured shapes into holes in the lid of a small plastic post box. Some people will do their utmost to make the shapes that you give them fit; others need exactly the right-shaped piece before they will accept what you say. Of course, the latter are much more difficult to teach, and the responsibility to find the right-shaped piece lies with the teacher – not the pupil.

When I meet a rider who is as keen as Katie to argue a point theoretically, I usually find that she is assessing different schools of thought through an *intellectual* process, and not through her body perceptions. She is thinking about riding, instead of feeling the horse – who will himself tell her which of these many alternatives is right. *When you put the right key in the right lock you open the door*, and the horse will leave you in no doubt about which the right key is – although, as Katie and I agreed, this is much easier when his response is instantaneous. To wait even a few minutes for it can be extremely hard! But the experience of feeling him change puts an immediate stop to arguments like, 'So and so says in this book that . . . and my trainer always tells me that . . . It seems that what you are saying contradicts the theory that . . .'. It creates a knowingness which encompasses both body and mind and is beyond dispute.

Lesson 2

Gail: The Leg Aids, Rising Trot and the Transitions

Gail arrived for her lesson with the kind of tale of woe that I hear all too often. Her horse, Frankie, is a fifteen-year-old mare, a thoroughbred/Irish cross who is just over 16 hands. Gail has owned her for six years, and bought her after she had been riding for only two years. Frankie had previously competed at club level in dressage, show jumping and eventing, but had done very little in the two years before Gail bought her. It took Gail quite some time to improve her own riding enough to feel that she had some influence over a rather fat, stiff Frankie, but they gradually progressed enough to be able to do club-level competition with some success. However, about three years ago, Gail had a bad fall in which she knocked herself out and damaged her back and neck. As a consequence, she was unable to ride for four months.

When Gail brought Frankie back into light work, she rode wearing a supportive collar round her neck. After some time, however, she decided to put the mare in foal, but this was not successful, so Frankie had a year off. This has been followed by another unsuccessful attempt to get her in foal this year. Gail did some initial fittening work with Frankie before she went to stud, but once there, she had to have two weeks of box rest whilst she was treated for an infection. Between then and our lesson Gail had given her three weeks' work – the first serious work they had done together for three years.

The first thing that struck me as they warmed up was how lazy Frankie was, and how hard Gail was working – kicking and shoving and putting in tremendous effort which achieved almost no result. That Frankie should be so lazy is perhaps not surprising given her history, but Gail had fallen head first into the trap which lazy horses set for their riders – and undoubtedly she was due to start sweating an awful lot sooner than Frankie! Their walk was reminiscent of a funeral march and the trot was little more than a shuffle. In her desperation, Gail was practically throwing herself around: Figure 13 shows what was typically happening in walk and Figure 14 shows one of her worst moments in trot. In both cases, if we could whisk her horse out from underneath her, she would undoubtedly land on the arena on her backside. But – amazingly, given what has happened in Figure 14 – she has managed not to grab the rein as a compensation for her inability to support her own weight.

My starting point was to rearrange Gail's body in the same way

13. Gail is riding in walk, early on in the lesson. The pronounced lean back that you see in her body was accompanied by very large movements in her seat. Notice also how she is using her leg.

14. This was not a typical moment in Gail's trot, but it shows what can happen when the rider is not well balanced over the knee and foot.

that I did Katie's, bringing her legs up over the front of the saddle, as you can see in Figure 15, and asking her to scoop her backside more underneath her so that it came further forward in the saddle. (Lifting the backside up to bring it forward without bringing the legs forward does not work so well, as nine times out of ten the rider puts it back down in the saddle in exactly the same place as it started from!) I then took hold of Gail's leg and brought it back down into place, as in Figure 16. This is well worth doing whenever you begin a session – but be sure that your horse will be sensible, or that you have someone to hold him for you. When you bring your leg back into place, grab hold of your thigh from the underneath so that you pull the bulk of the hamstring muscles around to the back, leaving a much thinner layer of flesh (the adductor muscles) lying against the saddle. This is a wonderful feeling, which gives you a much clearer contact with the horse's side, which is vital if the thigh muscles are to work correctly. However, not many people find that their leg automatically stays here, and you may have to train your muscles over quite a prolonged period of time by pulling them round to the back again at regular intervals.

I then taught Gail about the pinch, and about bearing down. These were much easier for her than they had been for Katie. My first priority was to help her to use them and her correct body alignment to change her relationship with Frankie. Instead of Frankie being the brains in their relationship and Gail being the brawn, I wanted them to reverse roles. In shoving her seat backwards and forwards in the saddle, Gail had done what practically every rider instinctively does when she becomes desperate about sending the horse forward. Unfortunately, many people believe that this instinctive response is the correct one; but I believe that they have misinterpreted the influence of the continental riders who have talked about 'the driving seat' or about 'using the back'.

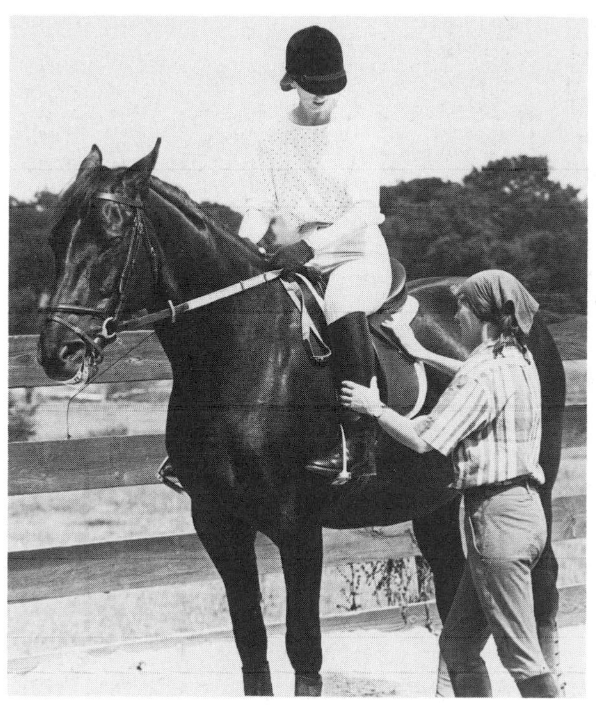

As an experiment, exaggerate this 'driving' action of the seat when you next ride your horse and find out how he responds. It may surprise you to discover that most horses slow down, or even grind to a halt! Horses are much happier when the rider sits *still* and the driving aids come predominantly from the leg. (See Lesson 6 with Sarah for a much fuller understanding of this.) In effect, Gail was using her leg to work against the resistance which she was simultaneously creating through the over-use of her seat: this wastes energy – just like treading on the brake and the accelerator both at the same time. Furthermore, the use of Gail's leg was so monotonous and predictable that it had become like background music to Frankie and she had 'switched off' to it. Since Frankie knew that Gail was not about to use her stick to back up her leg aids, she knew that there was no price to be paid for not obeying. In effect, Frankie and Gail had an unspoken agreement that it was fine for Gail to continue to shove and kick, and equally fine for Frankie not to respond. I am tempted to conclude that Frankie was demonstrating far more common sense than her rider!

Firstly, I showed Gail how to use her leg so that it would be effective. In their desperation, many riders attempt to use strength not just with the seat but also with the leg, so that the aid becomes a prolonged forceful squeeze against the horse's side. Some riders even think that they should squeeze all the time. Over recent years, 'squeeze' has become a part of our everyday vocabulary, and the idea of 'kick' has become thoroughly discredited. In my childhood,

15. Gail has brought both of her legs right up over the front of the saddle – just as you do when tightening the girth. In this position, it is easy to scoop the backside more underneath you.

16. I have taken hold of Gail's thigh from the underneath, pulling the hamstring muscles around to the back and bringing the leg slightly further back than it will eventually sit. Then I can slide it onto the saddle from the back towards the front, keeping the bulky thigh muscles out of the way. It is important that the rider keeps her pelvis in place throughout this manoeuvre, so that she does not hollow her back. If you help somebody else by doing this, be firm, but respectful of her physical limitations!

'kick' was the norm, and although I am not sure where 'squeeze' originated, I suspect that it was a part of the general move away from old-fashioned army teaching and ideas. However, if you look at the way in which good dressage riders use their legs, you will see that they do not squeeze, they *touch*. When a sharper aid is required, the touch becomes a slap, with the leg rebounding as soon as it touches the horse's side. In the stronger aid, the leg makes a particular sound, a 'thunk', which only happens when the calf muscles are under stretch and the whole lower leg acts as one unit – like a stretched elastic band rather than a wavy one.

To help riders get the idea of this, I begin by holding the inside of their leg and their foot as I ask them to give an aid. By the way they squash my hand, I can assess how they use their leg naturally. Then, I touch the outside of their calf, firstly in the way that they touched me, and secondly in the way that I want them to touch the horse – with a slap, and not a squeeze or a nudge. This makes the contrast between the two leg aids very clear to them. Then, to help them make the aid more effective, I often suggest that they think of the whole of the calf and foot as like a wooden boot tree within their boot. Then there can be no twisting of the foot outwards from the ankle or drawing of the leg back and up. (You can see this happening in Figure 13.) Instead, the whole of the lower leg acts quickly, remaining independent of the rest of the body so that nothing from the knee up is affected. The rider who uses a squeeze is rarely able to maintain this independence – particularly when her aid becomes prolonged and forceful – but it is vital that the leg aid utilises a mechanism which offers no disturbance to the rider's sitting and the horse's back.

If the rider is to maintain credibility with the horse, it is very important that she does *not* use her legs when he is already moving impulsively, otherwise she falls straight back into the background-music syndrome. The leg must be used sparingly, so that the horse can differentiate between the times when the rider effectively says, 'This is OK,' when she should leave him be, and the times when she says, 'This is not OK,' and she takes action. When a rider has spent years squeezing the horse at every stride, she usually does it on 'automatic pilot'. (Interestingly, the rider perceives the problem as being the horse's laziness; but in reality, each of them is just as 'switched off' as the other, and there will be no change from the horse until there is change from the rider.) It requires constant conscious attention for the rider to *stop* herself from using her leg, and this is usually much more difficult for her than learning the new leg aid.

It is remarkable how easily the horse who is naturally lazy lulls the rider into over-using her leg, so that the agreement 'leg means go' becomes negotiable. Only when this is *unequivocal* can the leg maintain its effectiveness, and the horse must know that the rider will back it up with stronger measures if necessary. Firstly, think of using a touch, and then if that does not work a slap. (Trainer Baron Von Blixen-Finecke calls the extreme version of this 'the penalty kick'!) If that does not work, you need your stick. Only when *you* know you mean business, and the horse knows that you mean business, will your legs have any effect: if you use the leg you have to mean it, and conversely if you do not mean it, do not use it. Otherwise, you will train your horse to be dead to the leg.

Thinking like this did indeed help Gail to make the change I wanted. She did not find it easy to stop herself from shoving and squeezing too much, but she was not as reluctant as many people, for whom 'kick' seems like an unwelcome return to their Pony Club days. I often find myself assuring them that this crude version of the aid can be refined to the degree that it becomes practically invisible. Its effectiveness is such that Frankie suddenly found herself at the receiving end of an unwelcome surprise, and she could no longer maintain her position as the brains of the partnership; despite her initial unwillingness, she was forced to become the brawn! Gail's body alignment was, however, still rather precarious, and I realised that she was under several other important misconceptions.

Figure 17 shows the way in which Gail's leg was lying, with her knee well away from the saddle and her calf rather firmly against

17 and 18. Gail's calf lies very snugly by the horse's side in Figure 17, but her knee is rather loose. Compare the amount of the knee patch on her breeches which is visible in each picture. Gail has a better contact with her calf in Figure 18 than you might expect, considering the change she has made in her knee and thigh. However, I am not happy about the way she has rounded her ankle outwards (see the jumping lesson for more about this), and the correction for this lies in getting a better inward rotation of the leg from the hip joint.

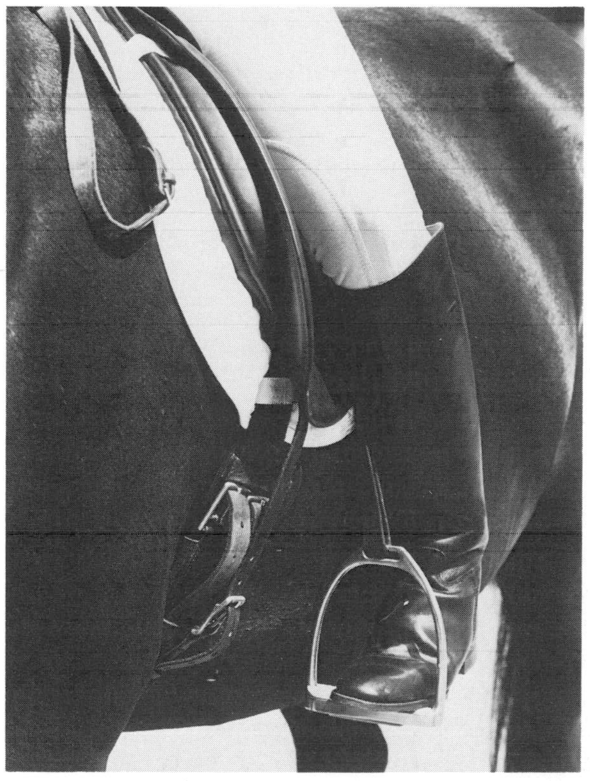

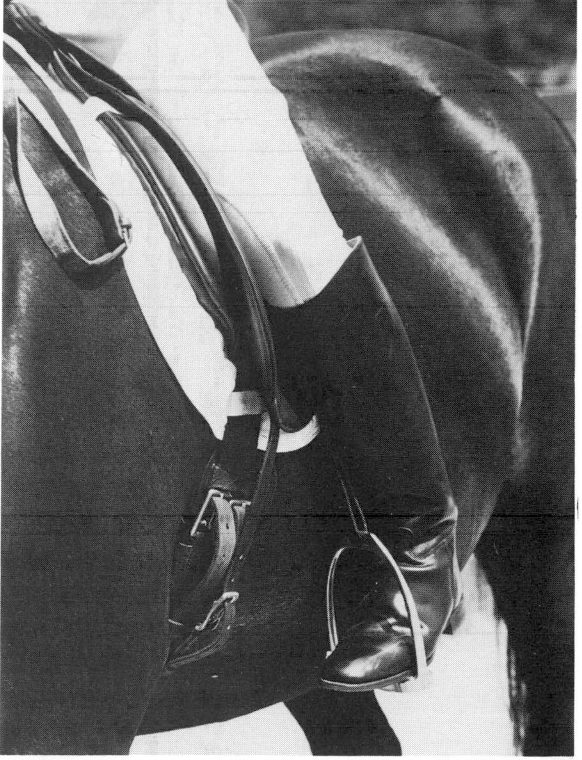

the horse's side. Her previous teachers had told her: 'Relax your leg. Take your knee off the saddle,' which is another modern-day response to the old army dictum of 'grip with your knees'. However, I have yet to see a top class dressage rider who does not have the knee lying on, or at least much closer, to the saddle, as Gail's is in Figure 18. (Sometimes it is not possible to get the knee actually on the saddle flap. This completely depends on the design of your saddle, the length of your thigh and whether the saddle fits you correctly.) So I persuaded Gail to put her thigh and knee much more closely onto the saddle, even if this meant that her calf was not so close to the horse's side. Over time, it will become easier for her to get a whole-legged contact with the horse: the idea of having a little gap in the hip, knee and ankle joints is important here, and we will come back to this in Lesson 8 with Carol. But if contact with either the thigh or the calf has to be sacrificed in the meanwhile, I am sure that the calf should be the one to go.

To help Gail to understand the correct relationship of the knee to the saddle, I used the following image: 'Imagine that there was a little hook lying on the bony part of the inside of each knee, hooking onto the ends of an iron bar which passes through the horse's belly. This holds the knee in place so that it cannot move; but it does not act in the same way as a piece of elastic, which would pull the knees inwards and create the wrong type of 'grip'. The little hooks enable the knee to become a stable *anchor point* for the pelvis. Without this kind of stability, the body is too prone to the kind of mishap that has happened in Figure 14.

The rider's thigh muscles can work in one of two ways. Either the pelvis is the fixed point, and the muscles contract to move the knee (this happens when you stand on one leg and swing the other), or the knee acts as the fixed point, and the muscles contract to move the pelvis (which happens when you get up from a chair). In riding, if the pelvis acts as the fixed point and the knee acts as the mobile point, the thigh becomes wobbly and the knee tends to come up. But if *the knee acts as the fixed point and the pelvis acts as the mobile point*, the thigh is pulled down around the horse and the body becomes much more stable. The pelvis is also free to make the subtle movements which are required in correct sitting, so that the rider can 'go with' the horse and change her positioning for circle left, circle right, the lateral movements or a transition.

As long as this structure is in play, riders in sitting trot get away with having a rather wobbly lower leg – in which the knee is the fixed point and the ankle is the mobile point. But in really good sitting *the ankle acts as the fixed point for the knee*, which in turn acts as the fixed point for the pelvis, stabilising the whole leg and offering great stillness and control. Both thigh and calf muscles then act like stretched elastic bands which are fixed at both ends (remember, however, that elastic bands come under tension by pulling their ends apart, whereas muscles come under tension when their fibres shorten, drawing the two ends closer together). There is a sense of weightedness in the way the legs hang – the German Master Seunig once said that they should be like 'wet towels'! However, this is a tremendous demand on the muscles: it is a great deal easier for us to use the pelvis as the still point and the lighter, more mobile parts of the body as the moving points. If the muscles work the other way round, the little, lightweight, mobile parts are responsible for anchoring the big, bulky, heavy parts. We rarely do this in everyday life and very few people naturally stumble across this way of using the muscles. But even if the vast majority of people knew what they were supposed to be doing, it would be no surprise to find that they did not immediately have the muscle power and control to do it! The answer is to maintain this way of working for short periods of time, resting in between whiles until your strength improves.

Correct use of the thigh and calf muscles is one of the first things I set out to teach, and rising trot is the best medium in which to teach it. It is in rising trot and walk that the rider first begins to understand how her body should work, and how it interacts with the horse. Her neurology is given a 'blueprint' from which it can work in more taxing situations. This is why I initially place so much emphasis on slow work. Later, when her horse's back is carrying her well, the rider can take what she has learnt into sitting trot and canter. With her knee and her thigh muscles well in place, Gail was getting much closer to maintaining the correct body alignment and to being an effective rider – but there were still several problems. She was under the impression that her upper body was supposed to be upright in the rising trot, and this was one of the major reasons why she tended to come behind the movement. Also, every time she rose out of the saddle her lower leg stayed fairly well in place, but every time she sat again, it shot forward. (Compare this with Sarah's rise in Figure 43. Her lower leg came forward on the rise rather than the sit. Which does yours do?)

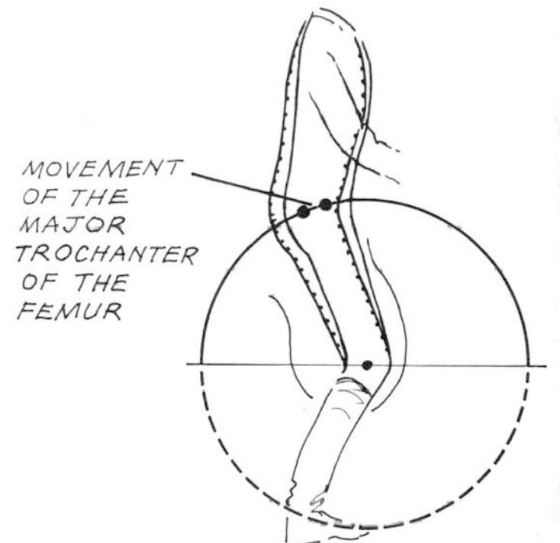

Diagram 3. The mechanism of the rise. The rider's lower leg serves to stabilise her, and movement occurs only from the knee up. The knee acts as the centre point of a circle and the thigh as a radius of that circle. The pelvis then moves on a small arc of the circle. This is like an inverted pendulum. Notice how the angle of the upper body changes but how the shoulders barely move.

I asked Gail to put her stirrups up one hole – just as I did with Katie – to help her to stabilise her lower leg. In Figures 19 and 20 I have asked her to do the rising-trot movement standing still, and I am holding her knee and ankle to check that they are functioning correctly. To understand the mechanism of the rise, think of the knee as the centre of a circle and the thigh as a radius of that circle (see Diagram 3). The pelvic movement is then forward and back along a small arc on the circumference of that circle. This means that the pelvis does not go *up*, but moves *forwards* towards the pommel, coming almost underneath the shoulders, which barely move. Each rise brings the rider towards the vertical; and as she sits, the pelvis moves *backwards* so that it comes behind the shoulders and the upper body is inclined forward. Her lower leg remains completely still throughout the movement. But many people straighten their knee as they rise, pushing harder against the stirrup and displacing their foot forward. Others, like Gail, displace the foot forward on the *sit*, when they should instead just bend the knee. Either way, their muscle system loses its power, and their foot cannot provide a stable base of

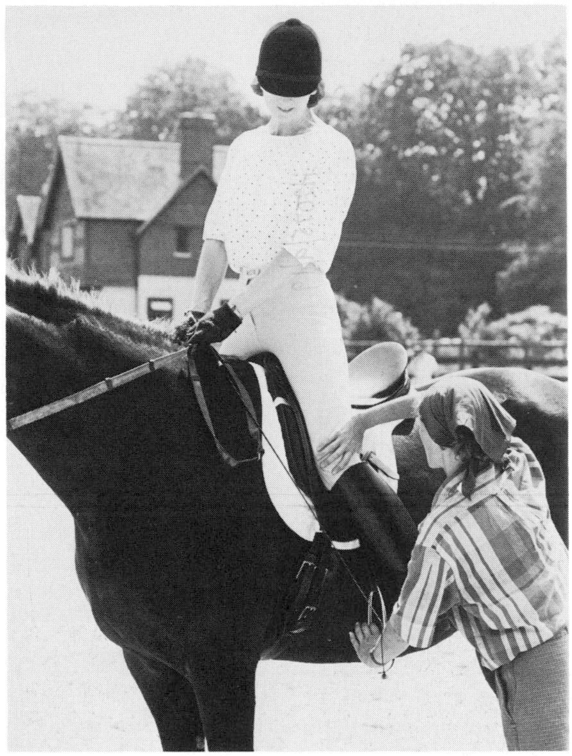

19 and 20. I have my hands on Gail's knee and foot, making sure that they work correctly as she rises and sits. In Figure 19 I am emphasising the way in which the knee cap must point more down as she rises, with her foot staying back underneath her, so that she feels as if her weight passes down through her thigh and knee towards the ground. In Figure 20, I am making sure that her foot stays back underneath her as she sits, keeping in place whilst she bends her knee.

support throughout the movement, acting as the anchor point for the knee. As a result, the rider loses control of her body weight, and on landing she thumps down into the saddle.

I cannot overestimate the importance of this correct mechanism for the rise, and I have been known to spend up to twenty minutes of a lesson helping the rider to get it right in halt! Experienced riders are often horror-stricken by this, but once they have 'got it' they understand why I was being so insistent. When they are in trot again, I make them fine-tune the movement by asking these test questions: 'How would you land on the riding arena if we could take your horse out from underneath you?' and, 'Would you balance on a diving board?' This second question is my favourite: the rider should be balanced over the stirrup as if it were the edge of a diving board and she was standing on it preparing to do a backward dive. When the heel is *down and back*, our diver/rider can be in perfect balance, but as soon as she pushes the heel down and forward, she catapults herself into the water. Most people can instantly diagnose when they are about to fall off backwards, and they usually find the thought of this so horrible that they become very determined to hold the correct alignment!

Gail was now beginning to get the measure of Frankie and of her own balance, but she was also starting to experience the discomfort and disorientation which go hand-in-hand with these profound changes. She felt as if she was gripping with her thighs and knees, tipping forward and riding with her heels up. Again, I reassured her that her body was simply registering differences and not giving her absolute measurements. If I had had access to a mirror I could have proved this to her, but without one it is often difficult for the rider to believe me! The worst design fault in the human body is, I think, its lack of a built-in spirit level. This means that we have no instinctive knowledge of vertical, and can veer off it by leaning too far forward, too far back and/or off to one side. You only have to look at people walking along the street to see how common this is! Gail was correct in her perception that she was now leaning forward, but her bodily sensations were telling her that the lean was very much greater than it actually was.

By now Frankie was much more responsive to the leg, and her trot was much more impulsive (see Figure 21), but this created two new problems for Gail. Firstly, she was so determined to maintain impulsion that she was over-doing her rise and thrusting her pelvis

21. Frankie's trot is much more impulsive and Gail has a great deal more body control. Although Frankie is not yet 'on the bit', her carriage has improved enormously from that shown in Figures 13 and 14, and she is beginning to come into the seeking reflexes. Gail's outside leg could be slightly further back behind the girth, but if we could whisk Frankie out from underneath her, I think she would land on the riding arena on her feet.

too far out of the saddle. This happens very often, and I find myself telling riders that it is the horse who is supposed to have the impulsion, whilst they remain cool and calm! Gail had become so fast and furious that she had lost control of the tempo, i.e. the speed of the horse's steps. In extreme cases of this, the horse has to run along extremely fast in order to keep up with the speed of the rider's up-down! However, few people in this situation realise that *they* are creating what appears to be the horse's impetuousness. It is always so much easier to blame the horse than it is to acknowledge the problem as one's own.

The second difficulty arose whenever Gail regained control of her rise (there is more about how to do this in Lesson 5 with Janet). For when Frankie's steps slowed down, she slowed *too much*, losing impulsion very quickly and forcing Gail to use her leg. Gail was unused to Frankie's new responsiveness, so she tended to slap too hard, and Frankie responded with such gusto that she accelerated out from underneath her, speeding up her steps again! The trot took on a 'start – stop – start – stop' quality, with Frankie reacting strongly to all of Gail's rather unrefined aids, regardless of whether they were intended to maintain the tempo or to send her forward. In this stage of the rider's learning, horses typically respond in this way: they are happy either to go fast, taking short, quick steps, or to slow down their rate of stepping whilst also losing power. The trot becomes either a run or a shuffle, and it is hard for the rider to stabilise it, creating an athletic gait between the two extremes. The key to this lies in learning to *keep thinking about the tempo whilst sending the horse forward*, and to *keep sending the horse forward whilst thinking about the tempo*. It is much easier to think only of 'go' or 'slow', without having every aid include its opposite, and I regard this as one of the watersheds which separates the rider who is in reality a passenger from the one who is actually riding. Few horses naturally volunteer to maintain impulsion as they take a slower step or to maintain the slowness of the tempo as they make a bigger, more powerful one. The rider has to extract from the horse much more effort and athleticism than he naturally wants to offer.

The difficulty of this is compounded by the fact that the 'start – stop' trot is so tricky to ride and the rider is easily thrown around by it. Each time Frankie decelerated, Gail held her balance quite well and did not tip forward as many other riders would have done. (Had she done this, I would have suggested that she thought of her thigh bones being like solid, strong iron bars, which could act like buffers.) But when Frankie accelerated in response to Gail's driving aids, Gail was 'left behind'; her foot shot forward and her upper body fell back, throwing her back into her old balance so that she landed in the saddle with a thump which was not appreciated by Frankie. In effect, it was her reward for obeying Gail's leg aid and going forward from it, so it was extremely important that Gail learnt to counteract this tendency. Many riders fall back onto the horse's back like this when they use their leg or ask for an upward transition. This is one of the few things which can make me quite angry (on the horse's behalf); for why should the horse go forward when he knows that this will be the result?

I explained to Gail that whenever Frankie accelerated suddenly, it was just as if she (Gail) were standing on a rug which was being pulled out from underneath her feet. Unless she was prepared, she would topple over backwards – just as she was now doing on her horse. So whenever she asked Frankie to go forward, she had to be ready to 'go with' her. This requires the equivalent of doing a little jump which would hold her upright on the rug. It is hard for the mind to work out how to do this; but the mental effort is wasted, for in practice the body instinctively knows how to hold itself in place and the secret lies in *being prepared*.

The trot which Gail had produced in Figure 21 was a vast improvement from her starting point in Figure 14. Although the circuit is not yet complete, there is much more energy flowing around it, which is an important first step. On the next day she did even better, and Frankie showed some genuine work in the seeking reflexes. Gail also rode some walk to halt transitions. I regard these as the prototype for all other downward transitions, and I use them to imprint the right pattern into the rider's neurology. So until she has mastered walk to halt, and mastered the art of riding her horse in good carriage, I never expect the rest of her downward transitions to be good. Gail found that she tended to lean back, push her feet forward and pull her stomach in whenever she thought about stopping. Any transition down always tempts the rider to water-ski, and inevitably the horse responds to this change in her balance by becoming the motor boat. Both parties then become entrenched in a pulling match which can seem never-ending; the attempt to halt drags on, and the horse's walk 'winds down', looking like the last few painful movements of a clockwork toy.

The secret of the halt lies in maintaining an *upright* body, for without his 'water-skier' the horse suddenly finds that he cannot play the role of the motor boat! It is also vital that the rider prepares for the halt by pretending that all she wants to do is to walk on. Most riders stop bearing down and stop breathing the moment they even think about halting. Then, they no longer take the horse – and without this push forward through their body, he immediately begins to decelerate. This is the beginning of the end. To counteract your ingrained reactions in these early stages of the halt, it is important *not* to think of stopping, and *not* to grow tall, for this tends to make you hollow your back, draw your stomach inwards and restrict your breathing – so it is much better to think of *keeping your ribs dropped down towards your hips*, of actively bearing down and of timing the halt to coincide with an outbreath. If the halt is to be a direct, clean transition, the rider must keep the horse marching forward. She must stop herself from preparing for the halt her old way – and then she must surprise herself with her new-found aids: she holds her body very firmly in place, stops the walking movement of her seat bones (see Lessons 6 and 9) and then closes her hand.

The correct halt has the quality of a knife passing through butter; the horse 'sits down' instead of pulling against the hand. But initially, he may fall against the bit, expecting the bit to pull back, and as he does this, the rider feels him make a strong contact. Like Katie in the last lesson, she has to learn the difference between *passive resistance* and pulling back – because if she plays his game and becomes the water-skier, all is lost. It is a myth to think that the horse who wants to 'motor boat' will halt without the rider using her hand – this is only possible after he has come to expect and accept the correct interaction with her. So the hand must play a part, and initially the rider may have to hold it, closed, for several seconds whilst the horse leans into it in the hope that he can tempt her to water-ski.

Unfortunately, many riders do not have the confidence and the courage to sustain the correct position of body and hand during this time. The horse is deliberately testing them, and often they fall into the trap of bringing their hand back towards their body so that their body is forced to come back too: then they are water-skiing again. Or they may bring their hand back and down, which creates a pull on the rein and tends to make them lean forward. Both of these are particularly tempting when the reins are too long – so hand, rein, body and the horse's walk must be well set up before the halt. If the hand moves at all, it must come *up* a little, so that the elbow bends more and the finger nails turn slightly upwards: only then can it be independent of the body, which as a result can remain still and vertical until the horse has halted. There is a tremendous difference between a clean, clear, direct halt and one which is long, drawn out and based on pulling. The horse offers the rider such clear feedback that she cannot fail to perceive the difference between the two – and this makes the halt a tremendously useful teaching aid. It is often frustrating for the rider, however, because the correct positioning is so precise that probably only one out of ten will work well to begin with. But no rider who experiences this difference *even once* can fail to be convinced of the profound effects which her body position has on the horse.

Gail had told me at the beginning of the lesson that she had thought it would take about a year before she achieved correct basic work from Frankie, so she certainly surpassed her expectations. ▪

The change she found the hardest to make was the snugging in of the thigh and knee onto the saddle, but as her stability improved, she realised why this extra effort was necessary. (It is, as you will learn later, only the first half of the story – but it remains a vital starting point.) From my perspective, it seemed that there were two particularly profound learnings for her. One concerned a way of generating impulsion which produced a much more convincing result for much less effort. This was based both on a technique which was new to her and on the belief that she did indeed have the right to insist on obedience to her leg. The other was an understanding of balance as an active rather than a passive phenomenon, in which one has to make small corrections and adjustments with each passing moment. Gail was surprised to discover how difficult and intricate rising trot is, and how precise one has to be during any transition. The use of the body in rising trot, or in a halt transition, is a very precise and powerful mechanism, which, as you have seen here, can have tremendous influence over the horse. When the rider can use that influence to her advantage, she gains tremendous power. She interacts with the horse so well that she makes riding look easy and the horse's response seem natural and inevitable.

Lesson 3

Jan: The Positioning of the Body and an Introduction to Asymmetry

Jan came on the four-day course at West Wilts Equestrian Centre with her Welsh Cob mare, Ropewalk Pride. Jan has owned Pride since the horse was three and although she is now seven she is still very novice and has not done a great deal of work. This is partly because she is Jan's second horse, but Jan also confessed that she has all but 'given up dressage', and this is why Pride has mostly just hacked out. Jan had reached a stage in her riding where she was continually feeling depressed about her apparent inability, whilst simultaneously becoming desperate in her attempts to 'get it right'. Finally, the struggle felt so futile that she lost heart. So she decided to take up long-distance riding in the hope that 'letting herself off the hook', combined with long hours in the saddle, might somehow give her the seat and the abilities for which she longed. She is not the first person I have met who has made this transition; however, she is also not the first to have admitted that although long-distance riding is great fun, it is for her a substitute – and if she felt competent enough she would really prefer to do dressage. She was also well aware that her horse would be less stressed by long-distance work if she were more correctly ridden.

In her disillusioned state Jan had not had any proper riding lessons for quite some time, however, through reading *Ride With Your Mind*, her optimism had been rekindled, and she hoped that I would be able to help her in an empathetic and constructive way. In her notes to me, she wrote, 'I am so confused from trying various seat and leg positions that I really don't know what is right any more. . . .' Her body was just as confused as her mind, and in the lesson she joked with me that she felt so wobbly in the saddle that she had no sense of having a normal position which felt like 'home'. She was, however, horribly aware of a problem with crookedness, which made her feel that she had very little control of her right leg.

Most trainers revel in the kudos of working with talented riders on beautiful horses, and whilst I also enjoy this, I take particular delight in working with riders like Jan. From her position of having given up in despair and confusion, the only way she can go is up, and since she has not recently invested hundreds of pounds in lessons, and she does not have an established belief system, she has nothing to lose by changing. She professed herself very willing to leave behind her rather limited sense of 'home': this is a tremendous help to me and it allows our work together to go much faster. (The same correction can easily take me four times as long with someone who holds their 'home' more dear!)

Figure 22 shows Jan's starting point, which admittedly looks more out of balance on this right rein than it did on the left. However, it shows the now familiar loss of the correct balance over the feet, and this is at least partially responsible for Pride's rather hollow carriage.

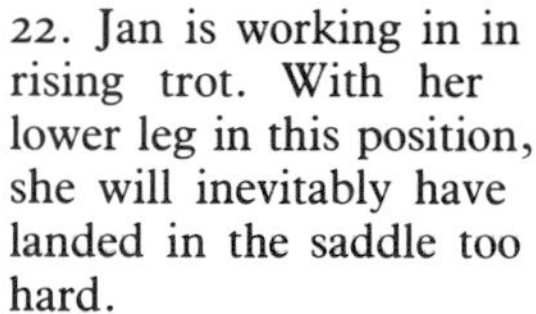

22. Jan is working in in rising trot. With her lower leg in this position, she will inevitably have landed in the saddle too hard.

I began, as I always do, by bringing Jan's legs up over the front of the saddle. Whilst they were there I asked her, 'Are your seat bones on the same level as your pubic bone, are they lower down, or are they higher up?' She felt that they were lower down, and I asked her to keep them just this much lower as I brought her legs back down again. This is a very useful diagnostic tool, which helps to establish the correct angle for the rider's pelvis as it rests on the saddle. In good sitting, the back and the front of the body look like two parallel, vertical lines, and the seat bones point directly down towards the ground rather than towards the horse's hind or fore feet (see Diagram 4). If the rider's backside begins to slip out from underneath her as she starts riding (especially in sitting trot), her pelvis rotates so that her seat bones slide back and her back hollows. This height differential between the seat bones and the pubic bone is then lost, and the seat bones point *backwards*, bringing the rider into the 'fork seat'. This is all too common in our riding schools, and it is the stance taken by riders who are determined to get their leg long at all costs. It is also a particular danger for women, whose pelvic structure gives them a naturally more hollow back than men.

Interestingly, Jan had just the opposite problem, and she tended

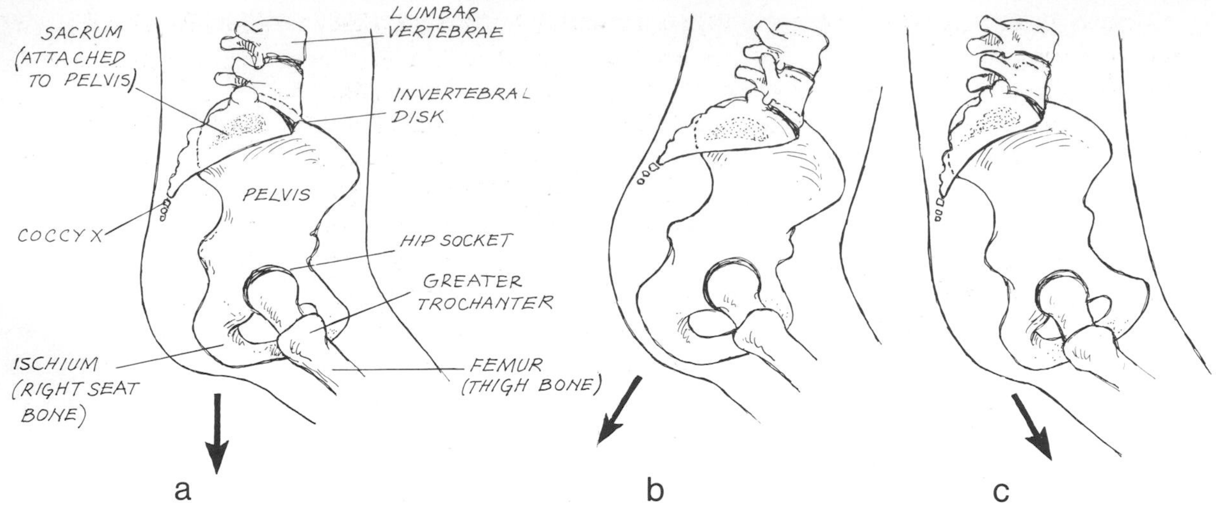

Diagram 4. When the rider's seat bones point straight down (a), the back and the front of her body become vertical and aligned, and her sitting is correct. When the seat bones point backwards (b), she comes into the fork seat and her back hollows. When they point forwards (c), she comes into the armchair seat and her back rounds. This is also influenced by the adjustment of the stirrups: when they are too short, the rider tends to round her back, and when they are too long she is forced to hollow it.

to lose the correct parallel alignment by rounding her lower back and tucking her backside *too far* underneath her, sitting towards the back of the seat bones so that they pointed towards Pride's front feet. (In this respect, she is very different from both Katie and Gail.) As this happened, the front of her body caved in, so that she appeared very hunched. So I suggested that she imagined having flashlights on the tips of the seat bones which she must keep pointing straight down towards the ground. (This image is the brainchild of the American teacher Beth Jenkins.) This helps the rider who would like to fall back into the 'armchair seat' to avoid the temptation to sit on the back of her buttocks. Holding herself upright seems difficult and stressful at first, but it has a dramatic effect on her lower leg; for once the pelvis is positioned as if in an armchair, it becomes *impossible* to hold the heel back under the hip. If you find yourself struggling in vain to bring your leg back underneath you, it may well be your pelvis which needs to change.

It is important to understand this relationship between the pelvis and the leg: if you fall into the armchair seat your seat bones point forward, your thigh and your calf come forward and up and you round your back too much. But if you try hard to stretch your leg down long, you will sit towards your fork, so that your seat bones point backwards and you hollow your back too much. Neither way can the knee act as the anchor point for the pelvis, enabling the thigh muscles to be used correctly. (See the last lesson with Gail.) The hip joint is bound by the collateral ligament, the length of which determine the degree to which the joint can open – so it restricts the angle between the torso and the thigh. If you are not aware of your own limit, you will reach a point when you can only make your knee go further down on the saddle by *hollowing your back*: in reality, you have not opened the hip joint more (even though you probably think you have!).

The correct alignment of the thigh and pelvis is very precise, and in order to achieve it I often have to alter a rider's stirrups. The idea that the rider should 'stretch her leg down' is so prevalent that I more often have to shorten the stirrups than lengthen them – especially as so few people are aware of the limitation imposed by the collateral ligament. To find the right length for stirrups, quit them and let your legs hang comfortably. Then check on the direction of your 'flashlights' as you sit and place your hand against your front, and against the small of your back, to feel whether they are rounded or hollowed. Adjust your stirrups so that your feet rest in them *without you having to stretch your legs down*. This challenge only comes later, after your pelvic positioning is well established and the collateral ligament has lengthened a little.

Jan has the disadvantage that her posture is rather hunched, and, along with a shortening of this ligament, all the flexor muscles at the front of the body have lost flexibility and become shortened. It is this which creates the tendency for Jan's pelvis to angle itself so that her legs come up and her shoulders drop forward. I set my priorities differently from many riding teachers, and I like to work from the middle of the body outwards, so I decided to leave her shoulders alone for the time being. Unless a rider specifically asks for help with them (as Val did in the next lesson), I usually let them be in the early stages of our work. When Jan's pelvis is aligned correctly, she will slouch less, but because of her muscle use and development, there will still be a residual rounding of her shoulders and she may need skilled help from an Alexander or other body work teacher. She will certainly need a good deal of commitment – off the horse as well as on it – since this is how she walks about, sits in her office, drives her car and how she sleeps in bed. One of the reasons that I am unusually successful at creating change with riders is that I tackle it in 'bite-size chunks', and I never ask them to bite off more than they can chew!

I also showed Jan the pinch and the bearing down. She had read about these in *Ride With Your Mind* and had tried them for herself, but she was surprised to discover the degree of narrowing in and pushing out for which I was asking. I have yet to meet a rider who has overdone these when attempting to work them out for herself, so do not be afraid to 'go for it', especially if your muscle tone, like Jan's, is rather low in the extensor muscles of the body. In her case, whilst the flexor muscles at the front of the thigh have shortened, the extensor muscles at the back of it have *lengthened*. When Jan came into the correct position, she felt a pull in the flexor muscles of the front of the thigh, and she will need to keep feeling this if her knee is to act as an anchor point for the pelvis, stopping her from falling back into the armchair seat. One of the tricks in helping her, however, lies in realising that whilst she has to feel this pull in the muscles at the front of the thigh, she also has to *hold more* in the muscles at the back of it. The pinch helps here, bringing more tone into the hamstring muscles: we are balancing the springs in Diagram 1 (page 40) and helping her seat bones to point in the right direction. To bring her muscle system into balance, she needs to feel that she is pinching and bearing down, lengthening the front of the thigh and holding in the back of the thigh to the ultimate extreme and she is still unlikely even to approach the natural muscle balance and level of muscle tone which a talented rider would take for granted.

Jan had queried the pinch feeling, and I wanted her to understand why it is so important, so I asked her to walk on, repeatedly making the pinch feeling and then letting it go, so that she could discover how it affected the position and orientation of her seat bones. (Do this for yourself next time you ride.) She found that it made them come further forward, further up and closer together whilst still pointing down. (Whilst the feeling of their moving closer together is extremely convincing, the distance between the bones themselves cannot vary. You are actually feeling the top of the hamstring muscle moving inwards to cover the bone, providing a cushion which protects both your seat bone and the horse's back.) As I explained to Jan, the saddle rises towards the pommel with both sides coming further forward, further up and closer together, so making the pinch naturally helps the rider to mould onto the saddle and prevents her from slipping backwards.

However, the idea of drawing the seat bones forward, up and in often surprises people, especially when they have been taught to press down with them, and to spread their seat out over the saddle. Pressing down creates two pressure points which can cause discomfort to the horse – and whilst the seat bones should feel clear, the rider's weight must also be distributed *down her thigh*, i.e. forward over the horse's rib cage, where he has the strength to support it. The sitting surface then encompasses the whole of the area of the backside and thigh which are in contact with the saddle – the weight-bearing surface includes almost the entire area of suede on a pair of suede-seated breeches. If you think of bringing the knee down and the heel back, the thigh and the calf become shaped like an arrowhead which has the knee as its point: this makes it easier to distribute your weight down your thighs. It also helps to think of pointing your 'flashlights' straight downwards as you sit, and to imagine that you are sitting on one of those chiropractic posture stools which are good for your back. If you sit on a slope and rest your shins on a slope, there is much less strain on your lower back – and much less temptation to slouch – than there is if you sit in an ordinary chair.

Sitting like this gives the rider that enviable, elegant line in her thigh – and contrary to popular belief, she can achieve this without having the long and thin body shape which we all admire so much (see Figures 23 and 26). It also makes her far more stable because she utilises a much larger base of support. If her horse stops suddenly, her thighs act like buffers which hold her body back in place, whilst the rider who sits only on her seat bones is much more likely to topple forward. Sitting correctly draws the rider's centre of gravity more forward: few people realise how important this is – despite the fact that our ultimate aim is to transfer the horse's weight backwards so that he carries more of it on his hind legs (there is more about this in Part Three). But before we can do this we have to align our centre of gravity with his, and then we have to bring the *combined* rider/horse centre of gravity further back. If bringing a horse off his forehand simply required that we should sit further back, we would all succeed in riding collection by sitting on his croup!

Common though it is in our riding dogma, thinking of widening the seat bones apart has some very undesirable effects. It encourages them to slip backwards, and at the same time it also takes them off their correct positioning on top of the horse's long back muscles (the longissimus dorsi). These lie very close in to his spine on either side (see Diagram 10). I believe that whoever originally said that you should 'spread your seat out' was *already* making the pinch feeling, although he did not realise he was doing it. The spread then happens concurrently, and it involves the area of the backside lying between the seat bones and the lesser trochanter of the femur, which lies on the underside of the thigh beneath the greater trochanter. The lesser trochanter is the bony lump which stops you from falling over if you sit on the floor with your legs bent round to one side, and the part of your backside which rests on the floor is the part that should be spread (see Diagram 5). (Try this now, or lie on your side, and poke around under the greater trochanter, feeling the difference between it and the seat bone.)

The underneath of the pelvis and thigh have a structure similar to a child's two-wheeled bicycle when it is used with small stabiliser wheels. The two seat bones are narrowed in together, and they act like the edges of the central tyre. The stabiliser wheels are like the lesser trochanters of the femur, attached into the main wheel (pelvis) via a connection which is like the neck of the femur. When the seat bones lie close in to the horse's spine but the backside is also spread, one gains both precision and stability. But problems often arise for the rider when one or both 'stabilisers' are held up and away from the saddle: this always affects the whole leg right down to the foot, and if you have one heel that is always above your toe – with a supposedly stiff ankle – a raised 'stabiliser' is usually the cause. This means that the solution to the problem lies up near the hip joint and not in the ankle. (Test this by standing and putting your fingertips on the greater trochanter of the femur on one side. Now raise it; what happens to your foot? What do you have to do to put your heel back on the ground again?)

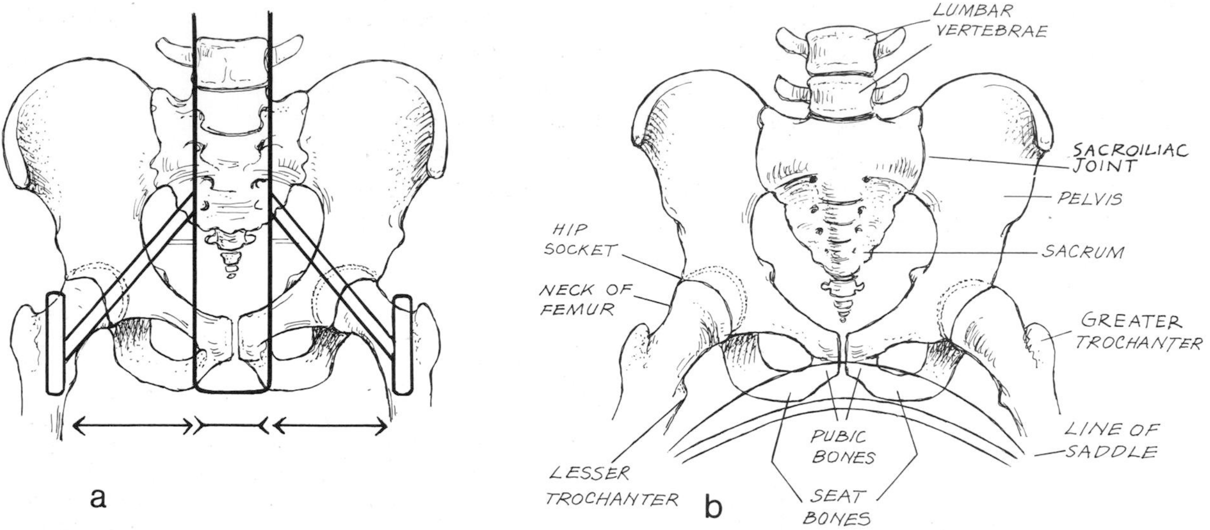

Diagram 5a. The structure of the pelvis mirrors a child's bicycle with stabiliser wheels. The pinch makes the seat bones feel as if they move inwards so that they lie snugly each side of the horse's spine and act like the edges of the centre tyre. The rider then spreads the part of the backside between them and the 'stabilisers', the lesser trochanters of the femur.
b. The pelvis seen from the front.

The idea of pinching and spreading both at the same time is extremely subtle. I would recommend that you become very familiar and comfortable with the pinch, and with the feeling of having your seat bones correctly angled, before you even begin to think about dropping your 'stabilisers', or about making corrections to a permanently raised heel. Bear in mind, however, that if you attempt to spread *between* the seat bones you will actually lose stability and feel as if you are floating off the sides of the horse. Many people who feel nervous find an immediate sense of security when they narrow their seat bones inwards. When they later drop their 'stabilisers', they completely change their leg position, adding the elusive quality for which teachers are searching when they ask the rider to 'stretch the leg down long'.

Firming up Jan's pinch and increasing her pelvic muscle tone made many of her wobbles disappear. Like Gail, she also needed to think of sitting still rather than moving her backside in an exaggerated attempt to follow the movement. She gained much more stability than usual, but there was then one more basic change which she needed to make, and this involved snugging in the thighs. I suggested that she thought of hooking her knees onto the end of an iron bar, just as Gail had done, and then I realised that she also needed to narrow in the thighs higher up. I told her to think of her thighs making a 'V'-shape as they spread out around the horse, with her pubic bone as a bar across the 'V'. If the bar (her pubic bone) became shorter, the whole 'V' would narrow inwards, bringing the adductor muscles of her inside thigh into play. To make sure that Jan knew what I meant, I put my hand between her thigh and the saddle and asked her to squash it!

Figure 23 shows Jan's body very well aligned in walk on the left rein, and it also shows the beginning of a change in Pride's carriage. They both held this unusually well as they went forward into trot, and Jan was well able to maintain her balance over her feet – this was largely because she was undeterred when her feel sense told her that her heels were up around her ears! However, when she changed onto the right rein, it was apparent that the correction I had made to her thigh had not stuck. Since Jan was so willing to risk the unfamiliar – and since there was so obviously a problem – I decided that we would tackle her asymmetry.

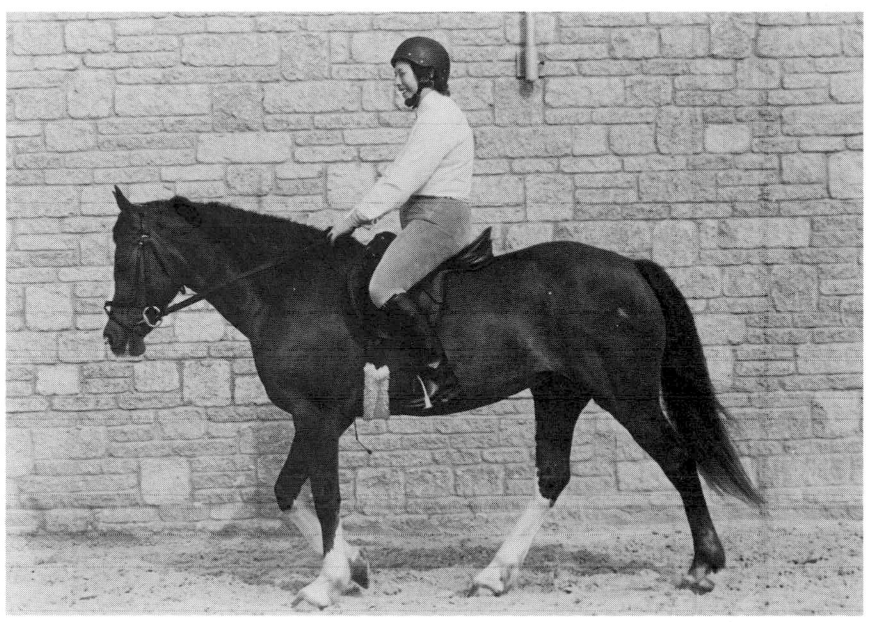

23. Jan has made a great shift in her way of sitting. She would now balance on a diving board and Pride has responded to this by beginning to come into the seeking reflexes. Although her shoulders are still rounded, the line of Jan's thigh has begun to look elegant.

I began this work by checking the length of Jan's stirrups, and I found that the right one was a hole longer. So we shortened it, and I then asked her a series of questions to make her more aware of her starting point. In a very gentle way, these forced her to become conscious of her incompetence. Jan answered these whilst walking her horse, first on the right rein and then on the left, and the answers were consistent in each case. My first question was: 'Do you have an even weight in both stirrups?' to which her answer was: 'No, there's more in the left.' I then needed to know, 'Do you have one foot where the heel is more down, and one where you are more on tiptoe?' Jan replied that her right heel felt higher than her left, and that both of her heels were up inside her boots, which were falling down! She also realised that her toes were curled up – a common problem which destabilises the foot as a base of support and creates an unhealthy tension in the calf muscles. I also asked, 'If you feel your two inside thighs, all the way from your crotch down to your knee, does one lie more snugly on the saddle than the other?' Jan responded that the left one was definitely more snug, and she realised that her right knee literally waved away from the saddle at each step of the walk. My last question was, 'Do you have one seat bone further forward and/or heavier than the other?' Jan was not sure about this, so I decided to work purely with the information she had given me about her thighs and her feet.

Firstly, Jan uncurled her toes, and this immediately made her feel as if her heels were lower than her toes – although to my eye they were not. Again, her body was simply registering the difference. I then used my body to demonstrate to her the mechanics of her asymmetry. As you can see in Figure 24, her pelvis is primarily positioned over her left leg, which supports most of her weight. It therefore lies close to the midline of the body and points straight forward. Her right leg carries less weight, and it turns outwards – away from the midline and the saddle – which puts her right foot on tiptoe, raising her 'stabiliser' as well. Her weak right leg is the inevitable result of her weight distribution, and the chances are that Jan walks with most of her weight on her left leg and that she often stands as I am doing here. She would almost certainly kick a football by standing on her left leg and kicking with her right. (This idea of 'footedness' is much more relevant to the rider's asymmetry than handedness, and is a useful diagnostic tool. Which leg would you kick with?)

The correction lies as in Figure 25, where I have positioned my pelvis more over my right leg. This has made my right thigh come towards the midline and point more forward, so that I have, if anything, slightly more weight on my right foot than on my left. (To understand the correction more fully, try it standing up as I have done. Also try its mirror image and discover which position comes more naturally.) My left thigh now points slightly outwards, as indeed it needs to when the horse is correctly bent on the right rein. This displaces his rib cage *slightly to the left*, so that there is a bigger bulge underneath the rider's left thigh than under her right (see Lesson 7 with Margaret).

It takes tremendous concentration and commitment to make the change which Jan needed to make, even though she understood it clearly, and even though I had given her the key which I knew would open the door. This initial change can happen in a very small amount of time, but it can take years for it to become so ingrained that it feels natural and effortless. With every lapse of concentration, the rider tends to fall straight back into her old pattern – but at least she now knows how to redeem herself. Many people attempt to make a weight change or to correct an asymmetry

24. I am demonstrating Jan's asymmetry: my arms are pointing in the same directions as my legs in order to emphasise the difference in the angles of her two thighs. The rider's unweighted thigh always turns outwards like this.

25. I have slightly exaggerated the change which Jan needs to make. Although the angles of her thighs will be similar to the above when she is riding correctly on the right rein, her inside foot will carry only slightly more weight than her outside one.

in ways which cannot possibly work, and few people realise that the secret of the change lies in the positioning and angles of the thighs. If Jan can hold her right thigh parallel to the saddle and snugly against it, this will pull her pelvis over to the right and hold it there. This naturally lowers her right 'stabiliser' and heel, giving her control of her whole leg. But as soon as her right thigh weakens – which it will inevitably do to begin with as the muscles are not used to this added strain – her pelvis will slip back over again. To help Jan, I suggested that she thought of sitting in the middle of a clock face, in which the direction of twelve o'clock was straight forward towards the horse's ears. She then had to make her right thigh point towards twelve o'clock.

Jan made an extremely good effort, and, as you can see in Figure 26, the alignment of her right leg has changed completely, and Pride has responded beautifully with this change in her carriage. Jan could feel a distinct difference in the way she was moving, and she was so thrilled that when she changed to the left rein again, she wanted to try sitting trot. In Figure 27 her pelvis is tucked too far underneath her again and her shoulders are rounded, but she is sitting quite still with very few wobbles or bumps. She would probably not quite balance on a diving board, but at least her lower leg has not returned to its original position – this is quite surprising considering her extreme tuck-under. I asked Jan to demonstrate her normal sitting trot to me, and her body immediately became wobbly and spongy; but as soon

26. Compare Jan's right leg now with its initial positioning in Figure 22. The whole right thigh has rotated inwards, her foot is back underneath her and it is weighted more. Her whole position looks much more elegant, and Pride is moving very well.

27. Jan takes sitting trot on the left rein: she has her backside tucked too much underneath her, and as a result her upper body has crumpled. But her knee has remained well in place and her hand is light. Only when her pelvis is less tucked underneath her will she be able to open her shoulders. And as sitting becomes easier for her, she might even smile too! Pride has continued to move well.

as she began pinching and bearing down again, she became more solid and organised, as if her body were made of putty.

Jan made this change to sitting trot more easily than Katie or Gail would have done. Although Jan has the disadvantage of having much more 'spongy' muscles, she has the advantage that her back tends to round rather than hollow. It is when the rider's back hollows that she tends to actually bump – and this is why it is so counter-productive to set the stirrups too long. The *downthrust* of the rider's weight comes down her spine, into the pelvis, and down to the seat bones, which are its two lowest points. The *upthrust* from the ground (communicated via the horse's movement and the stirrup) comes up the front of each thigh bone and into the hip joints. So in order for there to be some give in the body, the seat bones must be below the level of the hip joints: otherwise the upthrust meets the downthrust and 'wham!', the rider's backside leaves the saddle. Jan may look rather hunched, but as long as she can stop herself from gripping up by keeping her knees in place (hooked onto the ends of their iron bar), she will sit quite well. If instead she tended to hollow her back, sitting trot would be far more difficult: she might look more elegant, but she would definitely bump!

Pride did not change her carriage or show any objections when Jan began to sit, so she obviously approved – and by waiting until Pride's back was already in good carriage Jan had stacked the odds in her favour. I would not have let her go sitting before this change had occurred, because the rider's success here is determined partially by her ability to sit, but also partially by how 'sittable on' the horse's back is. This in turn is determined by whether his movement shows the seeking or the cramping reflexes – and the horse who is just beginning to move well often cramps up very quickly when the rider first goes sitting. This blocks the impulse generated by the hind legs as it reaches the loin area, breaking the circuit and creating a very jarring gait. Jan was lucky that Pride was so willing to give her the benefit of the doubt, but I suspect that Pride would not have been so generous on the right rein. Here, Jan would have had the added problem of her asymmetry – since having her body weight predominantly to the outside, and her unweighted, wobbly leg on the inside, would make her much less stable. If Jan could have coped with all of this at once, *and* could have dealt with Pride's probable response on this rein, she would have gone beyond the normal range of parallel processing into the realm of the super-human!

As Jan came back to walk at the end of the lesson, Pride wanted to stretch her neck forward and down – the ultimate of the seeking reflexes. In Figure 28 you can see how her back is lifted up under Jan's seat, as if her whole rib cage were a balloon that somebody had put more air in. (Compare this with Figure 22, which looks as if someone has let all the air out.) This walk is a sure sign that our previous work had been correct – a vote of confidence from the horse, who now trusts Jan's way of sitting. Jan had demonstrated to me that she certainly was not lacking in ability, and her openness to learning will more than compensate for having a body which is not ideally shaped for riding. On the next few days she consolidated this change, and began to understand how her seat bones were also involved in her asymmetry. On the last day of the course, when I asked Jan what she needed to get from her lesson in order to leave feeling clear and satisfied, she responded that she wanted to be absolutely sure that she recognised her new 'home', and that she knew what to do whenever she lost it. Having found it as clearly as she has done, I do not think that she will ever feel so 'at sea' again, and I hope she now finds that dressage is not the mysterious, unattainable skill she used to think it was.

28. Walking forward and down – the horse's desire to stretch her long back muscles is a sign that they have been working correctly, and is a great vote of confidence in the rider. Notice how much more open Jan's upper body is in walk, and her pelvic angle is now more correct. Compare Pride's carriage with Figure 22.

Lesson 4

Val: Positioning the Body on a Circle

Val had to contend with the worst of a seeringly hot day when she came for her first lesson on the two-day course in Hampshire. Her horse, China, is a nine-year-old black mare who was originally bred to point-to-point. However, she did not grow big enough and was sold as a five-year-old to people who did very little with her. Val bought the mare from them two years ago, and her work was so incorrect and explosive that Val found herself *having* to become interested in dressage out of sheer necessity! She has ridden all her life, but her previous experience is mostly of hunting and jumping. However, now that her interest has been kindled, she takes regular lessons, including clinics with quite a well-known trainer. She has also been competing at riding-club level.

When Val told me how explosive China had been, I was quite surprised. Figure 29, which was taken early in the lesson, shows a rather dull-looking horse (although the heat could well have been a factor in this). To my eye, China and Val both look as if they lack 'stuffing': to understand this, imagine that they were a stuffed toy horse and rider. They do not have the look of brand new stuffed toys, which bulge with stuffing; instead they look rather elderly, as if the stuffing has worn thin. Along with this, their walk was

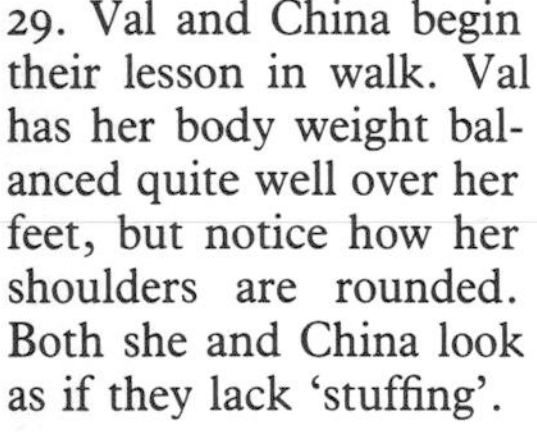
29. Val and China begin their lesson in walk. Val has her body weight balanced quite well over her feet, but notice how her shoulders are rounded. Both she and China look as if they lack 'stuffing'.

rather lazy, with Val using her legs at every stride so that they swung rather floppily backwards and forwards, mostly going past China's sides and not actually touching them! She was unaware of this movement, and had to exaggerate it deliberately before she realised what she was doing. (It is helpful to do this whenever you cannot feel a fault that is being pointed out to you; by making it bigger, you overcome the anaesthetic which has been created by familiarity. By learning how you do it, you gain considerable information about how *not* to do it.) Later on, Val found that whilst the physical aspect of keeping her legs still was not difficult, it required tremendous concentration. This was hard to maintain – but when she succeeded, she created the stable base which allowed her to balance as if on a diving board.

After a period of working in, I began the lesson with my familiar reorganisation, bringing Val's legs up over the front of the saddle, realigning her body and then showing her how to use her leg effectively (see Lesson 2 with Gail). During her working in, Val asked me for help with one of her major problems – sitting up straight. However hard she tried to sit up, she found that she always collapsed again, and that her shoulders inevitably rounded. So I suggested that she imagined two lines coming up the front of her body, starting at about the mid point where each thigh joins the torso – the place where you can feel several tendons at the top of the thigh. The lines then pass each side of the abdomen, over the breasts, and up towards the indentations which lie near the ends of the collar bones. The most important part of them lies in the region between the rib cage and the pelvis. I told her to think of pressing her body against these lines, as if they really were solid. (One of my pupils enriched the image by thinking of pressing his body against prison bars. Other people have pretended they were wearing braces. The choice is yours!)

When I originally found this helpful, I thought that these lines must be figments of my imagination; but I later realised that they are the edges of the sheath of the rectus abdominus muscle, and that they are often visible on muscular men (statues made by the ancient Greeks usually show them clearly). This push is really another aspect of the bearing down, which now extends all the way from the pubic bone to the sternum. Without it, the upper body inevitably crumples. Many people have found that the image gives them an instant solution to a long-term and difficult problem, although when the flexor muscles have become shortened, and the body habitually tends to crumple, this push can be quite difficult, and it can leave the rider with aching muscles. Figure 30 shows Val only a few minutes after she had begun to bear down this fully. She told me that it felt totally different from the feeling she had created in her previous attempts to sit up straight. These had involved her hollowing her back, and she had felt as if her shoulders and back were 'two separate parts'. With the correction in place, she also suddenly looks as if she is much more full of 'stuffing'.

30. Val is thinking of pushing the front of her body against imaginary iron bars. Notice how open her chest is compared to Figure 29.

31. Val is attempting to turn China on the left rein. Her body has twisted inwards and her inside hand is well behind her outside hand. If we could see her from the back, we would almost certainly see that she is leaning in.

When I first looked at Val working in, it was apparent that except for her slumped shoulders, her alignment was more correct than any of the previous riders. However, as I watched her on both reins it was immediately obvious that there was a significant difference between the two. She had responded so well to my initial corrections that I decided to make this the focus of our lesson, and I asked her: 'Which rein do you prefer riding on?' She answered that she preferred the left rein, which surprised me, so I asked her why. She felt that she had a much better bend on this rein. Figure 31 shows a typical turn as she comes round towards the fence, and as I looked at this I asked her, 'Do your horse's shoulders go exactly where you want them to go in these turns, or do they deviate from their ideal path?' She found this a rather strange concept, but gradually came to realise that her horse's shoulders were falling much further out than she wanted them to, drifting towards the fence. I asked her the same question as she worked on the right rein, where she realised that her horse's shoulders did indeed go exactly where she wanted them to, with no drifting either in or out. So I then asked her, 'Which rein has the more correct bend?' to which she initially answered, 'The left.' When I queried this, I saw a look of complete bewilderment pass across her face.

Val could feel that she had much more control of her horse on the right rein than she had on the left, but she was now totally flummoxed because she had been told that her horse's bend was more correct on the left rein than it was on the right. So which rein really was the better one? If we had a photograph taken of Val from the back it would help us, as observers, to reach a conclusion, for I am almost certain that we would see Val looking upright on the right rein and tipped in towards the inside on the left rein. However, Val was totally unaware of this, and was, I believe, under a common misconception: on the left rein, her horse was not *bending*, it was *jack-knifing*, and going round the corner like an articulated lorry. This meant that although her nose was coming round to the left, her shoulders were going out to the right. Val had responded in the way that riders usually do in this case, grabbing at the inside rein in a desperate attempt to pull the horse round. However, this only makes the jack-knife worse, exaggerating the difference in the directions taken by the nose and the shoulders. Doing this is rather like thinking that you can turn a bicycle by pulling at the inside handle bar. This is the fastest way I know to guarantee that you will land on the ground!

I could see how Val's asymmetry was contributing to her horse's evasive pattern, and to make her aware of what was happening, I asked her to walk her horse on a circle on each rein whilst I asked her the following questions – a fuller list than I used with Jan. Before you use them, always measure your stirrups to make sure you are riding level.

Does one of your feet have a firmer pressure into the stirrup than the other?

Is one foot more heel down and one more on tiptoe?

If you feel the inside of your thigh all the way from your crotch to your knee, does one thigh lie more snugly on the saddle than the other?

Is one of your seat bones more clear and firm on the saddle than the other – more like bone on concrete – and is one more rounded and fuzzy, as if it has disappeared within the flesh of your bottom?

Is one seat bone further forward and one further back?

Do your shoulders lie on a radius of the circle you are riding on: do they point in front of the radius (so that I, as an observer in the centre, tend to see your back); or do they lie behind the radius (so that I as an observer tend to see your chest)?

Are your hands on a level with each other, or is one further back towards your body than the other?

Does one have a stronger contact than the other?

The following questions, which I did not use with Val, are also useful. I will come back to some of the more complex ones later, particularly in Lessons 7 and 10.

Do you lean forward more on one rein than you do on the other?

In rising trot, do you land more heavily in the saddle on one rein than you do on the other?

If you think of your thigh bones like iron bars, is one more iron-bar-like than the other, and/or does one of them have bits that are rubbery or missing?

Is the central axis of your body aligned with the horse's central axis, or does it tip off to one side?

Is one of your 'stabilisers' up and one of them down?

If you were sitting in the middle of a clock face, with the horse's head and neck pointing out in front of you at twelve o'clock, what time would your seat bones be saying?

Val's answers to the questions I asked were as follows.

On the left rein (shown in Figure 31):

Her left (inside) foot pressed more heavily into the stirrup, with the heel more down.

Her right (outside) foot rested more lightly in the stirrup, with the heel more up.

Her left (inside) thigh was much looser in its contact with the saddle than her right (outside) thigh, which was laid firmly against it.

Her left (inside) seat bone was further back than her right (outside) one, and was also heavier, feeling more like bone on concrete.

The line of her shoulders lay behind the radius, and as you can see in Figure 31, an observer in the centre of the circle sees her chest.

Her left (inside) hand was further back than her right (outside) hand, and it had a stronger contact.

On the right rein (shown in Figure 30):

The difference in the weight taken by each foot was less than on the other rein. Her right (inside) foot was now slightly heavier, with a slightly lower heel than her left. (This is the mirror image of the above.)

Her left (outside) thigh was still looser in its contact with the saddle than the right (inside) one, which was firmer. (This is the same as the above.)

Her seat bones carried approximately equal weight, and felt much more equal in the quality of their contact. (This is different from the above.) The right (inside) one was now in advance of the left (outside) one. (This is the same as the above.)

The line of her shoulders now lay on the radius of the circle she was riding on. (This differs from the above.) Her hands were now level and the contact was more even. (This differs from the above.)

I always make a point of asking these questions because in the realm of asymmetries, each rider is unique, and whilst I can make inspired guesses at the answers, there is always the chance that I might be wrong. The rider also benefits tremendously from having to feel her body and answer them. If I simply told her my perceptions she could happily say, 'Oh yes,' without ever having engaged her feel sense. Two very different types of knowing are involved –

that which somebody else has told you and that which you actually experience for yourself. The weighting and positioning of the seat bones and the feet quite often change from one rein to the other, but the relative snugness of the thighs and the twist of the shoulders almost always remains constant, and these are the vital clues to the straightening.

In Val's case, the twist of the body is particularly obvious. (It was, for instance, apparently not a factor for Jan, even in Figure 22, although the majority of riders show some twist.) I asked her if she was familiar with the idea of having her inside hip in advance when riding on a circle, which apparently she was not. I was surprised by this, as I grew up knowing this to be one of the golden rules – not that this enabled me to understand it, or to do it! Val had, however, heard of the idea of riding the horse 'from the inside leg into the outside rein'. Whoever first coined this phrase is unfortunately not alive to tell us whether we are to interpret 'leg' to mean 'thigh' or 'calf'. Most people, I think, assume that it means 'calf', but from my own experiences of riding and teaching I am not so sure. If we take it to mean 'thigh', it is easy to understand that on the left rein these were the two of the aspects of Val's body which were missing. Her inside thigh was wobbly and the outside hand had given forward. In their absence, her inside hand had taken over the job of attempting to turn the horse.

I knew – from bitter experience on both sides of this fence – that I could tell Val to: 'Give way your inside hand around the corner, do not pull back with it!' until I was purple in the face, and that it would not make any difference to her. In fact, she would probably have the experience of feeling stupid and powerless in the face of my exhortations. Her pulling on the inside rein is only a *symptom* of a series of interactions with the horse, which have as their cause Val's pelvic positioning. In effect, she always has her right hip and

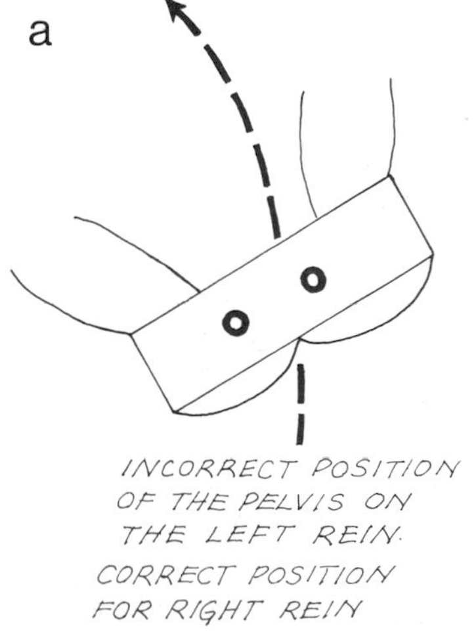

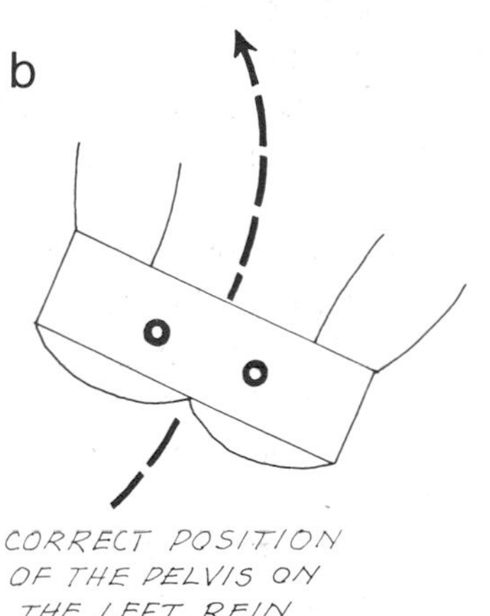

Diagram 6. Think of the rider's pelvis as a parallelogram. With Val's right hip permanently in advance, as in (a), it is easy to understand why her right thigh is always snug on the saddle and why her left thigh is always wobbly. It is also clear why her left seat bone is always behind her right. The correction she needs to make positions her pelvis in the mirror image to this, advancing her inside hip and seat bone and changing the angles of her thighs, as in (b).

her right shoulder in advance of her left. This means that she has no problem turning on the right rein but a major problem on the left rein.

If you think of Val's pelvis as a parallelogram, as in Diagram 6, you can see exactly why her thighs point outward in the directions that they do, and you can also understand the correction which will cause her work on the left rein to become a mirror image of her work on the right rein. (I do not mean to imply with this that the right rein is perfect, and it looks as if Val's inside hip and shoulder are *too much* in advance on this rein. But Val will almost certainly not make sense out of the more subtle corrections which need to be made here until she has come to terms with the left rein. As usual, we are working in 'bite-size chunks'.) My starting point was to explain to her the idea of her pelvis as a parallelogram, and to suggest that she thought of *advancing her left (inside) hip towards the horse's right (outside) ear*. Along with this, it is also helpful to think of keeping the point of hip in advance of the seat bone. In

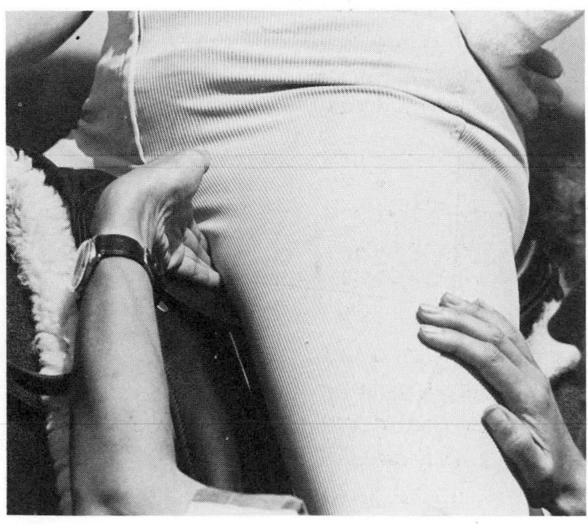

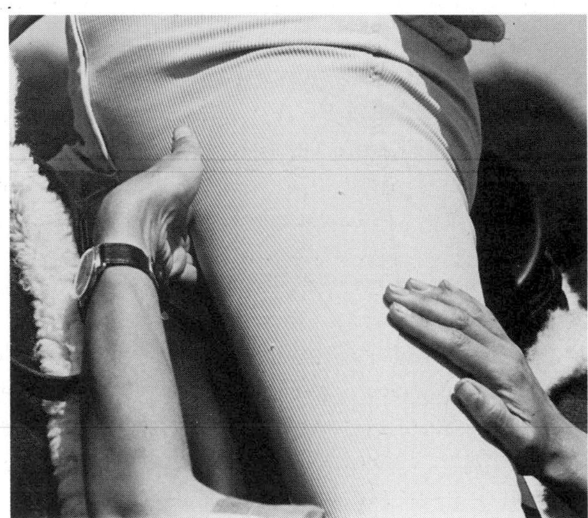

32 and 33. I have put my hand underneath the top of Val's thigh to demonstrate how it rolls against the saddle when she thinks of bringing her inside hip towards the horse's outside ear. Notice how it has covered my fingers in Figure 33, and how the whole of the left side of Val's pelvis has advanced, exposing more of the back of the saddle.

Figures 32 and 33 you can see the difference which this makes to her inside thigh, which has rolled forward to cover my fingers in Figure 33. This is a tremendously important correction. As these photographs were taken from exactly the same point, you can also see how the whole left-hand side of her pelvis has advanced, exposing more of the back of the saddle.

On their weaker side, most riders find it extremely difficult to hold their inside hip forward: gravity would have it drop backwards, and untrained muscles are no match for this. But instead of their inside seat bone supporting such a high proportion of their body weight, their *inside thigh muscles* must begin to support it (along with their inside stirrup and their outside seat bone). Previously, their inside thigh flopped outwards, and holding it against the saddle is an unaccustomed stress which usually causes pain. When riders complain, I assure them that this will prove extremely useful feedback when they are on their own and they need reassurance that they have indeed recreated the change they need to make! I like the idea that pain can be welcome and reassuring rather than unwelcome and horrible, and I am amazed that so many riders do not expect to feel pain (beyond their initial experiences as a novice). Like any athlete, gymnast or dancer, I expect to work out on the edge of pain, and I know that this increases my range and my effectiveness, strengthening the areas of my body which are weak. I find this pain a very satisfying and pleasant feeling – particularly as it is always accompanied by an increase in my body control and an improvement in my horse's carriage and movement. I welcome pain and work towards it: it is a huge limitation to think that you should always expect to feel comfortable and relaxed, without ever challenging your body's idiosyncrasies or putting it under stress.

Without this help from her inside thigh muscles, Val's left (inside) seat bone had protruded down into her horse's long back muscles, rather like a stiletto heel. The inside long back muscle is in a particularly vulnerable position on a circle, and the horse responds by retracting it. Bringing the rider's inside hip towards the horse's opposite ear is intended to lighten and advance her inside seat bone so that it does not cause discomfort to the horse. (In Lesson 10 with Jill it will become clear exactly how one determines its precise positioning.) To complete the change, the rider also needs to think of bringing her *outside* seat bone and shoulder further back and of weighting the outside seat bone more. The correction which enables the two seat bones to carry approximately equal weight is a combination of advancing and lightening the inner one, and weighting the outside one whilst drawing it further back. Previously, the outside seat bone would have tended to float forwards, up off the saddle and away to the outside – following the twist forward of the rider's outside shoulder and the displacement of her backside to the outside. The rider's outside 'stabiliser' would also have lifted, and the correction to this is even more subtle and difficult than the correction to the seat bone. For Val, it will lie in the next level of her learning. (To understand the change in the weighting of the seat bones, advance one shoulder and keep twisting your body round as you sit on your chair. What happens? Also make this same movement to the other side. Does one feel more familiar and comfortable than the other?)

Since advancing the outside shoulder begins the twist which lifts the outside seat bone, the correction to the seat bone must begin in the shoulder. As the rider brings her outside shoulder back, she brings her body onto the radius of the circle on which she is riding. (If this sounds strange to you, bear with me – I will justify it more later.) It then becomes much easier for her to bring her outside seat bone into contact with the saddle. (Again, try this in your chair: can you make your seat bones become equally weighted without moving the shoulder which has advanced?) As the rider brings her outside seat bone back it also comes *inwards* more, towards the midline of the saddle: to understand this, think of the way in which the inside seat bone advances, coming forward and in towards the horse's opposite ear. The movement of the outside seat bone is the inverse of this, as if they both rotated around a central point. There is now much more saddle underneath the outside seat bone, and it becomes far easier to feel it clearly. Instead of falling off the side of the horse, the seat bone is now securely placed on the top of his long back muscles. Again, the way to find the exact positioning for it will become clear later.

On a turn or a circle, the role of the rider's outside aids is to make a wall which prohibits the horse's outside shoulder from falling outwards as China's has done in Figure 31. In Figure 34 I am helping Val to get the feel of this by using my hands to hold her outside hand and the outside of her pelvis in place, so that they cannot advance in the way in which they have habitually done. (As you can see, however, I have not managed to prevent her shoulder from advancing!) At the same time, I am pushing her horse's shoulders around the turn. I want her to get the feeling of the horse turning 'in one piece', like a bus, instead of like an articulated lorry. As China comes into the turn, she will at some point take hold of the outside rein, effectively saying, 'Please give me more rein so that I can bulge my shoulders outwards.' Until now, Val has always unwittingly replied, 'Here you are,' giving not only her hand but her whole body as well. I want her to say, 'No deal,' maintaining a passive resistance with her outside hand and deliberately holding the whole of the outside of her body – the seat bone, hip, elbow, hand and shoulder – in place so that they do not budge. This will force the horse to accommodate to her, whereas in the past, Val has always accommodated to the horse. In this, she has become reactive rather than causal. Instead of the horse's weight falling onto her outside shoulder, it will now be displaced onto the inside (left) one. This is exactly what we want, because any turn or circle to the left is, after all, a controlled fall to the left, displacing the horse's weight in this direction so that he has no choice but to go there.

Whilst the outside of the rider's body has to form a barrier, the inside has to offer an invitation. If you look at Figure 31, it is easy to see that the horse could not displace her shoulders to the inside even if she wanted to, because Val's inside hand has become a barrier. The inside of the horse is completely scrunched up, and there is no room for the shoulder to step into. (Conversely, there

Positioning the Body on a Circle

34. With my help, Val is riding her horse on a ten-metre circle to the left. I am making sure that her outside hand and seat bone stay back in place, and I am pushing her horse's shoulders around the turn, to give Val the feeling of her turning 'like a bus'.

35. Val is working on the left rein showing a rather exaggerated but much more correct positioning. She is shown here at a slightly later point on her turn than she was in Figure 31, but notice how her horse has not jack-knifed and how light Val's contact with the inside rein has become. Both Val and China are much more full of 'stuffing' than they were at the beginning of the lesson.

is all the room in the world on the outside!) Only when her inside hip advances, will Val find it possible to advance her inside hand and give the inside shoulder the freedom it needs. In Figure 35, you can see how this has happened, and although you might criticise Val's position as being rather exaggerated, the difference in her horse is indisputable. To help her maintain her alignment, Val is deliberately looking towards the outside of the circle.

This change is one of the most disconcerting adjustments that one can ever ask a rider to make. There is a great deal of information to process, so often she has to struggle with overload as well as disorientation. Riders frequently begin a lesson by telling me that they want help with an asymmetry, and often it is something which they have cursed at and struggled with for years. But when they find out exactly what they have to do to straighten themselves, they can become markedly unenthusiastic. ('I wanted to be straight, but I didn't mean this! Surely it can't be right . . . .') Change always comes at a price, but not everyone wants to pay: Alexander teachers often find their pupils complaining that they have become 'all twisted up' since they began having lessons, and sometimes they hate this new feeling so much that they stop having them. Remember the strange sensation you had when you folded your arms in the opposite way from usual – and this is nothing compared to making a major correction with your pelvis! Val, for instance, does everything in her life with her right side in advance of her left: the pattern is deeply ingrained, and riding is only the thin edge of the wedge. To straighten her inbuilt twist, she must challenge her body and her sense of 'rightness' on the deepest level possible.

Unlike many riders, Val was quite restrained in the language she used to describe the changes in her body: she commented that she felt twisted towards the outside – which is not surprising as this is exactly what I was asking her to do. However, she also exclaimed, with a fair amount of horror, that her new way of sitting felt like the nearest she had ever come to riding sidesaddle! Other people have told me that they felt like Quasimodo, that they felt completely disorientated, or that they felt as if someone had wrung their body out like a dish cloth. However, almost all of them have soon realised the benefits of this seemingly peculiar contortion – which simply makes their body a mirror image of the way that it naturally sits on the other rein; for their horses have immediately and easily begun to bend and turn with no fuss, no fight and no pulling on the inside rein. Unlike Alexander teachers, I have the advantage of a powerful ally who always proves my point!

When the body is correctly positioned, it lies on the radius of the circle on which you are riding: this means that the horse's shoulders are on one radius, your body on another, and the horse's hips on a third. Like most of the people I meet, I was originally taught that my hips should be parallel to my horse's hips, and my shoulders should be parallel to his shoulders. This meant that I had to advance my outside shoulder, making a twist in my spine. Nowadays, some trainers teach the straight alignment of the body, and some still teach this twist: at the lower levels of teaching, most riders are taught to twist inwards. However, I was privileged to watch a Spanish Riding School performance recently, and to my eye, each of the riders had his body perfectly positioned on the radius of the turn or circle on which he was riding. When my pupils are sceptical about this, I often ask them to look at videos and photographs of the top riders and to judge for themselves. I invite you to do the same. Tremendous benefits lie in discovering what the top riders *actually* do, rather than naively relying on what they *say* they do.

I also rely on my observations of the many riders and horses who come to me for lessons – and I am convinced that they both work far better when the rider's shoulders lie on the radius of the circle she is riding. On the rider's weaker side, where her body naturally tends to twist inwards, deliberately advancing her outside shoulder compounds the twist, and almost inevitably causes her to lighten and advance her outside seat bone. This leads into the scenario that you see in Figure 31. Philosophically, it also seems wrong to me to advocate this twist in the spine, and I cannot believe that it is good for the body. Whatever school of thought a trainer upholds, however, it is a sure bet that his body has the tendency to twist inwards on one rein and not on the other – and if he looks superbly positioned on both, he has probably worked extremely hard. Regardless of the belief systems we hold in our heads, our bodies are inevitably asymmetrical: they do not mould themselves to match what we say!

Observing the rider on the rein where her body does *not* tend to twist inwards will tell you whether it is appropriate to ask her to advance her outside shoulder: she may need to in order to reach the point where her body lies on the radius of the circle. Perhaps, as it has passed down through the generations, a command which was once used with discretion has become a 'golden rule', always to be obeyed, regardless of circumstance. Confusion arises because both teachers and pupils rarely make a distinction between what the rider *feels* that she is doing – by comparison with her normal stance – and what she is *actually* doing: in the realm of asymmetries, the two can be markedly different. Bearing this in mind, it would – of course – be equally wrong to make a 'golden rule' that the rider should never twist inwards!

Confusion also arises because of the way in which teachers talk about 'the weight aids'. Many suggest that the rider should weight her inside seat bone as she moves onto a circle: but as the inside seat bone comes *down*, the outside seat bone tends to come *up*, leading to exactly the twist and collapse which Val is showing in Figure 31. Weight changes must happen by moving the pelvis *strictly in the horizontal plane*. Given the tendency of almost every rider to weight one seat bone in preference to the other, this is not as easy as it sounds – especially when the naturally heavier seat bone lies on the inside. Between Figure 31 and Figure 35, Val has moved her weight towards the inside. In Figure 31 her backside is actually sliding out across the saddle, and however much she leans in to counteract this, she will still feel as if she is slipping outwards. The key to moving her weight over to the inside lies in *weighting her outside seat bone, and bringing it towards the midline of the saddle*. Paradoxically, only this counteracts the effects of the centrifugal force. (The force which draws her backside outwards on a circle is the same force which sends the washing to the outside of the spin dryer.) Only when her outside seat bone is correctly in place can she hold her body vertical, weight her inside stirrup and hold her outside hand in place.

This is quite hard to grasp intellectually, but on a physical level, it is very disorientating to discover that one does not turn a horse as one would turn one's own body. If I want to turn to the left, I face left, turning my hips and my shoulders. If I want to turn a horse to the left, I face *right*, and position my body very much as if I were going to make a left-handed fencing lunge. (Conversely, a turn or circle to the right requires the rider to position herself as if making a right-handed fencing lunge.) In each case, the rider's outside seat bone must be distinctly further back than her inside one, and in this position it plays a key part in initiating the turn. The positioning of the seat bones *automatically* places the inside leg 'on the girth' and the outside leg 'behind the girth'. It is unfortunate that the Great Masters who wrote about this emphasised the position of the legs rather than the position of the pelvis: this seemed to escape their notice. (As Einstein once said, 'Everything should be made as simple as possible, but no simpler!' Their diagnosis is too simple to be very helpful.) The seat bones also become equally weighted – a point which helped Val to come to terms with the accompanying feeling of riding sidesaddle. Also, she found that she could lighten her inside hand with no problem at all and that she had also gained control of her horse's shoulders. By curing the cause, we had automatically cured the symptoms.

Val and China are now, in Figure 35, presenting a very different picture from their starting point in Figure 30. Val commented that she felt proud, and one could certainly say that her bearing had changed enormously. To put it another way, Val and China are now both much more full of 'stuffing'. Val was also able to hold these changes in sitting trot, although her brain was struggling to keep track of everything and her shoulders tended to round again. She wrote in her notes to me that she felt rather depressed after this first lesson, but very much better after the second, which consolidated these changes and added a few more points. She dealt with a tremendous amount of material in a very short time, and I think it was the shock of becoming conscious of her incompetence which led to her depression. However, she now has a much bigger repertoire of possible positionings and corrections, and instead of just following her old tramlines, I hope she will expand the repertoire even more.

Learning to adjust and maintain one's balance on the side-to-side plane is infinitely more complex and difficult than learning to adjust and maintain it in the back-to-front plane. I originally pieced together this correction – and my understanding of asymmetries – over quite a long period of time. Vague descriptions, 'golden rules' and incorrect teaching made my task very difficult. In your own quest, I suggest that you give this a fair trial, and then base your actions and beliefs not on what *I* say, or on what any other trainer says, but on what your *horse* says. (If you are able to work all this out on your own, however, and to get to the point where your horse gives you a resounding 'Yes', you will be doing extremely well!) This correction has been an important turning point for almost every rider I know, and nothing else I have ever tried has enabled my pupils to feel that they could sustain the correction and feel completely in charge of their bodies. At the same time, they have become able to ride the horse with an even rein contact and to feel that they can position him precisely into any turn. For many people, it has made the impossible become possible.

Lesson 5

Janet: 'On the Bit'

Janet came on the four-day course at West Wilts Equestrian Centre having previously had four lessons with me. When I first met her, she was doing a good imitation of the old 'English hunting seat', but she was able to establish a correct balance relatively easily. However, she felt that having one lesson every five weeks or so made it difficult for her to maintain the ground she had gained within each session. So she wanted to have a concentrated period of tuition to help her to ingrain all the new co-ordinations she was learning.

Mayday, her horse, is a threequarter-bred mare who is nine years old and just over 16 hands. Janet has had her for eighteen months, and with her previous owners she had hunted and competed in affiliated one-day events. As a child, Janet rode and helped at a rather down-market riding school and as an adult she has previously owned several horses. Only since buying Mayday has she become seriously interested in competitive riding, and she has had regular lessons on her. But she felt that she was not improving, and she was extremely disheartened to be told by a very well qualified instructor that her horse's temperament and conformation would never allow her to come 'onto the bit'. Janet does not have a background of disciplined riding and she keeps Mayday in a do-it-yourself livery yard where there are plenty of enthusiastic and potentially capable riders but where the whole ethos is rather anarchic. This means that she has no gauge against which to measure her likely improvements. In some ways this works to her advantage – in her naivety, she questioned the instructor's diagnosis where others might simply have accepted it.

When Janet started eventing Mayday, she found that her dressage scores were consistently letting her down, and as she wrote in her notes to me, 'I realise that I have subsequently become obsessed with getting the horse "onto the bit".' In our first few lessons we dealt almost solely with establishing Janet's balance, and she had so much else to think about that we circumvented this problem. However, I had realised in our previous session that the reprieve was over, and that the problem now needed to be addressed. When Janet came out to work in for this lesson, it obviously had to be our priority. The presence of the camera was affecting her in just the same way that I imagine a dressage judge might have done, and I was horrified to see her degenerate into a rider who was completely intent on positioning the horse's head!

Figure 36 shows Janet riding her horse in walk very early in the lesson. You might well look at Mayday's carriage and think, 'That looks nice,' but with my more experienced eye, I can see the fatal flaws, which are much more visible in Janet's body than they are in Mayday's. But in Figure 37, where Janet has gone on into trot, the problems have become blatantly obvious in both of them: Mayday has attempted to come above the bit and Janet has responded with a determined attempt to hold her head down – more determined than the restriction she is already imposing in Figure 36. This has resulted, as it always does, in an even greater evasion from Mayday, which has taken them both one step further into the spiral

of increasing tension. Look more closely at Figure 36, particularly at the front of Janet's body: I can see clearly that she is pulling in her stomach, and lifting her sternum in a way that is not correct. (There is more about this in Lesson 7 with Margaret.) She has also tipped forward, showing rather tense arms and shoulders, along with a hand whose primary function is to hold Mayday's head down. She is riding her horse 'from the front to the back'. Compare this with the attitude of her hand and body in Figure 38, which was taken later in the lesson. Here her horse is much more genuine in her desire to reach into the rein, and Janet is showing a stomach which bears down and pushes forward towards the hand – instead of a hand which restricts the horse by pulling back towards the stomach. Although there is still some tension in her elbow, Janet is riding her horse 'from the back to the front'.

36. Mayday's carriage looks quite nice here, but look at Janet's body. She is tipping slightly forward, with her sternum pulled up and her stomach pulled in. Her hand is also very restrictive.

37. Janet is now paying the price for attempting to ride her horse 'from the front to the back'. As Mayday went forward into trot, she hollowed her back. Janet is desperately trying to hold her head down and this is only making the evasion worse. Without Janet realising it, her pelvis has slid back down into the hollow of Mayday's back.

One of my first questions to Janet during this lesson was, 'If we took 100 per cent of your attention and divided it into two parts, what percentage would be focussed on your horse's head position and the feeling in your hand, and what percentage would be focussed on your pelvic positioning and the feeling of her back?'

Janet told me that 80 per cent of it would be focussed on her horse's head position and only 20 per cent on her own pelvic positioning. (What would be typical percentages for you?) I told her that this was exactly where her major problem lay. In focussing on the position of Mayday's head, she was relying on two things. The first was her eyes, which tended to stare at Mayday's ears to make sure they were in the right position. The second was her hand, which quickly resorted to force. When the rider stares, she becomes dogmatic rather than sensitive: using focussed vision cuts off the brain's ability to process kinaesthetic feedback, so the rider cannot know what she is feeling. This makes skilful riding impossible – and the more desperate the rider becomes, the more she tends to stare at the horse's ears, the more she resorts to brute force and the more she dooms herself to failure. I told Janet that these percentages would have to reverse for her to really begin to understand how she could best influence the horse, becoming much more reliant on the subtle feelings in her pelvis instead of the much grosser feeling in her hand. She should also be much less reliant on visual feedback, using her peripheral rather than her focussed vision.

38. This shows much more correct work, with Janet riding her horse 'from the back to the front'. Mayday's back is being held in carriage by Janet's pelvic positioning. Her hand (which had originally been trying to hold Mayday's head down) is now much lighter.

The stage which Janet has now reached is an extremely important phase of her learning. When I bring somebody on from a more novice starting point, I attempt to by-pass with them all the trauma and drama which accompanies this excessive need to get the horse 'onto the bit'. Fortunately, this has only become an issue for Janet in the last eighteen months, since she has been having lessons and competing Mayday. But I meet many other riders who have been in this stage for much longer, and almost inevitably they get stuck there. I myself spent years determinedly trying to get horses' heads down, and I was horrified by the thought that anybody should ever chance to see me with my horse's nose up in the air! Over recent years, I have cultivated the art of learning how to influence horses' backs rather than their noses, but I have also cultivated the art of saying to myself: 'It is now 11.15 on Thursday morning, and my horse is going round the school with his head in the air. So what?' This used to mean to me that I was no good, that I would never be any good, and that anyone who chanced to see me would probably write me off in the same way in which I was writing myself off. Now it simply means that at this particular moment, in this time and this place, things are going wrong. So what?

I do now have the advantage that I know *how* to make this change with the horses I ride – and if I cannot do it right now, I know that it is only a matter of time. Of course, it is not so easy for the person who does *not* know how to be so phlegmatic or so trusting. But I like to cultivate this attitude of trust in my pupils: to convince them that if they cannot do it now, then it is simply because they do not know how. Once they do, the problem will be solved. Being unable to ride horses 'on the bit' is not a reflection of any innate inability; it simply shows that the rider has her attention in the wrong place. *This* is the hard thing to change, and in my work with Janet, I had to make a two-pronged approach. I wanted her to learn much more about her body and its interaction with the horse: this, I knew, would teach her 'how'. But at the same time as I was showing her this, I needed to keep checking how much of her attention was focussed on bodily feelings – primarily on her pelvis and its contact with the horse's back. If I let her attention zoom in on her hand and her horse's head position, I ran the risk that my words of wisdom would only be received by 20 per cent of her attention, the other 80 per cent of it being busy elsewhere, holding Mayday's head down!

In the early stages of the lesson, Janet experienced similar difficulties in rising trot to those encountered by Gail. Both of their horses are rather lazy and although Janet's position is now much more established than Gail's, she was not initially very good at regulating her rise. She was 'going like crazy' whilst Mayday was being extremely 'laid back', and to help Janet improve the relationship between her rise, the tempo and the impulsion, I suggested that we used a numbering exercise. In this, five would signify the point where all these elements were just right, and the horse had a powerful, athletic step in a slow tempo; six to ten would mean that Janet was overdoing it, causing Mayday to run increasingly fast, with a corresponding loss of tempo and athleticism; and four down towards zero meant that Janet was slowing the tempo but losing impulsion, with zero itself signifying a complete stop. Whenever I said, 'Now,' Janet was to give me the number which corresponded with that moment, preferably without thinking about it. I explained to her that I was not going to give her marks for being right or wrong, and that I simply wanted her to give me the numbers 'off the top of her head'.

My reason for doing this was to improve Janet's concentration and to encourage her to notice changes in herself and the horse whilst they were still very subtle. It is much easier to make a correction at a four or a six than it is to make it at a two or an eight, and if the rider catches these changes early enough she can nip them in the bud so that they barely become visible to an observer. In riding, as in everything else, prevention is always much better than cure! This exercise is extremely useful in many situations (examples could be: how still you are sitting, how round your horse's carriage is, how much impulsion you have, how good you feel overall, etc.). The refinement it produces gives an interesting insight into how more skilful riders function: it usually shows you that you can achieve a lot more than you thought you could, giving you a taste of the horse's response when your body is more organised and you work with more sophistication. At the same time, the discipline involved shows what it feels like to pay attention all of the time instead of just occasionally.

I did this exercise with Janet also because I wanted her to understand exactly how her rise was influencing the horse: when she went too high and too fast, she not only tended to lose control of the tempo, but she also wasted energy and found it difficult to keep the horse 'in front of her'. (There is more about this later, particularly in the next lesson with Sarah.) When Janet thought of going lower and slower, Mayday immediately lost impulsion, just as Gail's horse had done. Janet's rise also tended to go 'mushy', and not to reach the point where she could be responsible for her own body weight at the top of it. (See Figure 19 in Lesson 2 with Gail.) When this happened she could not keep taking the horse, and she risked 'water-skiing' like Katie. It is both difficult and extremely important to maintain a 'punchy' quality as you make the rise lower, so that it is still a series of controlled thrusts. This keeps the muscles of the body acting like stretched rather than limp elastic bands. Then between each thrust you make a little pause in the air at the top of the rise, and a little pause in the saddle as you sit. It is this pause which gives you control of the horse's tempo whilst your legs maintain his energy level. The rising trot mechanism is a very precise one. When it works correctly, the horse has no choice but to trot along underneath the rider in the tempo which she has chosen.

It took Janet some while to discover the intricate balance which gave her horse no choice but to offer her a fairly consistent 'five' – the powerful step and the slow tempo which are so difficult to combine. Only by pinching more did she gain the body control which enabled her deliberately to pause at each end of the rise. She commented that she found this extremely hard work, not only in her muscles but also in her brain, which did not respond easily to the demand for constant concentration. In fact, Janet identified lack of concentration as being one of her major problems in learning. She felt that she had the kind of 'butterfly brain' which easily lost interest, and she often wanted to give up when things did not go well. Later on in the lesson she admitted that when they *did* go right she got so excited that she forgot to breathe! We both laughed about this, and I reminded her of what she already knew: that the rider does not have time to step outside her interaction with the horse and react to it in any way – not even for a moment, and not even to congratulate herself. As soon as she does this she is no longer in tune with him, and as soon as she stops keeping her half of the bargain, he stops keeping his.

At the beginning of the lesson, 80 per cent of Janet's attention was embroiled in a desperate attempt to influence Mayday's head position with her hand; she wanted to 'teach' (or maybe even force) her to come 'onto the bit'. But unbeknown to Janet, Mayday was already responding to her pelvic positioning, *which cannot help but put the horse into the seeking or the cramping reflexes*. Any rider who does not know how to use this natural interaction to her advantage always tries to override it by using her hand: effectively, she takes a horse who is already in the cramping reflexes and tries to make his nose vertical. This is a travesty of 'on the bit'. I have proved to my own satisfaction that any attempts to change a horse's carriage which are based on use of the rider's hand can never succeed; they compound evasions, piling them on top of each other and creating even more breaks in the circuit. This can only make matters a hundred times worse. My belief in this makes me something of a purist, but to convince Janet of the need for 'purity' – especially in the heat of the moment – was a different matter entirely! However, I knew that if I could teach her how to use her body so that it worked *for her* rather than *against her*, she would no longer feel tempted to position the horse from her hand: when she had access to the correct tool for doing the job, she would no longer want to settle for second best and to try and use the wrong tool.

Look again at Figure 37 where Mayday has come above the bit. Janet has reacted by lowering her hand and attempting to pull the horse's nose back down again. She has also tipped forward, closing the angle between her thigh and her body – the typical reactions of a hand-orientated rider. Equally typically, at the same time as Janet has brought her body forward towards the horse's neck, Mayday has brought her neck back and up towards Janet's body. They have both contrived to close the angle which lies between them. What Janet does not realise is that the more she tips forward and lowers her hand, the more her horse will raise her head – firstly because both of them are involved in the closing of this angle, and secondly because her hand and the horse's mouth tend to show the same inter-relationship as two opposite points on a wheel (see Diagram 7).

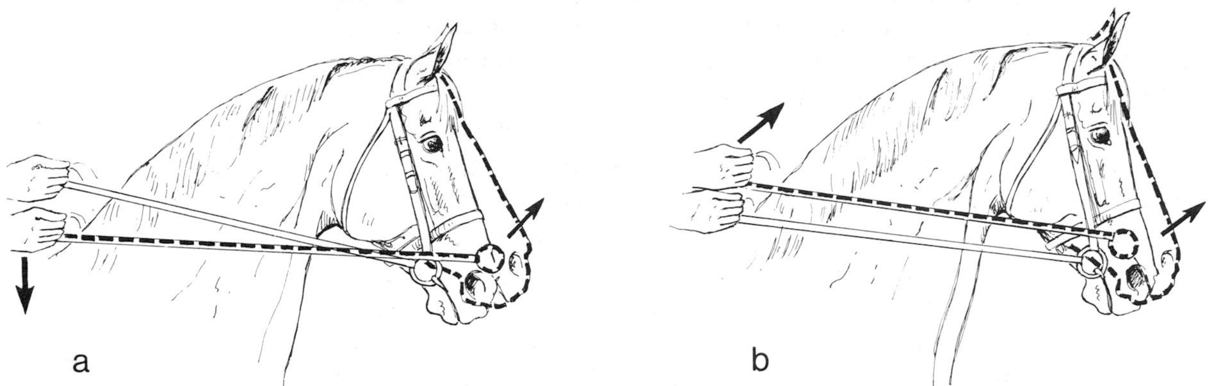

Diagram 7. The rider's hand and the horse's mouth usually show a wheel relationship. This means that when the rider lowers her hand, the horse's head comes up, and when the horse raises his head, most riders automatically bring the hand down, as in (a). The rider's aim is to maintain the hand as one point of a triangle, which is composed of the horse's crest, his nose and the rein. If the horse attempts to raise his head, she can maintain this triangular shape by raising and advancing her hand as well, as in (b).

When the rider responds correctly with the hand, she does not allow any change in the angle of the rein as it passes beside the horse's neck. When the horse is in good carriage, the rider's hand is always higher than the horse's muzzle. (Compare the angles of the reins in Figures 37 and 38.) I often tell riders that it is as if the horse's neck were *encased* above the rein, held as one side of a triangle which is formed by the neck, the horse's head and the rein. The rider must do nothing to disturb this triangle, and if the horse attempts to disturb it, her role is simply to keep it in place. This could involve raising and advancing the hand – the antithesis of pulling it down.

At the same time as Janet uses her hand incorrectly, she also reacts with her pelvis. By hollowing her back, Mayday has created a steeper slope underneath the saddle, into which Janet has slid back without realising it. She was thinking so hard about her hand and the horse's head that she completely missed this interaction. *But it is the nub of all the changes in herself and the horse which become so great and obvious once they have filtered out to the extremities of both their bodies*. Once Janet perceives this central interaction, she can correct the problem here, at its source. Then, all the other problems with the horse's head and hind legs, and with Janet's shoulders and hands, will simply not materialise. By curing the cause, she will have cured the symptoms.

When the horse hollows his back, he breaks the circuit in the loin area just behind the saddle, and depending on the way that he does it, the saddle can feel like an unending slope going down and back towards the ground, or it can feel more like the dip in a hammock. Either way, as the rider's backside slips backwards, her legs tend to come forward and up. This brings her into the 'armchair seat' and concentrates her weight down into this hollow, so that it is no longer spread along the length of her thighs (see Figure 37). The horse will then remain hollow until such time as the rider heaves herself out of the dip in his back, so that her thighs become weight-bearing again. Then, and only then, will the horse bring his back up again, 'filling her seat', as if his rib cage were a big balloon and the rider were some kind of suction pump which can draw it up underneath her and fill it up with air.

To understand how this works, kneel on the floor with your thighs resting against your calves and the upper surface of your feet against the floor. Then think of making the pinch feeling, and lift yourself *up* slightly, so that your backside still touches your heels, but you are supporting your weight with your thigh muscles. If you maintain this posture for only a little while, you will soon begin to feel a strain in the muscles. This is very similar to the way in which the rider remains in place even when the horse's back hollows, and it explains how she is able to keep a space available for his back to rise up into without her ever having to lose her contact with it. In effect, the rider has come into 'self-carriage', supporting her own body weight. *Only then* will the horse lift his back and lower his croup, coming into 'self-carriage' himself underneath her (the detailed mechanism of this is explained in Lesson 8 with Carol).

This explains why riders so often experience pain in their thigh muscles, and why it is such a natural, correct part of both learning and performing. In her notes to me, Janet wrote, 'When I become obsessed with getting the horse 'on the bit', I become tense in the shoulders, arms and hands – perhaps I am trying too hard. I now realise that (instead of trying) I have to concentrate to a much greater extent. I also must admit that I never realised before exactly how much you have to use your muscles especially in your stomach and your thighs. It was a revelation to me to realise how hard I had to work – I had always thought you were meant to relax on a horse!' One day, when her muscle tone increases and her horse is more inclined to offer 'self-carriage', Janet might well feel relaxed. She will even have magical moments in which it feels as if she is doing nothing. But meanwhile she has a choice: either she will feel the useful tension in the working muscles near the centre of the body, or she will feel the unhelpful tension in her shoulders, arms and hands.

To help Janet to maintain her body in the correct place so that her thighs remained weight-bearing, I used the image of the posture stool, which I had briefly introduced to Jan. I regularly use a whole family of images which essentially express this same idea: it is vitally important that the thighs support quite a large percentage of the rider's weight, reaching forward out of the hip joints instead of contracting back into them. So I suggested that Janet also thought of her thigh bones being strong and solid like iron bars, and imagined that there could be a little gap between them and the hip sockets. (There is more about this in Lesson 8 with Carol.) Figure 39, although it does not show fantastic carriage from Mayday, does at least show Janet (who is now in sitting trot) maintaining this correct relationship between the thigh and the pelvis. She has continued to keep this little gap between her thighs and her hip joint, and to sit as if on a posture stool. With any luck, she might just balance on a diving board. There is an element of 'limbo dancing' in her position, instead of the rather contracted posture of Figure 37.

One other idea was important for Janet. At the best of times she is weak in the muscles of the front of the body, and, like Val, she needed to think of pushing her body against imaginary iron bars. In Figure 38 her body is erect (and possibly a little behind the movement), and her shoulders are beautifully open, but in Figure 39 the added stress of sitting trot has caused her to round them again, making her balance on the diving board slightly suspect. As well as pressing forward against the bars, I suggested that she thought of making a particularly strong push at the level of her lower abdomen, at the point where I am touching Katie in Figure 9. She was then to aim this push so that it landed precisely at the dip in the horse's neck just in front of the wither – exactly where a breast-plate should lie. I explained to Janet that I was not asking her to move her lower stomach forwards towards this point; on the contrary, she was to feel as if someone had wedged a piece of wood into the gap between her body and the horse's breast-plate. She was to hold her lower stomach in its usual place, and to bear down, pushing forward through the gap.

39. Janet is riding in sitting trot. Compare her posture with that in Figure 37. Instead of contracting in the front of the body where the leg comes into the pelvis, she has maintained an open hip joint, sitting as if she were 'limbo dancing'. This enables her to keep a light hand.

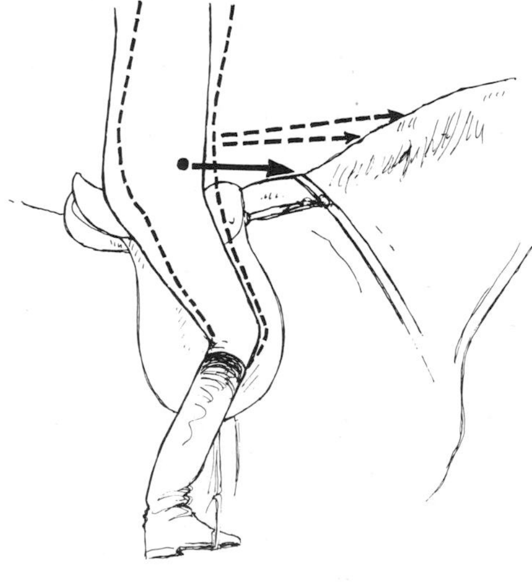

Diagram 8. The push out from the rider's lower stomach (about half-way between the belly button and the pubic bone) must land at the horse's breast-plate. If it lands too high up the horse's neck, the rider has to think of aiming better, of pushing from lower down or of moving slightly further back in the saddle.

This is quite a difficult concept to grasp, and its significance will only become clear to you later, when I explain it more fully in the next lesson with Sarah. But this push is tremendously important, and it is vital to aim it so that it lands in exactly the right place (see Diagram 8). I often ask riders, 'Whereabouts on the horse's neck is the push from your lower stomach landing?' and more often than not, it is somewhere up towards the horse's ears or even in the air way above them. I then suggest that they think of aiming better, of pushing from lower down in their body (so that the push lands lower down), or of moving slightly back in the saddle, so that the push again lands further back towards them. It is certainly landing too high in Figures 36 and 37, but in Figure 39 it is closer to being right, whilst in Figure 38 it is spot on. Only when the push lands exactly here is the horse truly 'in front of the rider'.

The burning question is: how long will it take Janet to begin to believe in the power of this correct pelvic positioning, even in those difficult moments when the horse begins to evade? Will she grab the rein as she has always done, or will she refuse to collude with the horse? This requires that she holds herself in front of the hollow in his back, keeps bearing weight with her thighs, pushes forward with them and her stomach, and thinks of drawing Mayday's back up underneath her. Most riders know nothing of this, and they are busily giving aids with their hands or their legs which are supposed to 'teach' the horse to come 'onto the bit'. In doing this, the rider has doomed herself to fail – and even if the horse's nose *does* become vertical, the carriage of his back and the freedom of his paces will never be correct. The rider has completely misjudged the level on which riders and horses communicate; she has also not realised how the carriage of the horse's back determines the carriage of the rest of his body, and how this is ultimately controlled by the way in which she sits.

In an attempt to convince riders of the power of this, I often ask them to imagine that the horse and rider interact like two pieces of a jigsaw puzzle, which have a correct way of fitting together. As the horse hollows, he changes the shape of his jigsaw puzzle piece, expecting the rider to collude with him and make a corresponding change. But if she refuses to do so, stoically maintaining the shape of *her* jigsaw puzzle piece, the horse has no choice but to reform his shape around the contours made by hers. By holding herself firmly in place, the rider can make it impossible for the horse to change the shape of his piece in the first place. This foils his evasion and is the way in which the rider remains causal even if the horse attempts to act like a wriggly worm underneath her. Lars Sederholm once said that the rider's role was to act like *a framework around the horse* rather than a load on top of him: by doing this, she holds his body in shape, holds the circuit complete and transmits the impulse of his step without interference. This is precisely what Janet, and all the other riders in this book, are struggling to do.

However eloquent I am, and however hard I argue my case, I know that neither Janet nor you, my reader, are really going to know what I mean until you have experienced for yourself the astounding degree to which the way in which you sit is responsible for the carriage of your horse's back. Really to believe it – and to trust it as well – you have to feel the horse's back disappear and then reappear underneath you again and again and again. I know very well how much easier it is to pay attention to the infinitely less subtle change which occurs in the position of his head and neck. You can, after all, see this with your eyes, and without training most people choose to rely on their visual rather than their kinaesthetic sense. It is very tempting to stare at your horse's ears, but the answer lies in using your *peripheral* rather than your *focussed* vision. Riding with your eyes closed can be a tremendous help if you need to break yourself of this dependence on visual feedback: when you open your eyes again, deliberately keep them defocussed. Look in the far distance: notice the full extent of the panorama that you can see and use this to help you develop your feel.

The next problem to overcome is the tendency to rely on your hands rather than on your pelvis. The hands are so light and mobile, so dextrous and so used to manipulating the world that it is not surprising that we are all so tempted to over-use them in riding. But I am asking you to give up both your eyes and your hands so that you learn to rely instead on the nerves and the muscles in the centre of the body, that little-known, inept, bulky area which is so difficult to manoeuvre. Am I crazy?

Fortunately, Janet knows that I am not: or if I am, she is too. For magic happened, and I suddenly heard her yell, 'She just grew up inside the saddle. It's almost like a mushroom!' Her horse also began to snort – a common response when the carriage of the back and rib cage changes, and the horse begins to breathe more fully. Janet did not yet have a consistent carriage from Mayday – but this is appropriate for her stage in learning, since the key for her lies in getting it and losing it, over and over again, until she understands exactly how it happens, and exactly how to respond to each little change in Mayday. The ultimate value of these good moments is limited by their *reproducibility*, and I would much rather see a rider make a smaller change which she can go away and reproduce at home than a greater one which she is unlikely ever to be able to make again. Anything, including riding horses 'on the bit', is easy when you know how; but the proof of the pudding is the ability to do it whenever and wherever you want to.

Janet had requested that we should work in canter, which we duly did. I had not seen Mayday's canter before, but I was correct in my suspicions that it might be rather wild and woolly, even though her trot is extremely lazy. In canter, we were immediately plummeted back a stage, where there was little hope of Janet maintaining her framework, let alone being able to process the subtle interactions which she was beginning to understand in trot. As soon as Janet went into canter, her stomach pulled in and there was an excessive rock in her shoulders. (Compare Figure 40 with Figure 57, page 156, which shows Carol sitting much more upright in exactly the same moment in the canter stride.) Janet did not bump, however, as many riders would have done, primarily because her backside remained well tucked underneath her, and her back did not hollow. This helped her enormously, and on the left rein at least, she was reasonably in control.

40. Janet in canter left. Again, her hand has become rather restrictive and she has an excessive rock in her shoulders.

41. The 'wall of death' in canter right. If Janet can count the tempo to herself, keep 'taking the horse' and maintain an even weight on both seat bones, she will in time have a slowing effect on the canter.

Mayday tends to fall onto her right (in this case her outside) shoulder, which Janet's asymmetry supports in much the same way that Val's did with China. However, here in canter Mayday's response (incorrect though it is) actually *helps* Janet, because when her inside shoulder is restricted, she cannot bound forward as impulsively as she would like to. On the right rein, however, where Mayday still falls onto her right shoulder (and therefore tends to fall in), the tempo speeds up and she careers round corners like a motor bike! On the right rein, it is harder for Janet to keep pushing out through her stomach so that she takes the horse, and this required her full attention. Figure 41 shows her in one of her worst moments on the open side of a circle, surviving what I call 'the wall of death' really quite well. Her only hope is to keep bearing down, keep pinching, keep equal weight on both seat bones and keep her thighs in place. If she could remain as if balanced on a diving board, it would be even better – but this is asking a great deal, and Janet has already done well not to pull back and start water-skiing. To help her keep control, I suggested that she counted the tempo of the canter to herself. (It is easiest to count 'two, three . . . two, three . . .', and not to verbalise the 'one' of the first beat, otherwise you run out of breath!) By some kind of magic, this synchronises the horse and rider, and it usually has a dramatic effect in slowing down the canter. It is also helpful to ride only short periods of canter, stopping if there is any indication that the tempo might speed up again.

As our lesson progressed, I kept asking Janet how much of her attention was where. In her trot work near to the end of the lesson, 60 per cent of her attention was on her body and 40 per cent on her hand, with relapses whenever she came to a corner or changed the rein, when she began again to rely on her hand and her focussed vision. In canter, she managed to maintain this 60/40 ratio, which I think was quite impressive. It took until the third day of the course for us to get a consistent 80 per cent of her attention on her body, and with this she achieved a much more consistent and at times very beautiful result from her horse. This 80/20 rule is tremendously important during the phase of gaining conscious competence and lowering the threshold which limits the subtlety of the rider's perceptions. With her attention in the wrong place Janet will blink and miss all the nuances of her interaction with the horse – just as Katie and so many other riders have done. But as long as she can hold it, she has a great deal going for her as a rider. Her body is nicely shaped and her backside does not go 'spongy' in sitting trot, so she naturally sits well. She has also begun to come to terms with her asymmetry, which is very similar to Val's. Her major problem is mental. She tends to be underfocussed: she loses concentration and her brain drifts off, thinking about other things. But then she panics and attempts to make up for this by becoming over-focussed: this causes her to use both her focussed vision and too much muscular tension, which results in her trying too hard. Paradoxically, each of these states implies the existence of the other, whilst being superbly focussed or correctly 'tuned' leaves space for neither of them. Janet's progress will depend on a disciplined attention, a 'relaxed concentration' which allows her to focus directly on the *process* of her interaction with the horse. She will then no longer become fixated on a need to conjure up the *product* – regardless of the cost.

Lesson 6

Sarah: The Rider's Seat and the Horse's Back

Sarah came on the two-day course in Hampshire bringing with her St Swithin, whose stable name is Swizzle. He is a 17.2-hand, home-bred, seven-year-old bay gelding by Ramiro, a Dutch warm-blood, out of an Irish mare. As a teenager, Sarah was a working pupil at a well-known training centre, subsequently teaching and schooling horses freelance. However, about ten years ago she changed career, and now she rides each day after work. Over a long period of time she has had occasional help from a well-known trainer. In 1989 Sarah competed Swizzle twice in affiliated dressage and in 1990 she won a Novice Qualifier after only three outings. She did not come to the lesson with any particular problem she wanted me to work on, apart from Swizzle's stiffness to the left, for which she felt she must be at least partially responsible.

The situation in which Sarah and I found ourselves is one of the most difficult which I ever encounter (as indeed was my meeting with Katie). Here in front of me is a rider who has had a great deal of experience, good tuition and a fair amount of competition success. She probably believes that she is doing well – and by some criteria she is. But as I watch her and her horse warming up, I think to myself, 'Oh dear, this is not correct.' I also know that the more subtle the incorrectness, and the more experienced the rider, the more difficult it is for her to become conscious of her incompetence. I often watch lessons given by very well-known and renowned trainers, and I am astounded that they do not challenge the rider on this basic level. Do they not see that anything is wrong, or could it be that they *do* see these fundamental flaws but do not know how to change them? If this is true – which I suspect it is – then the next logical step is to justify their inability by saying that remedial work on the rider's position is not within their sphere; they pass the buck – or simply leave it be. Or perhaps they *do* have the necessary skills, but leave well alone because they do not want to upset the apple cart by being so confrontative.

I believe so much in the ethos which I am teaching that I cannot help but tell the rider when I see an underlying incorrectness which permeates all her work. If I can also show her how to correct the problem, then I sincerely believe that I have given her the greatest gift that I can offer; but I do not always endear myself to my pupil by doing this. There are times when it almost seems as if a pupil has come to the lesson with the intention of showing me how well she can perform the various school movements! This is not a very helpful attitude (although I certainly know from my own experience how tempting it is to want to be perfect before even entering a lesson) and only goes to show how much we as pupils expect to receive damaging criticism rather than constructive help. But although I will not pander to the pupil, I take no delight in damaging anyone's ego, and I tread much more carefully on this rather delicate ground than any of my own teachers have ever done. However, my own popularity is not so important to me as the skill in which I believe.

When I first looked at Sarah's work I remembered an image which was once used by the husband of one of my pupils – who was totally naive to the horse world – to describe her horse's movement. He told me, 'You know, it used to look as if the horse was moving on square wheels, but now it looks as if he's moving on round ones.' I love the way in which untrained eyes are often so astute in their observations, until they become confused by all the ramifications of the ways it is 'supposed to be'. (This is one of the elements in the phenomenon of 'beginner's luck', which goes awry when the left brain interferes with the purity of this right-brain processing.) Sarah's horse did indeed look to me as if he were moving on square wheels, and as if the back end and the front end were like two separate pieces which did not join up. Figure 42 shows some of Sarah's early work in walk, but it inevitably cannot convey this quality, which was in fact more obvious in trot. It does, however, show an imbalance between the back and the front of Swizzle's body: it was taken in a particularly bad moment, in which his neck looks abnormally short. To be fair, however, Sarah felt that she did not have as much time as she would normally take for working in, and that Swizzle was not moving as well as usual because of this.

42. Sarah and Swizzle working in near the beginning of the lesson. Swizzle's neck looks much too short for the rest of his body, his back is hollow and his head carriage is very high.

Sarah's balance and her way of sitting were close to being correct but the subtle errors in it were having a profound effect on Swizzle. In walk, she was moving her backside backwards and forwards over the saddle, to a much lesser extent than Val or Gail did, but still to the degree that she was not 'plugged in' to Swizzle's back. This idea came from a pupil of mine, who having got herself 'plugged in', said that she felt as though her previous seat movements were like trying to put a bath plug into its hole, but finding that she only succeeded in sliding it backwards and forwards over the top! It is even better to think of an electrical two-pin plug, with the pins being imaginary extensions of the seat bones – or perhaps those plastic cowboys and indians, who have little bolts protruding from their backsides, which fit into holes in the horses' backs. Once the rider is 'plugged in', she and the horse move as one: this is a tremendously important idea, which I will develop more later. I explained this to Sarah by saying that I wanted her to sit 'still relative to the horse', meaning that she should have no extraneous movements in her seat which are not a complete match for the movements in the horse's back. (There is more about the detail of this in Lesson 7 with Margaret and Lesson 9 with Gina.) To help her, she could also think of sharing a common skin with him which she must not break – as if they were Siamese twins.

This is very much more still than most people sit, but it is appropriate, since the movements which take place in the horse's back are a great deal smaller than you might suspect. Next time you lead your horse, put your hand on his back just where your seat bone would be so that you can feel the movements. A large movement in the hind foot becomes a very small one by the time it has passed through the fetlock, hock, stifle, point of buttock and croup to the back muscles. These act like the pivot point for a series of levers which together operate as a very complex pendulum. Most riders insist, however, that their excessive seat movement is correct: 'But I'm going with him,' they tell me, 'and I've really worked hard to make myself this supple!' Although this idea of 'following the movement' or 'using your seat' seems to be encouraged in our riding schools, I am sure that any extraneous movement in the rider's seat acts rather like the interference in a radio set when it is not correctly tuned. It reduces the clarity with which the rider and horse can tune into each other; but instead of making the necessary refinements, it seems that most people would rather take the easy way out and turn up the volume!

The idea of sitting 'still relative to the horse' expresses a very strange paradox between stillness and movement, which a child – who had got it superbly – once described to me by saying, 'I feel as if my insides are moving, but my outsides are still.' This is the quality which riders from the Spanish Riding School demonstrate so beautifully. Sarah's 'outsides', however, were moving far too much, including a phase of going *backwards*. As I explained to her, there is no backwards in the movement of the horse's back, so at some point in the stride she was going against him. To stay with his movement, you have to do the equivalent of 'bottom walking', where you sit on the floor with your legs straight out in front of you and walk your seat bones along. Of course, on a horse's back you do not have to lift them up and down in the same way, and instead their movement follows the shape of the seam lines of the saddle: this means that the seat bones move rather like the forelegs of a horse who has bad action and 'plaits'. This brings the seat bones towards the midline of the saddle each time they come forward and up, which reinforces the pinch feeling. Try it on your horse and find out what effect this has compared with moving them in a straight line.

Sarah found it difficult to grasp this idea of sitting 'still relative to the horse', so to make it really clear to her I asked her to stop and to bring her chest down onto the horse's mane. I then placed one of my fingers on each side of her spine and moved them backwards and forwards in much the same way that she had moved her seat bones on the horse's back. She did not find this a pleasant sensation! I also contrasted it with the much more slow and subtle movement which enabled me to induce fractional movements in her muscles underneath my fingers so that we both moved together. When we plonk our backsides down on the saddle and ask the horse to walk forward, I feel that we do the equivalent of going up to someone, shouting, 'Hello!', slapping her on the back and rubbing our hand around rather vigorously. This is not how I like to be greeted, nor is it how I want to greet my horses!

At one time I did some training with Don McFarland, an American body-work teacher who trained originally in Rolfing and as a chiropractor before going on to train in many other body-work systems. He teaches 'Body Harmony', his synthesis of the underlying elements which enable a body to release its patterns of tension and regain its natural equilibrium. His work is similar to cranial osteopathy, and there are very few techniques involved; mostly he teaches a quality of touch, respect and of listening – through your hands – to your client's body. As you do this, you gradually learn to interpret its messages, and to honour its innate rhythms and timing, so that *the body itself* begins to trust your touch and to use you as a catalyst for its own releasing. I learnt more about riding on that course than I have ever learnt from riding teachers. Whereas Don influences a human back through his hands, I influence a horse's back through my pelvis and thighs, but the scale of the two is not dissimilar, and neither is the quality. When riders appreciate this, we will view our art very differently, our whole way of teaching and understanding it becoming very much more subtle.

Sarah is a rather small person on a very big horse, and when I taught her about the pinch and the bearing down, I asked her to take her stirrups up one hole – as I have done with almost all the other riders. In particular, I see many short riders like Sarah who attempt to make up for their lack of leg by riding very long; but I am convinced that a five-foot rider should ride like a miniature version of a six-foot rider, so that she has the same angles at the knee and at the hip. I recently went through the photographs in all of my riding books and measured these angles whenever they were clearly visible. Interestingly, all of the Spanish Riding School riders had angles of 140 degrees at the hip and 120 degrees at the knee. The greatest variations on this shown by other riders were 10 degrees either way. However, many of the riders I see – whether they be competing at the lower levels or learning in riding schools – attempt to ride much longer than this, so that the angle behind the knee comes much closer to 180 degrees. This is much longer than the successful riders who take part in top-class competition. This supports my idea that most teachers have gone overboard in telling the rider to 'stretch her legs down'. Having a longer leg makes it harder for her to balance on a diving board, and it increases the likelihood that she will hollow her back.

I also spent some time showing Sarah about the correct mechanism for the rising trot, where she was showing a much more common mistake than Gail. In fact, Sarah was demonstrating one of the faults I most frequently see. In Figure 43 she has pulled herself up into the rise from her stomach muscles and has also pushed herself up from her foot, so that her knee has straightened and her heel has moved down and forward. As a result, she is barely able to stop herself from falling back into the saddle. The correction

43 and 44. In Figure 43 Sarah has brought herself up into the rise by pushing her foot forward and pulling herself up with her stomach muscles. This upsets her balance over her feet, hollows her back and interferes with her bearing down. In Figure 44 she has remained correctly in balance over her feet; however, in attempting not to pull herself up from her stomach muscles, she has pulled herself up from her shoulders. She corrected this easily later.

she needs to make utilises the mechanism I explained in Lesson 2 with Gail. Compare Figure 43 with Figure 44, which shows a more correct balance – although when I stopped Sarah from using her stomach muscles in the old way, she attempted to pull herself up from her shoulders! If you are sitting in a chair reading this, think of standing up and make just the beginnings of the movement, firstly by pulling up from your stomach, and then by pushing up from your backside and thighs. (In the style proposed by Alexander teachers, you can also lead the movement by thinking of your head coming 'forward and up'; but make sure that you do not strain with your stomach muscles as you do this.) It is amazing how much work the thigh muscles must do to get you up – and riders who make this change in their riding are often shocked when they discover aches and pains which they have never felt before. This difference is vital, because if you pull yourself up from your stomach, you cannot maintain the bearing down. Since this is essentially a pushing out, the two are mutually exclusive.

As an accompaniment to this change, Sarah also needed to think of sitting as if on a posture stool, with her thigh bones snugged in against the saddle more and feeling as if they were iron bars. Swizzle's carriage made Sarah feel as if the saddle was a big slope backwards which she tended to slip down, and thinking of these images helped her to redistribute her weight so that she stayed nearer to the top of the slope. Not surprisingly, she was disconcerted by the feeling of being 'tighter', but this, I told her, was a sign that she was beginning to turn her body into a framework around the horse, giving her the power to hold him in the correct shape. In order to influence Swizzle's carriage and to send him forward, Sarah needed to be absolutely precise in her balance: when she was unbalanced at the top of the rise, she tended to come down into the saddle rather hard and rather far back, and she *deliberately pushed down harder* whenever she needed to give a driving aid. Her leg was also used in a rather prolonged and forceful way. (These two usually go together.) She thought that this combination was correct, and that she was being powerful with her seat, but in fact it is incorrect, which is why it was not working for her.

To understand why, think of the horse as a trampoline, giving the rider a rhythmic impulse with each step. Some horses are very enthusiastic trampolines, tending to catapult the rider out of the saddle the moment she lands in it, and sending her sky-high on each rise! (If her back is hollow, so that her own shock absorption is already bad, it can be extremely difficult for her to counteract this. The secret lies in having the correct pelvic angle, with a strong pinch feeling and the seat bones slightly lower than the pubic bone.) Other horses are rather dead trampolines, extremely happy to have the rider deaden their impulse even more. If you have ever trampolined, you will understand the difference between landing and bouncing up again and landing in a way which stops the trampoline

– and if you have not, you can probably imagine it well enough. Swizzle is a rather dead trampoline, especially on the right rein, where his right hind leg appears almost to glue itself onto the ground momentarily instead of pushing off actively. Sarah's rather forceful landing, with its prolonged squeeze from her seat and her leg, actually tended to *dissipate* Swizzle's energy and to *stop* the trampoline. This is the usual result when the rider thinks of 'using her seat' or 'driving the horse forward' – and it is the opposite effect to the one she wants to achieve. But very few riders realise this: the exceptions are people who ride rather fast, 'bomby' horses. Often they instinctively discover how to deaden their horse's energy like this as a way of staying in control!

I explained to Sarah that she must hold herself responsible for keeping Swizzle's impulse alive and flowing around the circuit. This requires her to land lightly in the saddle so that she is ready to spring out again. She then becomes able to counteract Swizzle's desire to deaden the impulse. In all our riding, the quality the rider puts in is the quality she gets out: if she puts in 'Uuugh . . .' she gets out 'Uuugh . . .', and on a lazy horse this can become an increasing spiral in which they both wind themselves into complete paralysis! (This can seem funny when written on paper, but in real life it is one of the most devastating things which can happen in a rider/horse relationship.) But if she puts in 'Ping!' she gets out 'Ping!', which can be dangerous on a horse which is 'pingy' already! Thinking of the trampoline helps to balance these two, and the idea describes beautifully the way in which horse and rider exchange energy in rising trot. It helps the rider to define how much rise and how much thrust is just right. As I explained in Lessons 2 and 5 with Gail and Janet, very few people show this quality, but it is an essential part of the ability to regulate the impulsion, the tempo and the horse's carriage. Without it, the rider's work can never be absolutely precise.

When Sarah understood this quality, and could push herself up from her thighs rather than pull herself up from her stomach, Swizzle's trot came alive. Much less effort was required from Sarah, since she was no longer working against her own resistance, and the horse immediately lost the look of moving as if he was on square wheels. His movement became fluid, and with this came the possibility of correct carriage. Figure 45 shows a vastly improved carriage. Although Sarah thinks she needs a lot of working in, I suspect (as I always do in these cases) that what she really needs is a change in technique, since with the correct tools it becomes much easier to extract the movement she wants from her horse with less time and effort.

When Swizzle breaks the circuit in his habitual ways (in the loin area, the base of the neck and the poll), he looks as if his head is too big and as if his neck is too short and too straight in its top line. (A well-known trainer has amusingly described this attitude of the neck as looking as though the horse had been sword swallowing!) One sees this very often and it is tempting to believe that the problem lies in the horse's conformation. Figure 45, however, shows that this is not true, and that it is simply a matter of carriage: for when the circuit is complete, the whole horse appears to change shape and to come into proportion. I often explain these changes, as I did in Lesson 4 with Val, by suggesting that the rider thinks of her horse as a stuffed toy. In an older, well-used stuffed toy, the stuffing wears thin, and in particular the horse's neck goes rather limp so that it is not solidly joined onto his body. But in a brand-new stuffed toy, the neck is much more solid, bulging with stuffing and arching out of the wither.

45. Some of Sarah's best work in trot: compare Swizzle's carriage with Figure 42. His neck no longer looks too short for his body, although he is still not quite 'coming through from behind'.

The rider's job is to fill the horse up with 'stuffing', so that more and more of it passes forward into his rib cage and neck. This brings him into the carriage of the seeking reflexes, so that he literally feels bigger and more solid underneath her. However, the horse would rather not be this 'full up', and he attempts to make the stuffing pass *backwards* between the rider's legs so that he does not have to take on this posture. In reality, 'stuffing' is muscle tone, and the idea of having the horse 'in front of you' implies that there is more 'stuffing' in front of you, or that the horse 'carries himself' more, with higher toned muscles. With less muscle tone he flops, just as China and Val were rather floppy at the beginning of their session. Once the horse is truly collected he is so full of 'stuffing' that he can feel as if he might burst! (Whenever your horse dances about underneath you, feeling as if he has grown a hand higher, you are experiencing the effects of high muscle tone. If this energy were under your control, you could probably piaffe with it, and demonstrate the collected movements far better than many riders show them in dressage tests!) Riders who aim for relaxation as their first priority often undermine their efforts to achieve power and collection. They do not realise that the only place in which a completely relaxed horse and rider could ever be found is flat on the floor of the riding school!

Sarah and Swizzle were not floppy in quite the same way as Val and China, but they definitely lacked 'stuffing', with the most obvious lack being in Swizzle's neck, particularly at the base of it where he likes to break the circuit. To help Sarah counteract this, I suggested that she thought of pushing out from her lower stomach towards the place on the horse's neck where a breast-plate would sit (see Diagram 8, page 112, in Lesson 5 with Janet). Initially her push was landing much further up the horse's neck, and only on the second day of the course was she able to redirect it so that it landed back down by the breast-plate. This can involve aiming better, pushing from lower down in the abdomen or moving slightly further back in the saddle. Sarah had to move back slightly, which meant that she also had to be extremely careful to maintain her balance as if on a diving board, so that she did not slide back into the hollow of the horse's back. There is only *one* correct place in the saddle for the rider to sit, and it varies from horse to horse (I explain more about the physics of this in Part Three). I often help people to find it by suggesting that they think of sitting *in front of the dip in the horse's back and behind the bulge of his neck*.

Only when Sarah had succeeded in this apparently rather strange endeavour could she really understand its importance. But whilst she was struggling I explained its significance as follows: 'Only when the push from the rider's stomach lands just in front of the wither is the horse truly "in front of her". If it lands a few inches further forward, then effectively the horse has managed to push those few inches of "stuffing" back behind her. If it lands further up the neck, then he has succeeded in pushing correspondingly more "stuffing" back behind her. If it goes way out above his ears into space, then the horse is well and truly behind her.' (This image is more difficult to work with than most. If you cannot make any sense out of it when you are actually riding, then this is probably what is happening to you. It will only make sense when your push is already landing in approximately the right place; so only introduce the idea when you are very well established in your basic balance and your horse is going well forward.)

Sarah had no hope of aiming her push correctly until she already had the correct mechanism for the rise in place, otherwise she undermined her own efforts by pulling in her stomach. She also understood the idea more clearly when she thought of bringing her thighs more snugly in against the saddle. They and the lower belly form a *barrier* which stops the 'stuffing' passing backwards, so they need to be firmly in place. At the opposite end of the horse, the bit provides another barrier. If there is no contact, the stuffing can leak out of the front, and it never builds up within the horse's body. On the other hand, if the rider pulls *back*, she colludes with the horse and joins him in squashing the stuffing backwards: she is riding the horse 'from the front to the back'. It is as if the horse's body were a tube of toothpaste, the rider's contact representing the lid on the end of it. With no lid, the toothpaste leaks out; but if the tube is squeezed backwards from the front it becomes crinkled and loses the beautiful look that it has as a brand-new tube. Horses often lose this look too, and many of them become 'crinkled' as their riders attempt to get them 'onto the bit'. This also happens with more ambitious riders as they move up through the competition grades and attempt to shorten the horse's frame and bring him into collection. The rider's hand must act like the lid on the end of the tube, which by its very nature can never pull back. As soon as the hand 'fiddles' or pulls, the price paid is the loss of the horse's natural beauty.

In Figure 45 Swizzle's carriage has improved enormously, but he is still not completely 'in front of' Sarah. The horse's movement is only correct in trot when the angle of the hind cannon bone matches the angle of the forearm (from the elbow to the knee). (See Figures 12, 27, 35, 38, 55 and 58.) He is then 'coming through from behind'. I find that the rider has most influence over this, and the horse's hind legs, when she thinks of *influencing the parts of his back with which she has direct contact*. She then fills him up with stuffing (or blows up the big balloon) so that his wither lifts, his rib cage fills out and his neck reaches and arches away from her. This creates the space for the hind legs to step well underneath the body. It is not so helpful to think the other way round, as if the push of the hind legs was responsible for creating the lift in the body: if all you needed to do was to kick harder to create this effect, we would all have succeeded years ago! The vital keys lie in the precise positioning of the body, the creation of stuffing, and in the exchange of energy which maintains the bounce of the trampoline. Many of the riders who are desperately kicking or squeezing are *at the same time* deadening the horse's energy and squashing him in the middle so that he drops his back. Their efforts are doomed.

It is interesting to see less visible change in Sarah's body than in almost all of the other riders. This is because the major changes she made were in the deep abdominal muscles. (Interestingly, trampolining is reputed to be the best way of exercising these!) At the end of this first lesson Sarah still felt uncomfortable with these feelings, which seemed so strange and different from her norm, but they 'clicked' much more on the second day. We were also then able to look at her asymmetry, and we found that her left thigh was always looser than her right. She also tended to lose her outside seat bone on both reins and to put more weight on her inside seat bone and inside foot. She might well have been doing this in an attempt to bring her weight to the inside on a circle, but when the rider does this, there is always a danger that her outside seat bone loses its contact with the saddle (see Lesson 4 with Val). However, it is interesting that Sarah's wobbly left thigh led to Swizzle falling *in* on the left rein, whereas both Val's and Janet's horses responded to their wobbly thighs by falling out. The precise positioning of each rider's seat bones accounts for this difference in the horse's response.

Usually, the rider diagnoses the side of the looser thigh as the 'bad' side. Whether the horse falls out away from it or in against it, he is always less stable on the rein where the looser thigh lies on the inside. Figure 46 shows Sarah on the left rein, and although we are not seeing her from the mid-point of her circle, it looks as if she has twisted inwards. She certainly has her inside hand behind her outside one – always a tell-tale sign. Finding her right (outside) seat bone on the left rein and lying her left (inside) thigh more clearly against the saddle immediately gave her a correct bend –

46. On the left rein, Sarah's body tends to twist inwards, advancing her outside shoulder and hand and causing her inside thigh to lie less snugly against the saddle than her outside thigh. She has difficulty creating a bend to the left, and in an incorrect attempt to do this, she is drawing her inside hand backwards, thereby pulling the bit through Swizzle's mouth and bringing his nose behind the vertical.

although the cure is not always this simple, and riders usually find it harder to make the necessary corrections when the horse is falling in than when he is falling out. (Lesson 10 with Jill explains more about this.) As this change happened on the second day, I do not have a picture of the correction she made, but Sarah felt an immediate change which was easy to see.

Sarah did not find it easy to change her established ways of thinking and working during our two lessons together, and although her horse's movement improved enormously, I left feeling that she was probably not convinced by my ideas. I regret that I did not have more time with her; like Katie, I think she might have needed about four lessons to really understand in her body as well as her mind what I was saying, and to appreciate the benefits of 'undoing her knitting'. She has told me since that she too would have liked more time to consolidate the new feelings she was getting. But I had obviously underestimated her commitment, and her understanding of what we were doing, and I was pleased to hear that the work we did together has made a profound difference to both her riding and her teaching. She feels that she is now understanding the rider/horse dynamic much better, whether she is looking at it or feeling it.

When she wrote to me after reading the first draft of this lesson, she said, 'I am the kind of person who needs to take on board information or instructions, try it, analyse it, shuffle it around and try again, and then go back to an instructor for further discussion and training . . .' I can understand this very well, because I am too – and this work is designed to be assimilated in this way, over time, and through experimentation. I was extremely pleased to hear that Sarah has taken this process on board, for only by doing this can the rider begin to *own* the knowledge I am imparting, and to know it 'in her bones'. (It is always nice for both of us, however, when she takes to it more easily!) Swizzle has now upgraded to Elementary after only a few more outings, and fortunately Sarah's success in the external world is going hand-in-hand with an increased understanding of her internal world – the subtle internal pieces which fit into the rider/horse jigsaw. I wish her luck in the external world; but even more, I wish her fruitful explorations of this internal world, because I know that this will yield the keys which will enable her to become a more powerful, precise and sensitive rider. As she achieves all this, she will win in competition too!

Lesson 7

Margaret: Becoming Causal

Margaret was the only participant on the clinic in Hampshire who had worked with me before, this being her twelfth lesson. The previous ones had taken place over a period of about six months. When I first met her it seemed that I was her last hope, and that if I could not help her to ride Saffron, then Saffron would have to go.

Margaret was given her first pony at the age of twelve, and between then and the arrival of Saffron, her riding experience had extended little further than quiet hacking on her increasingly elderly mount. Since her childhood riding lessons in the Pony Club, Margaret has been terrified of riding teachers and has rarely succeeded in doing what they have told her. She admits to being a nervy type of person, both on and off a horse, and she certainly does not have the kind of long thin body which riders are supposed to have. Although the odds would seem to be stacked against her, her response to my right-brain teaching techniques has been tremendous and her improvement has been a delight to see. Despite her history, I find that she is extremely skilled at learning, and I am sure that she has been helped in this by her training as an artist, which has included a long-term apprenticeship to a teacher who worked in a similar way to myself.

Saffron is a 15.2-hand mare who is seven years old. Margaret and her husband bought her as a two-year-old from her breeders, who were carriage driving enthusiasts. She is by National Trust out of a Postier Breton mare, and was the first stage in an attempt to recreate the Norfolk trotting horse. However, her breeders lost interest in the project and she was sold very cheaply. She was extremely easy to break in, and her first year's work went very smoothly. Margaret remembers enjoying her canter and likening it to the slow movement of a rocking horse. But Saffron then discovered that she could go fast, which left Margaret feeling absolutely powerless. A series of upsetting experiences followed to reinforce this feeling. The two worst occurred in a riding arena: in the first, Saffron lost her footing and fell in a canter which was already out of control. In the second, she failed to take a turn and crashed into the fence, giving Margaret a bad fall. Almost all of Margaret's riding, however, is done in a field or in the New Forest. Because of her work commitments, it is sporadic at the best of times, but Margaret found herself riding more and more infrequently and becoming increasingly scared even at walk. Several local instructors had attempted to help her, but she felt that no one had been able to make an inroad through her fear.

When I first saw Margaret, she looked almost paralysed with fright. Her back was extremely hollow, her stomach was clutched in and she had almost stopped breathing. She pushed her feet hard against the stirrups and hung onto the reins – a classic water-skier, as she remembers me saying, being pulled along by an equally classic motor boat. I spent quite some time in that first lesson helping her in walk before I dared to send her forward into trot, and when I did, I saw the whole scenario acted out before my eyes. Saffron's first step was like a bullet out of a gun, effectively pulling the rug out from under Margaret's feet so fast that she was left behind, falling into the water-skiing position. When the rider leans back like this and pulls against the rein, she may think that she is telling the horse to slow down, but in reality she is forcing him to play the role of the motor boat, thus encouraging him to go faster. It is as if the rug is on a polished floor, so that leaning backwards sends it out from underneath the rider even more.

In actual fact, Margaret had no idea what she was doing to Saffron, because her brain had gone numb and she was caught in the grip of a panic so intense that it stopped her from thinking straight.* In that first lesson, my major task was to bring her and Saffron back from the madness of their respective 'panic zones'. Sports psychologists differentiate between the 'panic zone', the 'stretch zone' and the 'comfort zone'. No learning takes place in the 'panic zone' – it is far too frenzied, and horse and rider are run by the adrenalin which fuels the instinct of 'fight or flight'. But in their 'stretch zones' they both have access to higher brain functions and to the state of conscious competence which enables them to choose learned responses over brute instinct. Initially this is very difficult (a 'stretch' for all concerned), and it is in the 'stretch zone' that the hard graft of learning takes place. Over time, these learned responses become easier, and eventually they become ingrained as part of the rider's and the horse's natural repertoire, taking place in their 'comfort zones'. This aspect of learning is now complete, for by the time they reach this stage, horse and rider are functioning on 'unconscious competence'.

Margaret is the first to admit that it is she who has frightened Saffron, and she has a good deal of sympathy for the horse's plight, especially as – when they are not out riding – they have a tremendous trust in each other. (She does not think, as many nervous riders do, that Saffron is 'out to get her'.) So Margaret knows that

* If you too are a nervous type of person with a tendency to panic, I recommend Joseph Chilton Pearce's beautiful book, *Magical Child*, which may well give you an insight into the origins of your fears.

she must master her own fear before there is any chance of getting a positive response from Saffron. However, I firmly believe that this cannot be done through will-power. The change can only take place once the rider has access to, and faith in, a whole new set of co-ordinations within the body. As she learns these, she must stay within very controlled conditions, and only gradually can she be allowed to test the boundary of her 'stretch zone', reclaiming ground which was once in the area of panic.

I am sure you can predict by now how Margaret's body alignment needed to change. I took her stirrups up two holes, taught her the pinch and the bearing down and made sure that she had a correct shoulder/hip/heel alignment. This changed the angle of her pelvis as it rested on the saddle so that her lower back was no longer hollow. I made her take great care in the upward transitions, so that she 'whispered' to her horse about trotting and stood a chance of being able to keep 'going with' her. I also made her pretend that she really did want to go at Saffron's rather fast pace, so that instead of attempting to slow down, Margaret kept taking her, thrusting her pelvis forward at each stride. Otherwise, her trot would very easily have degenerated into 'water-skiing'. The change in the angle of her pelvis enabled her to make little pauses at each end of the rise, which gradually gave her control of the horse's tempo. She remembers very clearly that I had her thinking of her thigh and calf as an arrowhead, with the knee at its point. As she did this, she felt like a jockey . . . a feeling which was so exaggerated, I am sure, because of its contrast to her normally long leg which was stretched – and often braced – down into the stirrup. By the end of the lesson, she also found that she was using her thigh muscles in a completely new way, which gave her considerable discomfort.

The corrections I wish to cover here concern Margaret's hollow back, her sense of 'up' and 'down' and her almost non-existent breathing. Whenever she perceived herself as being in danger, Margaret's body folded up so that her feet and shoulders came forward and her backside came backwards. As this happened, she took a quick, shallow inbreath and then did not breathe out again. We all tend to do this when startled (try it now), and it forms part of the 'foetal crouch' reflex. (I write about this at length in *Ride With Your Mind*.) Margaret held her breath with her sternum lifted and her stomach pulled in, which in turn made her back become hollow. When I had her bear down and drop her sternum, she actually felt hunched and collapsed, as if she was 'squashed into a little ball'. I often tell hollow-backed riders to imagine that I am punching them in the stomach, and I also pull backwards on the waistband of their breeches at the small of their back. This makes the back and the front of the body look like two vertical, parallel lines (it is miraculous how even large backsides suddenly disappear!), but it usually upsets the rider's sense of 'rightness', and her understanding of our riding dogma, so much that I often hear cries of 'but surely this can't be right'. . . .

From her Pony Club days, Margaret had taken very seriously the advice that she should 'sit up straight and push her heels down'. So from her waist she stretched *up*, lifting her sternum and upper body, and at the same time she stretched *down*, pushing her feet down hard into the stirrups (see Diagram 9). Riders who do this cannot make the pinch feeling, so they lose the security and power which this brings. Their waists also become a separation point between the upper and lower halves of the body, which causes a major break in the circuit. In my corrections, I made Margaret feel as if she was squashing both halves of herself in towards her middle. This now comes easily to her in walk and trot, but she still has to feel an exaggerated sense of it in canter, otherwise she pushes down into the stirrups again, which produces an equal and opposite force which pushes her *up*, straightening the hip and knee and causing her to bump way out of the saddle.

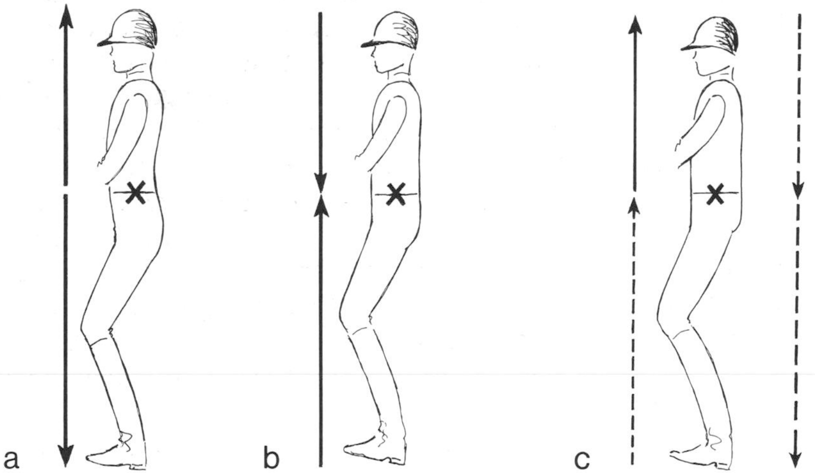

Diagram 9. Most riders stretch up from the waist and stretch down from the waist as in (a). In doing this, they hollow their backs and push down into the stirrups. In learning how to counteract this tendency, they have to feel as if they are doing the opposite, bringing both halves of their body in towards their middle, as in (b). When they establish correct carriage from the horse, they go through a sequence: initially they drop down, bringing their ribs towards their hips and resting their foot in the stirrup. Then they think of the horse coming up underneath them, and bringing them up, as in (c). It is this sense of coming up that good riders talk about.

The rider sits much better, thereby influences the horse much better, when she thinks of *dropping down*, so that her ribs come down towards her hips and her backside comes down onto the saddle. Her feet are then just *resting* and not *pushing* on the stirrups. (After all, when you stand on the ground you just rest on it, you do not push on it, and in riding, the stirrup replaces the ground as your base of support.) Then, and only then, can you think of the horse coming up underneath you, as if he were a big balloon being filled up with air. He then lifts you up, giving you a feeling of being tall and elegant; but the 'up' can only come after the 'down', and it begins from the pubic bone and not just from the sternum. It often amuses me to recall the story I was told by a pupil of mine who went to watch a demonstration given by a well-known dressage rider. A member of the audience asked him, 'How do you do piaffe?' to which he replied, 'I just grow taller.' *I* know that his sense of 'taller' begins from the pubic bone and includes the horse coming up underneath him, but most people in the audience who went away to try their luck at piaffe would probably have thought of growing taller from the *sternum*, separating the upper body from the lower body and leaving the horse well and truly stuck to the ground underneath them!

I also made Margaret become very conscious of her breathing out so that she could not simply hold her breath. I told her to think of breathing out through that famous point to which we keep coming back – the top of the bottom segment of the rectus abdominus muscle, about half-way between the navel and the pubic bone – as if there were a little tap there (see Figure 9, page 57). I often suggest to people that they make an 'Ah' sound on the outbreath, or even that they think of growling on each outbreath. This image – which I have found a tremendous help in my work – was invented by one of my student teachers in her work with someone who was asthmatic and had enormous problems with breathing. Try making a growling sound now (silently in your throat if necessary) and feel what happens to your lower belly. You will almost certainly find that it pushes out, and that it is difficult, if not impossible, to make a powerful growl with the belly pulled in. Tennis players exhale as they serve, and often grunt at the same time, simply because they are bearing down strongly to ensure that the power of their pelvis is transmitted through to their upper body. Martial artists too make dramatic yells, not to frighten their opponents but to help them to access their own power. This means that telling your horse in no uncertain terms to, 'Get on you rotten little . . .' has a beneficial effect on *you*, and perhaps it is this as well as sheer volume of sound which has the beneficial effect on him!

If instead you have trouble on the inbreath, which many people do, this signifies that you normally breathe only in your upper chest, with a habitual holding pattern in the diaphragm itself which makes bearing down impossible. This is often not easy to release; however, the rewards of full, deep, breathing and a strong bearing down make it well worth the effort. It is helpful to think of breathing through your mouth and feeling the coldness of the air as it passes down the front of your windpipe into your belly. Also think of putting your breathing into a rhythm with the horse's gait: each inbreath and each outbreath should last for at least two strides of walk and three strides of trot. If you cannot make them last this long, you have some work to do!

As Margaret worked in that day in Hampshire, she still had to be very aware of bearing down, pushing outward with her lower belly as if she could push her guts against her skin. Paradoxically, at the same time she had to think of her waist area and her belly button coming *backwards*, so that her pubic bone lifted and her seat bones and coccyx dropped down onto the saddle. (Her body has exactly the opposite tendencies to Jan's in Lesson 3. Margaret habitually hollows her back and pushes the waist area and belly button forward *in the wrong way*. Hence this rather strange paradox. Experiment with your own body to make sure that you clearly understand the difference between bearing down and hollowing your back.) As Margaret has learnt about bearing down, a series of changes has happened within her body, causing her to go through a stage of feeling sick. 'I'm sure I've been sick with fright all my life,' she told me, 'and I have been holding in my belly to try to hold back that feeling.' I am happy to report that she has not actually been sick and that the feeling has passed; but it is interesting to realise how the internal organs are influenced in their functioning by our posture and breathing.

Saffron now works quietly, and at times extremely well, although the canter is still a cause for some concern. We have rated Margaret's panic level out of ten, and it has reduced from being eight out of ten to zero at walk and usually about four out of ten in canter. I insist that she does not canter at home unless she thinks she can keep the panic level down to a four, and she has had some quiet canters in the forest which have really delighted her.

In this particular lesson, we focussed on steering. Margaret had done some basic work on this before and had made a correction similar to Val's with her own asymmetry. Saffron is extremely 'rubber necked' – she can go from jack-knifing in one direction to jack-knifing in the other remarkably quickly – which does not give Margaret much leeway in terms of the correctness of her sitting. On this particular day we found that she was tending to fall outwards on the right rein and as this happened Margaret's right hip was dropping back and her foot was coming forward. Figure 47 shows me with my hands on her pelvis and her foot, indicating the way that they have the same relationship as two opposite points on a wheel: so only when the hip advances is the foot able to come back into place.

This helped Margaret somewhat, but I decided to take the bull by the horns and to offer her a fuller explanation of what was happening. This is illustrated in Figures 48 to 50. Supposing that you, represented by my hand, go up to the top of your rise in rising trot, and whilst you are there the horse, represented by my body, falls onto his left shoulder (Figure 49). You are a naive rider who comes straight down into the saddle without making any corrections. Which side of the saddle do you land on? As you can see in Figure 50, it is the right side. (This is somewhat complicated.

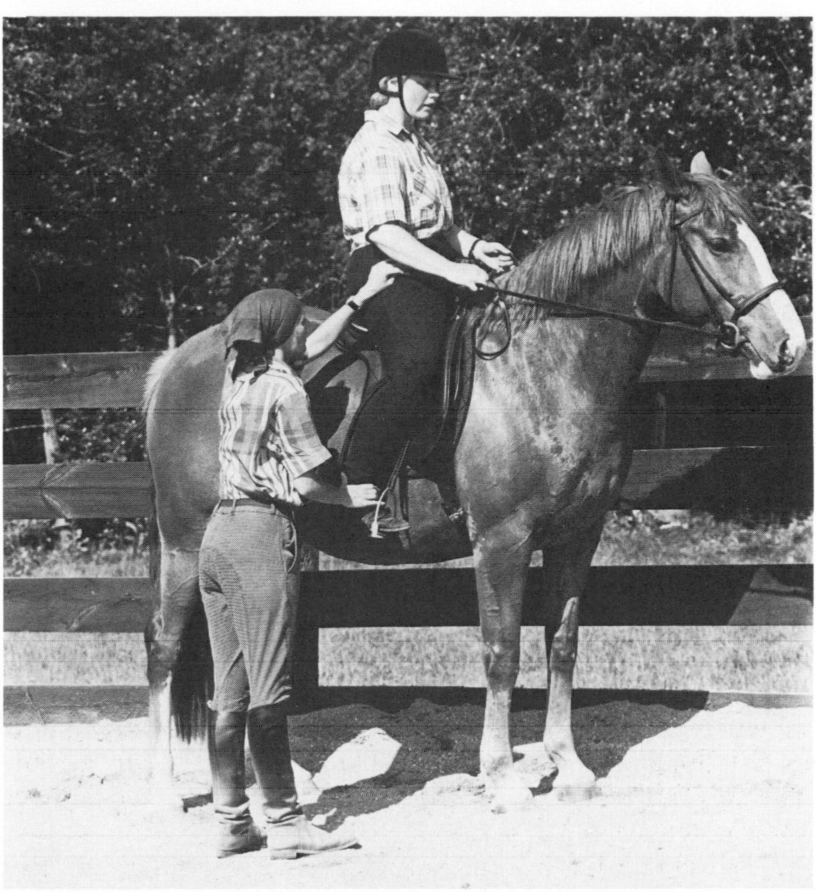

47. I am holding Margaret's right point of hip and right foot to show her how they are always positioned like the two opposite points on a wheel.

48, 49 and 50. I am using my body to demonstrate the positioning of the rider and horse relative to each other on the side-to-side plane. (See text.)

Please think about it clearly, so that you really understand.) You are then sitting on the right side of the saddle and, relative to you, the horse's shoulders are bulging out to the left. The converse could equally well be true, so if the horse fell onto his right shoulder and you made no correction, you would land on the left side of the saddle. How must you sit if you want the horse's shoulders, relative to you, to bulge out to the right? The answer is the way in which Margaret must sit in this case so that she counteracts the horse's tendency to fall left and positions Saffron's shoulders to the right instead.

If, relative to Margaret, the horse's shoulders are to come towards the right, Margaret must sit more to the left. This is different from the usual idea of sitting to the inside on a circle. It is much more sound to think of positioning the horse's shoulders *relative to you* than it is to think of positioning your body *relative to the circle*. The first renders you causal in a way in which the second does not: you can change the positioning of the horse's body underneath you in very significant or very subtle ways, making adjustments as often as necessary. Compared to this, it is very crude just to sit to the inside because you are riding a circle. (You will understand the physics of this better after reading Part Three.)

The bottom line in this interaction was that both Margaret's seat bones kept falling off the side of Saffron's long back muscles. These muscles, the longissimus dorsi, are the largest muscles in the horse's body. They insert into the vertebrae in the root of the neck and pass each side of the spine to the horse's croup (see Diagram 10). Everything in riding begins to work when THE RIDER'S LEFT SEAT BONE IS ON TOP OF THE HORSE'S LEFT LONG BACK MUSCLE AND HER RIGHT SEAT BONE IS ON TOP OF HIS RIGHT LONG BACK MUSCLE.

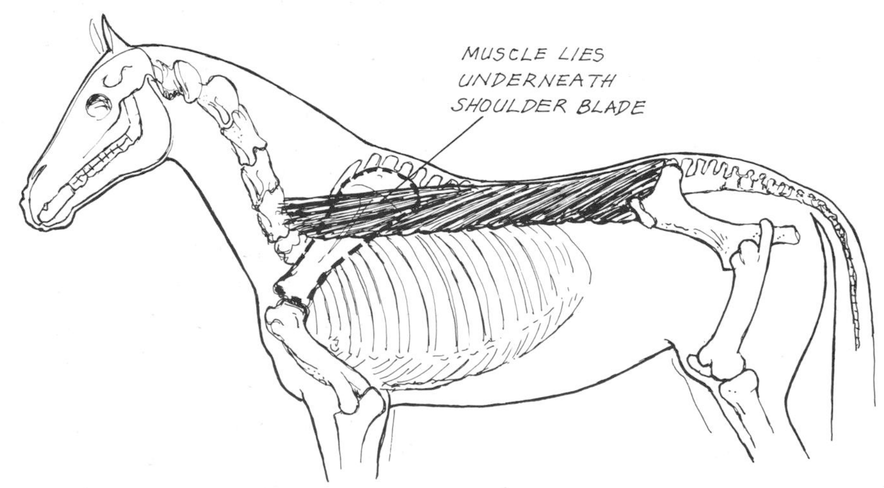

Diagram 10. The horse's long back muscles are the largest muscles in his body. They run each side of his spine and connect his croup with the lower vertebrae of the neck. The diagram shows their individual segments, which can each contract separately, creating a ripple which passes forward from the croup with the movement of each hind leg. This happens in each of the muscles alternately.

(This is so devastatingly simple that I cannot think why it has taken me – let alone the rest of mankind – so long to work it out!) Unfortunately the distance between the rider's seat bones is rather too wide for them to sit comfortably on top of these muscles, so when one seat bone is correctly placed, the other tends to fall off its muscle (see Diagram 11(a)). In my body this distance is 5½ inches (14 cms) – much wider than the channel of a saddle, designed to keep weight off the horse's spine so that it is carried primarily on the long back muscles. When one seat bone falls off the long back muscle, this leads to a loss of control of that side of the horse. This happens very frequently and is one of the most significant yet undiagnosed problems besetting riders.

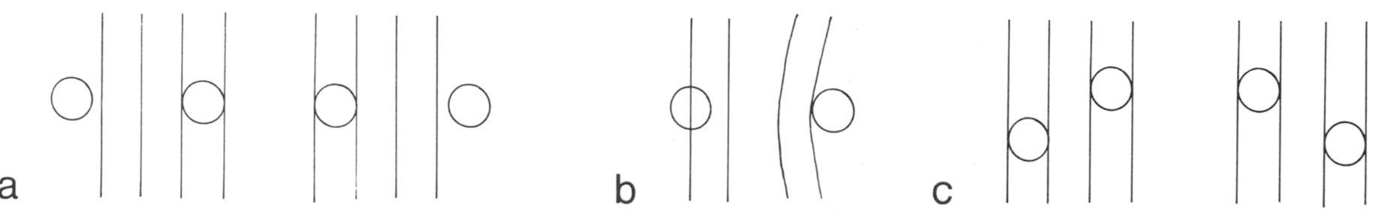

Diagram 11. The rider's seat bones and the horse's long back muscles as shown schematically from above. When one seat bone is placed correctly, the other one tends to fall off, as in (a). This is particularly likely in the female pelvis, where the seat bones are wider apart than in the male. The difficulty that Margaret was having is shown in (b), where the horse's right long back muscle has moved in towards the midline and the left long back muscle has dropped, making it hard to feel. In order to hold both seat bones in place on top of each long back muscle, they must come onto a diagonal, as in (c): on the right rein the correct positioning is usually on the ten to four axis and on the left rein it is usually on the ten past eight axis.

The need to place each seat bone on top of the horse's long back muscles is one of the major reasons why thinking of spreading the seat bones apart is so detrimental. The pinch feeling plays a vital part in holding the seat bones in place and is perhaps even more important for women than it is for men, since the seat bones are further apart in the female pelvis than they are in the male. (However, although I teach fewer men than women, I have yet to meet one who does not have the same problem.) Through the pinch feeling, the seat bones exert a gentle pressure in towards the horse's spine, which encourages the muscles to lift up and become more defined. Instead of lying flat, they then stand out from the muscles of the rib cage, like two pieces of rope which run on either side of the spine (see Diagram 12). They also then work independently from the rib cage, instead of acting more as if they were glued onto it – and this changes the whole quality of the horse's movement. At the same time as the long back muscle becomes defined, the rib cage fills out, becoming rounder, so that the rider can feel it more clearly under her legs (there is more about this in Lesson 8 with Carol). When you are riding the horse in the correct carriage, the effect you feel in the long back muscles can be seen in the muscles which run each side of the crest. They stand out, making the top of the neck look flatter instead of wedge-shaped, and giving it that beautiful arch which is relished by us all.

It is very interesting here to make a comparison between human and equine anatomy and movement. Put one hand just under your sternum and the other so that your finger and thumb lie on either side of your spine, just by the small of your back. Then bear down and feel for any change which happens in your back as well as your front. If you have reasonable muscle development, you will feel your own long back muscles stand out against your fingers, feeling, again, like two pieces of rope. (If this is not clear in your own body, try it on someone else's!) This is an *isometric contraction*, which firms up the muscles to gain stability rather than to move the bones, and it mirrors the way in which the horse uses his back and belly when he is in good carriage.

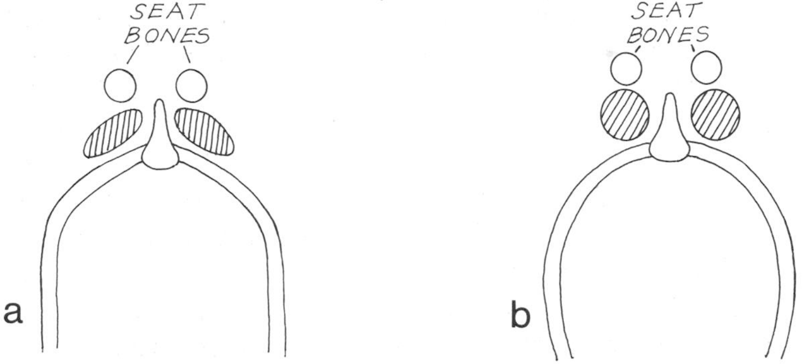

Diagram 12. When the horse's long back muscles are dropped, his rib cage is slab-sided, as in (a). The muscles are then difficult to feel and to stay on top of. When the back muscles become defined, they are like two pieces of rope, and at the same time the horse's rib cage fills out, as in (b). This makes the horse's carriage and movement become correct, and makes it much easier for the rider to feel the back muscles and to keep both of her seat bones on top of them.

Interestingly, a rider's first awareness of changes in the horse's long back muscles usually happens when he does a dropping, and bears down to the extreme. When I am teaching, I rarely miss an opportunity to point out this change to less experienced riders! It is also interesting that when the horse first begins to show the seeking reflexes, he often does a dropping, and also often grunts – a sign that he, like good tennis players and powerful martial artists, is transmitting the power of his pelvis through to his forehand. He also often snorts, instinctively wanting to clear his nose because his breathing is now so much more full and deep than it was before he began to bear down.

When the horse is 'swinging through his back', he adds movement to the action of bearing down. (You too can bear down and walk at the same time.) Each of his long back muscles is composed of segments which are individually wired, and from this base of high muscle tone each one contracts in turn, creating a ripple which passes from the horse's croup towards his wither as each hind leg moves (see Diagram 10). The American researcher Dr Deb Bennett likens this to playing a *glissando* on a piano, in which the pianist runs his hand over the keys from one end of the keyboard to the other. Difficulties arise when a part of one or both back muscles is 'locked' so that it moves *en bloc* – as if a group of notes are played at once. This is very common, but in my experience the pattern can usually be released by good sitting. (This is something I usually do rather than teach. Essentially the release happens when the rider sits so still that she moulds onto the 'frozen' part well enough to match its stillness, and then to begin to induce movement in it. The moment of release is often quite dramatic, and some horses shake their heads for the next few minutes, as if they are shaking out the tension.)

Many people misunderstand the correct feeling in a horse's back, just as they misunderstand the way their own back works in correct sitting. When the horse's long back muscles become more defined through isometric contraction, the movements in them become *smaller* than they are when the muscles are slack, for the muscles gain the resilience of stretched rather than limp elastic bands, and they are much less 'wavy'. But the correct movement is also *bigger* than the movement you feel when the back is hollowed and the muscles make an isotonic contraction. They then pull the croup towards the lower part of the neck, shortening the distance between these two points and making the back drop downwards. At the same time, the horse becomes pot-bellied – just as the rider does when she hollows her back. This makes his back muscles much less easy to feel under the rider's seat, and it minimises the movement they make. In fact, it feels like the nearest thing to sitting on a block of wood!

Once riders have felt a tense, contracted back come alive with movement, they immediately realise that this must be more correct. But many riders whose horses have slack backs assume that because the movement feels big, it must be right, and the term 'swinging through the back' seems to reinforce this idea. But in his evasive pattern the horse typically does one of two things: either he is so jelly-like in the loin area that he *dissipates* the impulse from the hind leg, weakening it so much that it cannot pass forward around the circuit, or he *blocks* it by hollowing his back isotonically and/or by 'locking' some segments of the long back muscle. When the horse bears down and the long back muscles act like stretched elastic bands, they make a '*glissando*' alternately with the movement of the corresponding hind leg, transmitting the impulse of the horse's step very cleanly.

When the rider sits well, she also stabilises the middle portion of her body by bearing down, which makes her very precise in her 'bottom walking'. She 'goes with' the horse by moving each seat bone forward in turn; this involves her back muscles in a different way from the way in which she uses them if she creates a wave-like action in the middle of her back. I spent years cultivating my 'wiggle in the middle'; but top-class riders do not sit like this. The 'wiggle' allows the rider to sit fairly comfortably, but not to be causal. It drowns out the more subtle movements in the horse's back that she must feel and mould onto, and it interferes with the passage of his impulse around the circuit. To understand these different ways of using the body, put your hands against your back muscles and feel the difference in them when you bear down and 'bottom walk' as opposed to when you swing your back and belly forward.

My first thought when I get on a horse is to 'plug into' his long back muscles and lift them up underneath me so that they become more defined. Margaret has done very well in learning to sit 'still relative to the horse' – a problem with which all the other riders so far have been struggling – and this gives her the sensitivity which lets her know what these muscles are doing. She had not, however, previously thought in terms of whether she was falling off one or both of them. This is an extremely important idea, which I usually introduce by explaining the basic principle and then asking the rider, 'Are each of your seat bones on top of the horse's long back muscles or has one of them fallen off?' Interestingly, *almost everyone I have ever asked has been able to give me an immediate answer*: the placing of the seat bones on the horse's long back muscles is quite obvious once the back muscles themselves are raised, and once you know what it is that you are supposed to be feeling for.

Only about five out of probably several hundred riders have not understood me when I first introduced this idea – although I always stack the odds in my favour by choosing my timing very carefully. Most of those who did not immediately understand have been riders who have been working, rather incorrectly, at quite a high level. I remember one of them looking at me and saying, 'But how could one possibly feel that?' in a voice tone which expressed the idea of, 'How ridiculous!' Meanwhile, the sixteen-year-old girl with whom she was sharing her lesson was saying, 'Help! I've just fallen off. . . . Ah yes, I've got it again . . .' She was riding extremely well, was thoroughly intrigued by the whole idea and was producing tremendous changes in her horse. It does not take talent to feel this, nor is there any mystique involved: it is well within the scope of the 'average' rider. The secret lies in knowing what to pay attention to.

When the horse falls onto one of his shoulders, the rib cage is usually displaced to that same side. (Do not confuse this with the change in its shape which happens when the long back muscles become defined.) To make Margaret aware that she was sitting on an asymmetrical horse, I asked her to walk on whilst she answered the following question: 'If we were to bisect you and Saffron down the middle through both of your spines, so that each of your buttocks and thighs lay on either side of this imaginary line, would you have an equal bulge under each side, or is it bigger under one side than it is under the other?' The bulge was, as I suspected, bigger under the left side. When Saffron falls outwards to the left, her left long back muscle drops away instead of lifting up, and Margaret's left seat bone easily slips about on top of it. At the same time, Saffron's right long back muscle moves to the left, feeling as if it moves in underneath the spine. (In reality, I think it must move under the supraspinous ligament; see Diagram 15, page 152.) Margaret's right seat bone is then positioned too far to the right of it (as in Diagram 11(b)). With both seat bones out of place, Margaret loses the correct connection with the horse's back, becoming reactive rather than causal. (This is the mirror image of the problem which Val had in Lesson 4. There I worked more simply, unravelling the twist in her body rather than dealing with its precise positioning on the horse's back. She will come to this later.)

When Margaret can keep each of her seat bones on top of the horse's long back muscles, she will be able to hold the muscles in place – for if the rider will not take her seat bones away from the horse's long back muscles, he cannot take his long back muscles away from her seat bones! When one of the long back muscles moves in under the supraspinous ligament, the rider has to move her seat bone towards the horse's midline so that she keeps contact with the muscle. By carefully moving her seat bone outwards, she can draw the muscle back out again. This sounds very difficult but it is surprisingly easy to feel and do. No one to whom I have ever taught this has failed to understand me and to do it. Once the rider has control of these muscles, the rider can then *choose* to position the horse's rib cage and shoulders to the right or left, and she becomes truly causal. But right now, Saffron chooses how *she* will place her rib cage and her back muscles, at the same time choosing where Margaret will sit. This keeps Margaret reactive. Almost all the riders I meet are reactive in this way, this whole interaction being beyond their awareness: for in their wildest dreams, it never occurs to them that these variations might be possible. They are doubly hampered because they do not know what they do not know, and they have no idea how precisely and strongly they must position their framework in order to dictate the position of the horse's back, rib cage, wither and neck. Only this gives them the power and control which they envy and admire in the most talented riders.

This asymmetrical positioning of the rib cage is, I believe, the determining factor in the horse's asymmetry, and by changing this, one changes the relative weight carried by each of his legs. This alters the way in which each hind leg steps, and the way in which the horse's weight is directed towards one or other shoulder. By influencing the horse via the part of his body on which you are sitting, you gain control of his whole body. *It does not work half so well to think of this the other way round*: one influences the hind legs via the rib cage, and not the rib cage via the hind legs. But first, the rider must have complete control of the positioning of her two seat bones and her thighs. Every person finds that she has her own idiosyncratic difficulties with this: I find, for instance, that my right seat bone is much less easy to position than my left, which I can easily move forward or back as I choose. The more mobile left seat bone has the disadvantage that it is more difficult for me to keep bearing enough weight on it. For years, it tended to float about, and it fell off the horse's long back muscle very easily. Conversely, the right one – if I let it – gets stuck down in its place, carrying so much weight that it does not easily budge, and can become an unwanted protrusion in the horse's long back muscle. Over the years, this has actually caused me the greater problem – leading to just the same scenario on the right rein which you have seen with Sarah on the left.

To help Margaret, we began by positioning her thighs. When the rider is correctly placed, and the horse's bend is correct, the rider's inside thigh usually points almost straight ahead. If she were sitting in the middle of a clock face, this would be towards twelve o'clock. When the horse falls outwards, I tell the rider to keep her inside thigh lying against him so that she can feel his rib cage pressing against it *continually*; for when this contact is lost even for a moment the horse seizes his chance to shift his rib cage over to the outside. Then, she loses the sense that, relative to her, there is an appropriate bulge of rib cage to the inside. The outside thigh, however, points more towards ten to twelve on the right rein and ten past twelve on the left rein, allowing the horse's rib cage to bulge out underneath it – since it is this which forms the bend. If, however, like Saffron on the right rein, the horse's rib cage is bulging out *too much*, the thigh may need to become a more active barrier, pointing in more towards five to twelve. (Until a few years ago, most riders thought that the horse's spine actually bent to follow the curve of a circle. However, researchers have proved that this is not the case, and whilst the spine remains almost completely straight, the rib cage bulges outwards. In effect, it pivots about the spine.)

Whilst all this is happening, the seat bones must stay on top of the long back muscles and not allow them to drop away or move in under the supraspinous ligament. In order to keep a narrow enough base of support on a turn, one must be in advance of the other, otherwise one of them will fall off (see Diagram 11(c)). Almost always, the inside seat bone must be in advance of the outside one, and we have already seen what happened to Val when this was not the case. Margaret too was in danger: Figure 51 shows her badly positioned on the circle, and you can see how the central axis of her body is not in line with her horse's axis. Her outside seat bone has almost certainly lifted and come forward, and her outside 'stabiliser' will have disappeared too. The correct positioning puts equal weight on both seat bones, aligning them on the ten past eight axis of our clock face. On the left rein, the correct positioning is the mirror image of this, which is the ten to four axis.

51. Saffron is falling out through her outside shoulder and Margaret is leaning inwards. She is almost certainly weighting her inside seat bone too much, and the horse's inside long back muscle has escaped the pressure by moving in towards the spine. Margaret's outside seat bone has lightened and lifted off the outside long back muscle. It may also have advanced.

52. The midline of Margaret's body is now aligned with Saffron's, and she has much more control of her horse's outside shoulder. Margaret's shoulders are close to the radius of the circle she is riding (although her inside shoulder may be a little far back). Her inside seat bone may still be weighted a little too much but both seat bones are on top of the horse's long back muscles.

Figure 52 shows Margaret very well positioned, with her central axis in line with that of the horse and the horse's shoulders coming much more correctly away from the wall. Margaret's outside leg is also clearly positioned behind her inside leg, as happens automatically when the pelvic positioning is correct. Margaret held this well when she went on into trot, but I was amused to hear a sudden yell from her as she came away from the wall one time. 'The rotten little worm! She just pushed herself out against me and shoved her rib cage out to the left!' Margaret had fallen off her right long back muscle again and had lost the correct placing of each seat bone and thigh. However, I was extremely pleased to find that she had felt all this happen, and that she was suitably shocked. As I told her, this was nothing new, but somehow she had previously contrived not to notice.

I like to encourage the rider in this benign sense of outrage towards the horse's antics. It is, I find, a very suitable attitude to have; there is no blame, and no intent to punish. There is humour, and an acceptance of 'what is', which is always an extremely good starting point for change. The rider has not drawn any conclusions about not being good enough, not having what it takes or about never being able to do it. Her ego and self-image are not at stake – as they usually are when she takes her riding very seriously and starts trying really hard. The damage which Saffron had done to Margaret's framework was repairable, although one has to realise that there is nearly half a ton of Saffron pushing determinedly against Margaret's left leg, and only about nine stone of Margaret attempting to be an impenetrable barrier! All Margaret had to do was to re-find Saffron's right long back muscle, put her right seat bone on top of it and then refuse to lose that contact. At the same time, she had to keep her right thigh in contact with the right side of Saffron's rib cage, so that this too could not disappear from underneath her. She also had to position her left seat bone *back* on its ten past eight axis, hold it on top of the left long back muscle, and to keep her left thigh in place as well. Not easy, but possible – when you know how.

That moment of feeling Saffron's determined repositioning of her rib cage was a very precious one in Margaret's learning, which I hope she will treasure. When we were talking recently, she told me that now, with hindsight, she understood what her previous teachers had been trying to tell her, and that she also understood why it had never worked. 'As soon as I picked up your book,' she said, 'I knew what had been wrong with all the teaching I had ever received. Nobody had ever helped me to define the point that I was starting from, so although I tried my hardest to do what they were telling me, it never worked. I firstly had to discover how I was pulling my stomach in and pushing on the stirrups etc. before I could learn to do anything differently . . .'

Margaret has made some wonderful changes in her walk, rising trot and canter, but it will be a while before I work with her in sitting trot. This will inevitably be hard for her, because of her tendency to tip forward, grow up tall, push against her stirrups and draw her stomach in. When her back hollows, she is highly likely to bump (which may upset Saffron), and she also has the kind of body which is naturally 'spongy' – so it will be difficult for her to exchange her wobbles for the stillness and security of putty. This will require the ultimate in bearing down. Margaret is tremendously sensitive, which, until now, has been her downfall; but it has recently helped her to learn a tremendous amount in a very short time, and despite a very difficult beginning, I am sure that she will overcome the odds and ride extremely well.

Lesson 8

Carol: Holding the Horse in Carriage

Carol lives quite close to West Wilts Equestrian Centre, and as her first introduction to my work, she came with a friend to a talk which I held there one evening. This was about six weeks before the four-day course, and it inspired her to come on an introductory day course and then to book two lessons during the four-day course, so the photographs here were taken during her second lesson.

Her mare, Tudor Queen, by Tudor Flame, is a pure thoroughbred who is home-bred, 16.2 hands and eight years old. Carol had her first riding lesson at the age of ten and owned her first horse when she was eighteen. She has subsequently kept horses throughout her adult life. She fits her riding in around the pressures of farming and a young family, and she also has an older horse, so she has brought Queen on slowly and has not competed her very much. She has, however, been extremely successful: she has frequently won in unaffiliated dressage, and in late 1989 she affiliated Queen and won a Novice Qualifier. I asked Carol what difference she felt our first lesson had made to her riding, and she told me that she felt much more effective than before and more solid in her body. Like the other riders, she had needed to change her position to bring herself into the correct alignment; her knee had come down and her heel back, and she was pushing forward much more, both in her rise and in the bearing down. This was the change which I remembered most, since without this push, Carol – with her very slender frame – gave the appearance of being a reasonably correct but rather weak rider.

I had found Carol very receptive and quick to learn in our first lesson and it seemed that it was enviably easy for her to translate thought into action. As she warmed up for this lesson, it was obvious that, although Queen's carriage had deteriorated, Carol had worked well on her own with the input which I had given her. Towards the end of that first lesson, the change in Queen and Carol had been dramatic and they had produced the kind of work that I almost drool over. ('Just my luck,' I had thought to myself, 'that I don't have a photographer here today!') Carol knew as well as I did that producing this work to order would be quite a different matter, and in the intervening time she had found that she was nearly at the end of each work session before she began to gain much influence over Queen's carriage. In particular, she had had difficulty with the walk. She wondered why that was and wanted some ideas which would make her more effective.

53. Carol warming up in trot: Queen's carriage is rather hollow and Carol has tipped forward. As with Janet and Mayday, both of them have contrived to close the angle which lies between them. However, Carol more often tended to be behind the movement in rising trot.

54. Warming up in canter: again, Queen is rather hollow and Carol has tipped forward. Notice how Queen's head looks too big for her neck.

Figures 53 and 54 show her warming up in trot and canter. Carol has tipped forward slightly too much in rising trot (although, like Gail, she more often tended to be slightly behind the movement). Her body has also rocked forward in canter, and in both, Queen's carriage is rather hollow. Like Sarah's horse, Queen gives the impression that her head is too big for her neck – although, as you will see in later pictures, this is really not the case at all. Firstly, I reviewed the basics with Carol and then offered her some new ideas, all designed to increase her push forward. In effect, Queen was compressing her body backwards so that her head pushed back into her neck and her neck pushed back into her wither. The fact that she could do this demonstrated that *her push back was bigger than Carol's push forward*. Queen was pushing the stuffing backwards, so that it passed back under Carol's seat and out through Queen's back end instead of Carol pushing it forwards so that it filled out Queen's rib cage and neck to create the seeking reflexes. At the same time, Queen was also pushing Carol's backside back and down into the hollow of her back, causing Carol to tip forward and guaranteeing that Queen could stay hollow until such time as Carol made the necessary adjustments.

To add more strength to Carol's push forward, I suggested that she thought of pushing the back of her body up towards the front as if she had no thickness and could make herself two dimensional – like a plane positioned at the front of her body. By adding this to her bearing down, she now had a push which went right through her body and was then directed out towards the point on the horse's neck where a breast-plate would sit (see Diagram 8, page 112). This gives the rider much more strength than the bearing down used alone – although in learning, it is best to begin with just this. When I am riding a difficult horse and I push forward to the extreme, I often feel the strain in two distinct lines which become defined as indentations in the muscles at each side of my sacrum, the bony part of the pelvis which constitutes the lower back.

To feel this, stand in an 'on horse' position and put your hands so that your finger-tips lie on the edges of the sacrum along the sacroiliac joints (see Diagram 5, page 84). Let your thumbs come around the sides of the pelvis. Then think of pressing forward through your body and of defining the indentations under your finger-tips as if you were pushing something through you. If you do this very strongly (much stronger than you might expect, and possibly to the degree that it hurts), you may feel the effect I am talking about. However, unlike almost everything else I advocate, this comes with a health warning; although I have never suffered any ill-effects, many people do have sacroiliac trouble, and you need to be careful not to stress yourself too much. After discussions with European riders about what they mean when they talk about 'using the back', I have come to the conclusion that this is it. It is *not* a pushing down, a movement of the pelvis in the saddle, or necessarily a leaning back; it is simply an increased push *forward*.

One more element is required to complete the push forward, which I explained to Carol as follows: 'Imagine the head of the thigh bone, which is shaped like a little ball, and which fits neatly into the rounded hollow of the hip socket. When the horse pushes back at you, it is as if the shortening in his body acts on your thigh, ramming the thigh bone home into the hip socket, which in turn rams your pelvis back in the saddle. To counteract this, you need to think of pulling your thigh bone forward out of your hip socket, as if you could make a little gap there which would in turn make your knee reach further away from you. When your thigh reaches forward out of your hip socket, the horse's neck begins to make a corresponding forward reach out of his wither; but if he succeeds in compressing his neck back into his wither, he will also compress your thigh back into your hip socket.' One of my student teachers recently thought up a brilliant way of demonstrating this idea: ask a friend to stand right in front of your horse's chest and to reach round, grab both of your knees and pull. Then you will understand what I mean. Most of the people we have tried this with so far have considered the prospect of generating this feeling for themselves and said, 'You must be kidding. . . .'! However, despite their shocked reaction, the vast majority of them have been able to do it.

The pulling of the thigh forward out of the hip socket obviously fits well with the push forward from the back of the rider's body towards the front of it and then out towards the breast-plate. (When I talked about bearing down in Lesson 1, I referred to some other elements which increase the rider's 'push': we now have the complete push forward from the back towards the front, as I understand it.) Thinking of the thigh pulling out of the hip joint also supports the idea of sitting as if on a posture stool, so that the thigh is weight-bearing all the way down to the knee. To put all these ideas together, I used one of my favourite images with Carol, which likens the hollow in the horse's back to the kind of pit which explorers in the African jungle used to use to trap animals for the zoo. (In my childhood there were many television films on this theme, but fortunately my younger readers will have grown up with more conservationist ideas! I hope they will still understand what I mean.)

When the horse hollows, the 'mantrap' which he creates lies just under the top of the rider's thigh and back towards the seat bone. The thigh acts like a branch placed over the trap (Diagram 13), but there is a little gap at the back of the trap where the thigh does not quite cover it. As long as there is sufficient weight at the knee end of the 'branch', it stops the rider from falling in. However, if the majority of the rider's weight is taken on her backside, she simply falls down the 'mantrap'. Either her body topples back, or her backside slips backwards and her body tips forward, and in each case her knee tends to come up. In rising trot, it helps to think of the thigh like one of those road barriers which are often used at the entrances to army camps. There is a heavy weight on one end, to which the pivot point of the barrier lies very close. The pivot is analogous to the knee joint, and the rider must weight her knee so that it is stable enough to counter-balance the weight of her thigh and body. This enables the thigh and hip joint to float up or down very easily, just like the long end of the barrier. The barrier never crashes down into its casing, and the rider's backside must never crash down into the saddle, even though it has the weight of her upper body stacked above it.

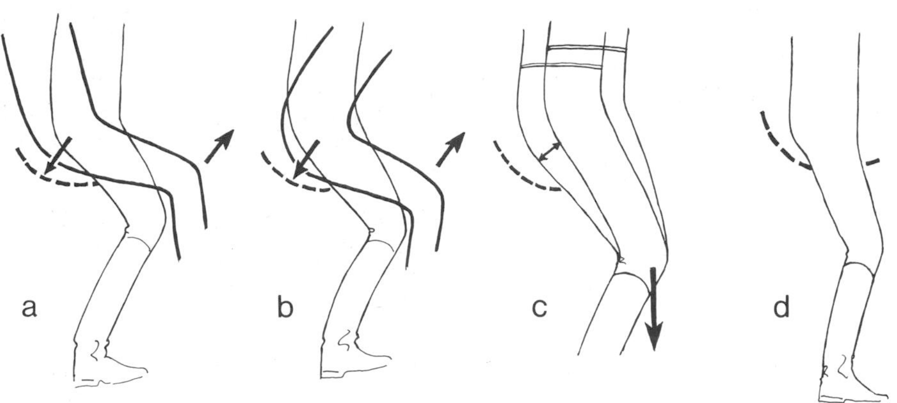

Diagram 13. The hollow of the 'mantrap' lies just under the top of the thigh and the seat bone. To hold the rider out of it, the thigh must act like a branch over the top of the trap and the knee must be weighted enough to hold it stable. Otherwise, the rider's body topples back, down into the trap, as in (a). She can also fall into it when her backside slides back and her body tips forward, as in (b). In rising trot, the thigh acts like an army barrier, hinged at the knee, so that the free end (the pelvis) can float up and down without ever crash-landing in the saddle, as in (c). If the stirrup is too long, and the thigh is too vertical, it does not cover the 'mantrap' and the rider inevitably falls down it, as in (d).

There is another way in which the rider can fall down into the 'mantrap'. If the thigh is nearly vertical, it does not reach forward enough to act like the branch and support the rider, so it too goes down the trap. This explains why it is important to ride young, green horses with a shorter stirrup than one would use on trained horses. Young horses make the biggest 'mantraps', so the rider needs considerable leverage in the thigh in order to support herself. This notion also explains why it is counter-productive in any situation to attempt to ride with the stirrups too long. Very many riders lose leverage and effectiveness this way: they cannot hold themselves out of the 'mantrap' and the horse's carriage inevitably suffers.

When Carol went out onto the track to try all this, we firstly had to check that the push out from her lower stomach was indeed landing at the breast-plate. Initially, it was going too far up the horse's neck, so Carol had to come fractionally back in the saddle in order to aim it correctly and to put Queen in front of her. It then became even more important that she thought of her thigh bones like iron bars (or branches), and snugged them more firmly into the saddle. She felt that her thighs were doing much more work than they had done previously, and although she was surprised by the amount required, I was not – after all, it is a huge demand on the muscles to counter-balance the weight of the body like this. (Remember the kneeling exercise which I gave you in Lesson 5 with Janet.) Carol's horse very soon produced the trot which you see in Figure 55, so she was instantly rewarded for her efforts, and when she went sitting she was able to maintain the same carriage, as you can see in Figure 56.

55. Some nice work in rising trot. Carol's body is well in balance and Queen is now reaching forward into the rein. The seeking reflexes have replaced the withholding which you see in Figure 53.

56. In sitting trot, Carol's upper body is very open and her front is pushing strongly forward. Queen could probably still lift a little more through the wither and the base of the neck. She also has her mouth open (as she does in most of the photographs), resistance here usually being symptomatic of resistance in the back.

So far, we have thought about the interaction between Carol and Queen in terms of 'forward' and 'back', and the need to make Carol's push forward bigger than Queen's push back. This required a greatly increased push from Carol, who paradoxically needed to be positioned further back in order not to over-shoot with it. If this happened, Queen was no longer in front of Carol, and Carol's weight was positioned too much over the horse's forehand, almost as if Queen had tried to wriggle out backwards from underneath her. But if Carol fell back into the 'mantrap', her weight was then too far back. To find the correct position in the saddle requires a very delicate balancing act. This obviously relates as well to the planes of 'up' and 'down'. (In fact, 'left' and 'right' are also often involved, since by holding her rib cage to one side and falling onto one shoulder, Queen can intensify her push back. But to consider the detail of this right now would make things far too complicated.)

I think of some riders as 'up' riders, who tend to ping up off the top of the horse – Katie, Gail and Margaret would be examples of this – whilst other riders are 'down' riders, who tend to squash themselves down onto the horse, and to squash the horse underneath them. Val and Jan would be examples of this. Carol has this up/down relationship more nearly correct (see Lesson 7 with Margaret and Diagram 9, page 132, for a fuller explanation of this), as do all naturally talented riders, who gain through this the ability to exchange energy with the horse without deadening the 'trampoline' or being thrown about by it. Carol's balance in the up/down plane was, however, slightly suspect, particularly in rising trot. She wrote in her notes to me that, 'I have to make a conscious effort not to bump when I land in the saddle', but it helped her to think of the army barrier landing very lightly in its casing. In walk, where Carol had experienced her greatest problems at home, she realised that she had been thinking too much of 'down', and had been bearing down for all she was worth without thinking of the horse then coming up underneath her, like the big balloon which she did not want to burst. The bearing down had been a new idea to Carol in the previous lesson, and not surprisingly she had gone overboard with it and not kept it within the context of the 'up'. This was the major reason for the problems she had been having in walk, so I suggested that she thought of sitting as if she wanted to levitate – as if I could whisk her horse out from underneath her and leave her serenely stranded in space.

Although Queen is a very well put together horse, with extremely nice movement, she does not have an easy back to influence, and she is extremely unwilling to make the definition in her long back muscles which I explained in the last lesson with Margaret (see Diagram 12, page 138). This change involves other muscles too, which form a ring, as you can see in Diagram 14: the rectus abdominus contracts to draw the horse's sternum closer to his pelvis, so that his belly hangs down much less than it would if his back were hollowed. At the same time the horse bears down, giving him a fuller

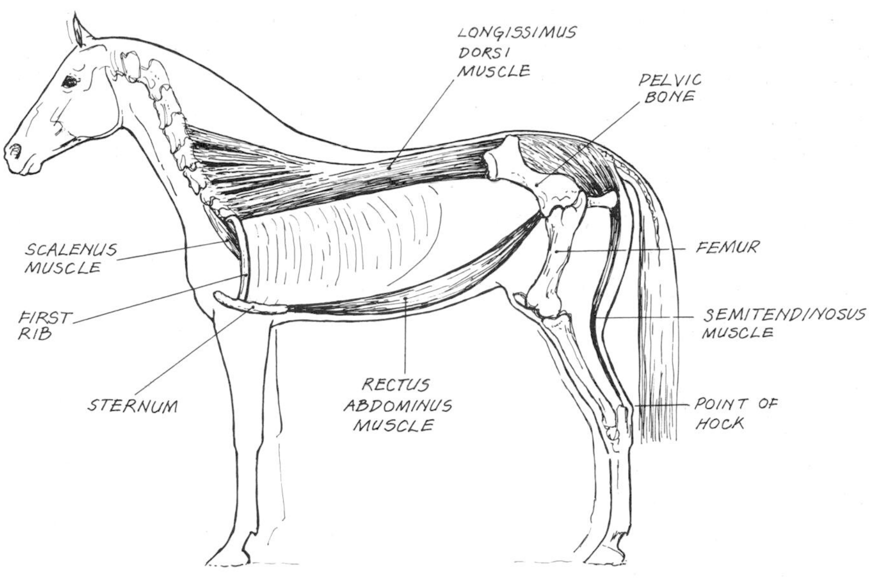

Diagram 14. The horse in correct carriage, who shows the seeking reflexes, utilises a ring of muscles. These create lifting in his back and the reach and arch of his neck out of his wither, and at the same time cause contraction in his belly muscles so that the belly no longer hangs down.

The ring of muscles is composed of muscles, bones, ligaments and tendons. The long back muscles join the lower vertebrae of the neck to the croup. The bones of the pelvis provide attachment for the rectus abdominus muscle, which runs along the horse's belly, also inserting into his sternum. The first rib attaches into the first thoracic vertebra, and it is also the seat of attachment of the scalenus muscle, which connects into the bottom two vertebrae of the neck. This completes the ring. When the rectus abdominus muscle contracts to draw the pelvis closer to the sternum, the back lifts and the long back muscles tend to lengthen. However, they also become more defined through the isometric contraction which occurs when the horse concurrently bears down. (This happens to the extreme when he is making a dropping.) As the neck reaches and arches out of the wither, the scalenus muscle at its base contracts. To understand these changes better, imagine them in your own body.

and more even breathing pattern and changing the way in which he uses his diaphragm. (This use of his abdominal muscles in correct carriage is rarely recognised, just as the use of the rider's abdominal muscles is rarely acknowledged, and in both cases we hear far more about the workings of the back.) The scalenus muscle which lies deep in the chest – joining the first rib to the base of the neck – also contracts, underpinning the way in which the top of the neck reaches and arches out of the wither. The longissimus dorsi muscles complete the ring, and although the contraction of the belly muscle causes them to lengthen, they contract isometrically at the same time, and this holds them so that they stand out, creating the definition which one can soon learn to feel.

The back is lifted by the contraction of the abdominal muscles, the holding in the long back muscles and also by the ligament system of the back and neck (see Diagram 15). When the horse lowers his head, the ligament which attaches in front of the poll and runs along the crest of the neck pulls on the spines of the vertebrae which form the withers. These in turn pull on the spines towards the centre of the back, via more connecting ligaments. These spines are angled backwards, making the pull more effective, and good conformation with a well-defined wither makes it even more efficient. The continuation of this ligament passes backwards from the centre of the back towards the croup and the tip of the tail. This pulls the back up and back when the horse flexes the lumbo-sacral joint at the croup and lowers his haunches. These ligaments act like the cables on a suspension bridge, which has the withers and the croup as its staunchions, and they pull up the centre of the back. Obviously this is the weakest part of the whole

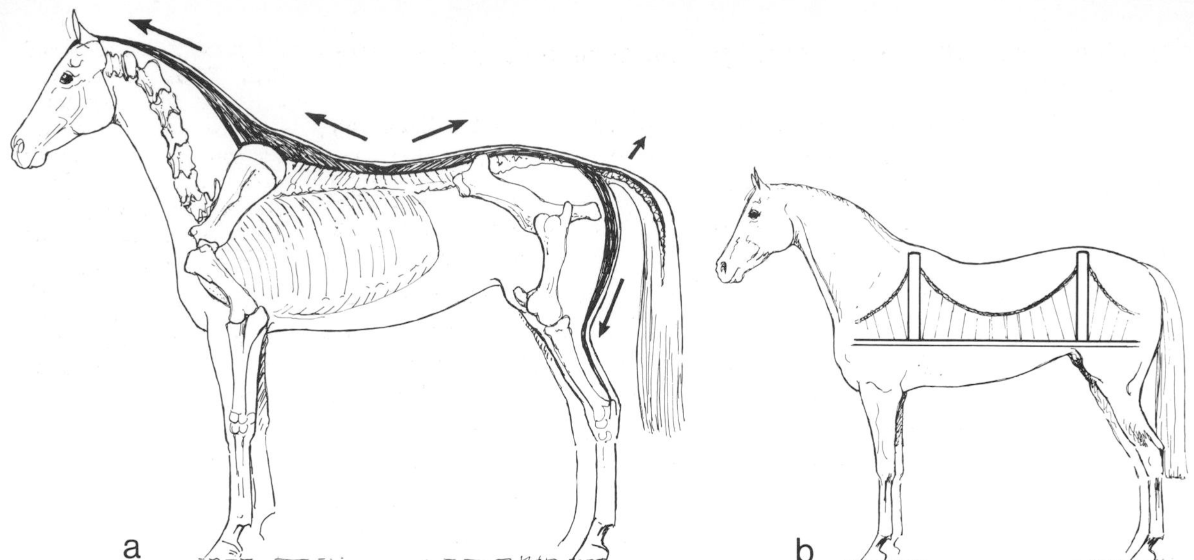

Diagram 15 (a). The ligament system which holds up the back. Ligaments (unlike tendons) are elastic, and they can be stretched by changes in the horse's carriage. The dorsal ligament of the neck attaches into the front of the poll, and as the horse lowers his head, the ligament stretches and then pulls on the spines of the withers. These in turn pull on the spines of the thoracic vertebrae. The supraspinous ligament, which is a continuation of the dorsal ligament, begins just before the end of the thoracic spine, extending backwards over the croup and the sacrum and on down to the tip of the horse's tail. A further ligament system runs from the croup to the point of the buttock, and then down to the hock, where it joins with the Achilles tendon. (This includes the smeitendinosus muscle, which functions much as a ligament.) When the horse 'sits down', flexing the lumbo-sacral joint at the croup, the middle part of

system, and if the rider's weight is concentrated here, down the 'mantrap', it is extremely difficult for this suspension system to function correctly. The working of the ring of muscles is also impaired, and the strain on the horse's back and belly muscles becomes immense. By weighting her thigh and sitting nearer to the front staunchion, the rider makes the horse's task significantly easier.*

Exactly where in this system Queen's reticence lies, I am not sure, but I began to appreciate how difficult she is after we had done some very good work and then stopped to talk. When Carol went out onto the track again afterwards it was like starting all over again from the beginning; Queen had dropped her back, and it took us quite some while to rescue the situation. I began to appreciate how Carol could feel that once she had got going in a work session, she did not dare to stop! However, there is a danger that long, hard periods of work within the correct carriage will make Queen progressively more reluctant to lift her back, as she will soon realise what she is about to let herself in for! To over-stress the horse like this can be very costly, so Carol's most important learning lies in knowing exactly how to move through the initial barrier so that she holds herself out of the 'mantrap' and creates a push forward which is bigger than Queen's push back. She will then be able to stop and start as she wishes, bring-

* This ring of muscles has been described most clearly by the American palaentologist Dr Deb Bennett, and I am very appreciative of her work. However, she believes that the long back muscles just lengthen as the abdominal muscles contract. My proposal that they are also under an isometric contraction comes from my experiences riding, where I, like many riders before me, can feel these muscles in action.

ing Queen into the correct carriage and then resting her before fatigue sets in.

One other element in this, which I explained to Carol that day, concerns the horse's rib cage. When the long back muscles have dropped, the rib cage becomes rather slab-sided, but as the long back muscles become defined, the rib cage also fills out (see Diagram 12, page 138). The rider's thigh plays a very important role in this. Firstly, of course, it has to snug inwards so that it makes contact with the rib cage in its rather contracted state. But then, with the inner thigh muscles still holding, the thigh has to attempt to draw *outwards*, and to bring the rib cage out with it, as if the rider had suction pads on the inside of her thigh. To attempt to draw the rib cage outwards before you have made contact with it makes no sense at all, but I believe that this is what most of the riding population are attempting to do. Whoever first suggested that you should not 'grip with your knees' but should 'relax your knee and take your thigh away from the saddle' was not, I think, giving us a very full or accurate description of his feeling. The confusion is not dissimilar to that which often arises when we are told to 'sit up' (see Diagram 9, page 132), for in each case we are only hearing about *the final stage in a process which actually has several stages*; unfortunately, the good riders who have influenced our dogma did not tell us about these previous ones.

Correct use of the thigh involves both the inner thigh muscles (to maintain contact with the rib cage) and the outer thigh muscles (to draw it outwards) – not the outer ones alone. Paradoxically, both schools of thought – the one which says that the thigh should lie firmly against the saddle and the one which says that it should be drawn outwards – are correct, *but each of them has only half of the truth*. In a similar way, anyone who says that the rider should either sit up or sit down has only half of the truth. She has to do both.

This simultaneous use of the muscles is very unusual, and it is something which few people would ever do naturally. It is equivalent to the simultaneous use of the muscles at the front and the back of the thigh which we covered in Lesson 2 with Gail. By using all the thigh muscles together, the rider keeps them acting like stretched elastic bands, which gives her tremendous control of her leg, especially when it is coupled with similar use of the calf muscles, and also with a little gap in the hip, knee and ankle joints. This makes the rider's body operate rather like a puppet which has strings attached to all its joints: the limbs themselves are not bendy but the puppet has tremendous flexibility, independence of all its limbs and very good shock-absorption.

Queen's reluctance to use her back well also showed up in several other ways. When she first came into the correct carriage, her step was not very powerful, and whenever Carol asked for more power,

the spine is pulled up and back. When he reaches his head and neck forward, the spine is pulled up and forward. These two pulls lift the middle of the back, holding it up much in the same way that the cables of a suspension bridge hold up the centre of the bridge. The staunchions of the bridge are the withers and the croup, as shown in (b).

Queen immediately hollowed again. I had to remind Carol that her first thought must be to maintain the correct carriage – using her bearing down, pinch, thigh muscles, etc. – and that she then had to *add onto these* the use of her lower leg. The physical challenge is to be able to do this without disturbing the body from the knee up, but the greater challenge is probably the mental one, even though this is a very simple example of parallel processing. If Carol just thought of sending the horse forward, and this thought *replaced* all others in her mind, she was bound to 'drop' the horse under her seat and effectively make her hollow. I see this happen time and time again, especially when the rider is giving the driving aids, and most commonly when she thinks to herself, 'I must shorten my reins.' She then forgets completely about holding the horse's back in place, maintaining the same contact, pushing out through her stomach, etc., and in one moment she can undo half an hour's good work.

Another example of Queen's reluctance to lift her back became obvious in the next lesson, when we began to work more with the school movements. Whenever she left the track to come onto a circle, she tended to hollow, even though Carol's turning aids were more correct than most. The scenario goes like this: the horse expects the rider to pull back on the inside rein, so he brings his head back and up, away from the rein contact, in an attempt to beat the rider to it. But in the process, he inevitably hollows his back, making a 'mantrap' which the rider promptly falls down into. As the rider tips back, she unwittingly pulls on the inside rein, fulfilling all the horse's worst fears. So next time he hollows more, making the rider tip back more and pull on the rein more . . .

Once I had pointed this out to Carol, she could clearly feel what was happening, although it was no easy matter for her to push forward through her body and thigh to the extent that she did *not* fall backwards and did not pull on the inside rein *even though the horse had effectively set her up to do so*. She also had to think of keeping the 'ping' in the trampoline, since Queen's hollowing also involved a slowing down and a loss of impetus, in which the inside hind leg lingered on the ground instead of springing off it. As far as the horse is concerned, the rider is guilty – and therefore likely to pull on the inside rein – until she proves herself innocent; so only preventative action from the rider can break this self-fulfilling prophecy. With a sensitive horse like Queen, who does not easily trust the rider's sitting, it is absolutely essential to *prove* to her that you will not upset her carriage.

To take the process one stage further, and to make sure that Carol was moulding onto Queen's back really well in sitting trot, I asked her, 'Do you feel your seat bones moving with the trot one side at a time or both sides together?' Carol felt the trot as a one-side-at-a-time motion, which of course it has to be, since the horse does not trot by jumping like a rabbit! But many people do not, so they have to go through a process of learning to separate their two sides in order to do 'bottom walking' at trot as well as walk. Carol wrote of her sitting trot that, 'I have to have a feeling of leaning back slightly. As long as I can maintain the pinching and bearing down and keep my seat bones moving alternately with her, sitting trot feels much more successful and under my control.'

After producing some good work in trot, Carol went on into canter. She then immediately became an 'up' rider, pushing down into her stirrups so that she was thrown up into the fork seat and came up off the horse's back as she had in Figure 54. Her back hollowed and as a result her upper body bumped and rocked forward with each canter stride. This made her heavier with her hand, and she also lost her pinch and the snugness of her thighs, so that she was unstable from side to side. All this is extremely common in canter – it happened to an even greater degree with Margaret – and of course it causes the horse to hollow and to become correspondingly heavy in the rider's hand. (This makes one appreciate how well Janet maintained her seat on Mayday's canter in Lesson 5, which was much more hollow and unbalanced.) Nine times out of ten, the incorrectness of the horse's movement makes the rider bump more, which in turn hollows the horse's back more, which makes the rider bump more . . . This creates a horrible vicious circle, providing one of the most frequent and obvious demonstrations of 'the spiral of increasing tension'.

The solution for Carol lay initially in leaning back more and squashing her ribs more down towards her hips, as if she could make her upper body shorter. (She must not, however, forget the big balloon this time.) Like Margaret, she also has to lighten her pressure into the stirrups, since her push *down* into them created an equal and opposite force which pushed her backside *up*. Once she thought of compressing both ends of her body towards her middle, she was able to drop the back of her backside down into the saddle, thinking of tucking her seat bones right underneath her. (It is often necessary to tuck under more to withstand the canter bound than it is to withstand the trot bound.) She then had deliberately to hold her thighs *out in front of her* – for with the change in her seat, they had begun to go straight down into the 'mantrap' instead of passing over the top of it.

Carol was tremendously surprised to find that I was literally asking her to bring her knee *up*, but this was necessary (as it often is in canter) to keep her out of the 'mantrap' and to create the necessary leverage in the thigh. So much had gone awry in the up/down plane that it was impossible for Carol to be correct in the back/front plane. However, she soon became able to bear down again, and then to lighten her hand, which enabled her to make the pinch feeling and to snug in her thighs so that she also became correct in the side/side plane and could draw her horse's rib cage outwards. You can see the result in Figure 57. Note how Carol's body is much more upright than it is in Figure 54, although she has a slight twist inwards.

57. This canter shows quite nice carriage from Queen. Carol is sitting well and she would almost maintain her balance on a diving board. Her backside is more tucked underneath her than it is in Figure 54, and as a consequence she can hold her body much more upright. But to sit absolutely still, and to be truly causal, she will have to tuck it underneath her even more. Her left hand is a little behind her right, pulling Queen's head to the inside. To correct this, she will need to bring her left point of hip towards Queen's right ear.

Whereas the movement of the rider's seat in trot is like 'bottom walking', the canter movement is different. The horse always has his inside hind and forelegs in advance of his outside hind and forelegs, and to mirror this, the rider's inside seat bone and point of hip must always be in advance of the outside ones. Many riders have *too large* a movement of their seat in canter (just as they have in walk), but the correct feeling must never 'unplug' them from the horse's long back muscles. Thinking of this makes them realise how small the movements in the horse's back actually are: it is more a question of bringing the seat bones *up* slightly in each canter stride, thus replacing an exaggerated forward-and-back movement. This also provides the key to the canter transition, for all that happens here is that the rider positions herself with her inside hip in advance and changes her seat bones from the trot movement to the canter movement. Again, the predominant change is a lifting *up* of the inside seat bone. As you do this, it is best to put your conscious attention on maintaining the pinch feeling and just to *think* of cantering. By positioning your pelvis correctly, you have automatically taken care of your lower legs – but the canter aid has much more to do with the changes in the seat bone movement than it has to do with the leg alone.

It must be obvious by now that there is tremendous intricacy involved in the rider's positioning, which this session with Carol demonstrates very well. In her walk she was too 'down', but in her canter she was too 'up'. In her rising trot she sometimes tipped forward and sometimes came slightly behind the movement, needing encouragement to lean forward just enough and to keep thrusting her pelvis forward. Only then could she keep 'taking the horse', and keep control of the way in which she landed back in the saddle. But in her sitting trot and canter she always had to lean back – otherwise her back hollowed and she bumped. In walk and trot, she had to come slightly back in the saddle in order to orientate her push forward correctly; but in canter, she had to bring her backside forwards and under. In each gait, she had periods of being 'just right' which she could easily recognise, but it will take her some while to establish this 'rightness' and to know how to make adjustments between the different gaits and movements.

Carol has the advantage that she is exceptionally quick to learn and to recognise different feels. Although she is working with the same feels as Katie, Janet and Gina (who you will meet in the next lesson), she has none of the mental interference which makes learning so much more difficult for them. She is not under- or over-focussed, so she does not lose concentration or try too hard. Her intellect and her body work well together so she can accept and try out new ideas. If she does something wrong, she does not perceive it as a sign that she will never be any good or as a reflection on her value as a person. This has enabled her to make very fast progress and in only a couple more sessions we have been able to explore the implications of this work in the lateral movements. However, I have been equally excited to see her twelve-year-old daughter watching each lesson with eagle eyes, and Carol has reported that just watching has enabled her to make significant improvements in her own riding. (I love to teach children at this age, before they have spent years ingraining their habitual ways of doing it wrong. By eighteen, when they have had six years' practice in doing it right, their understanding and skill can be tremendous.) Despite Carol's natural ability, she expressed a cry in her notes to me that I have heard all too often: 'I find it amazing that no one has been able to tell me these things before – not even renowned teachers who have helped me a lot, and who I hold in high regard. I really felt that my problems were just me – one of life's failures!'

Lesson 9

Gina: The Precise Positioning of the Seat Bones

I first met Gina in November 1988 when I ran a two-day course in Wiltshire. She was introduced to my work by a friend who was already a pupil of mine and who realised that Gina was particularly in need of my approach. Since that time, Gina has been on a number of courses in Wiltshire as well as a four-day residential course, so she has probably had about twenty-five lessons with me. Her horse, Andante, was nine at the time of this lesson, and Gina had owned him for five years. He is a 15.3-hand Welsh Cob/ thoroughbred cross with the kind of 'panic button' which I have often seen in Welsh Cobs. He is, however, a tremendously talented little horse, who has very nice movement and the ability to lower his croup to an unusual degree.

I have a very clear memory of Gina's first lesson, which sticks in my mind because she and Dante were both giving each other an exceptionally hard time. Gina was acting as if her life depended on getting Dante 'onto the bit' and her tactics included a fair amount of pulling back and fiddling about with her hands. Dante was acting as if his life was dependent on resisting. His body was very contracted and it was obvious that he was extremely sensitive and unhappy in his mouth and probably also in his back. He very quickly began to run away from this discomfort, which, of course, made Gina use her hand even more. Part of this was instinct, but lessons which Gina had had in the past had emphasised the role of her hand and her leg in bringing the horse 'onto the bit', and she had no idea at all that the real key lay in her pelvis – in drawing up the wither instead of compressing the horse from both ends.

When I first met Gina, I asked her to shorten her stirrups, and she still rides with them rather short. One of her longstanding arguments with riding teachers has centred around their insistence that she lower her heels. At the moment, however, this is a physical impossibility for her, even if she pushes hard against the stirrups. (As a result, she feels particularly unstable when she is jumping.) Like Jan, she is rather contracted in the flexor muscles in the front of the body and she has the added disadvantage that she cannot squat with her heels on the floor. (Try this for yourself now.) Both her calf muscles and her hamstrings are contracted, which reduces her stability over the stirrup. I have recommended that she squat for a little while each day, resting her heels on telephone directories until she can gradually reduce their thickness and lower her heels down to the floor. This will be a long-term project but the benefits for her riding will be immense.

It took Gina quite some while to begin to trust that her pelvic positioning could indeed make a much better job than her hand of shaping Dante; and only this faith, built up gradually over time, enabled her to become much more soft and quiet in her contact. The reactions of the compulsive 'fiddler' happen so far below the level of consciousness that it can seem almost impossible for her to sense them, let alone stop them. It helps to make a bridge with the reins – putting the free end of one rein under the opposite thumb: this makes it harder for the rider to move one hand independently of the other, which reduces the temptation to fiddle and to pull. The reins then begin to feel like solid rods which happen to have the horse's mouth at the other end of them, making it easier for the rider to feel as if she were pushing a pram rather than holding onto something which can be pulled about and manipulated. It also helps to imagine that the lower arm is an extension of the rein, so that the rider feels her contact with the horse's mouth in her *elbow* rather than her hand.

These techniques are helpful because will-power alone is rarely enough to stop a rider from over-using her hands. I once heard this put beautifully in a lesson given by Erik Herbermann, who likened the compulsive 'fiddler' to the person who talks of giving up smoking or chocolate bars. 'Just let me have one more,' they say, 'and then I'll quit.' Of course, after that there is just one more, and just one more, and an eternal promise that 'After this next one . . .'.

Gina has had her 'last' fiddle on many occasions, but she is now largely cured, except when she feels stressed by the more difficult work. The truth is that whenever the rider loses the correct placing of either seat bone on top of the horse's long back muscle, she fiddles about with her *hand* when she should in reality be fiddling about with her *seat bone* in a search to plug herself in again. It is as if there were a 'socket' in each of the horse's long back muscles which alone is exactly the right place for the seat bone and its imaginary extension to plug in to. (Think again of those plastic cowboys and indians!) It is no exaggeration or misrepresentation to say that the rider is faced with a task which is akin to trying to put a two-pin plug into a socket in the dark (with her seat bones). This means that ON EVERY HORSE, IN EVERY GAIT AND EVERY MOVEMENT, THERE IS *ONE* CORRECT PLACE FOR EACH SEAT BONE, which changes as the horse's hind legs move within each step. I speculate that this 'socket' is actually the end point of the thoracic part of the trapezius muscle (see Diagram 16). I am sure, however, that these points are not figments of my imagination: they feel so real that they must have physical form.

When the rider finds both of these points, and connects correctly with them, she had pretty much done her job: everything else she does seems to happen almost automatically, with no sweat and no hassle. An onlooker sees magic in action. As the rider moves her pelvis, she moves these connection points with her, placing the horse into just the bend and positioning that she wants, and making her hand and lower leg seem almost superfluous. But when the rider is unaware of this subtlety, and when she 'misses' with one or both of her seat bones, an entirely different picture is presented.

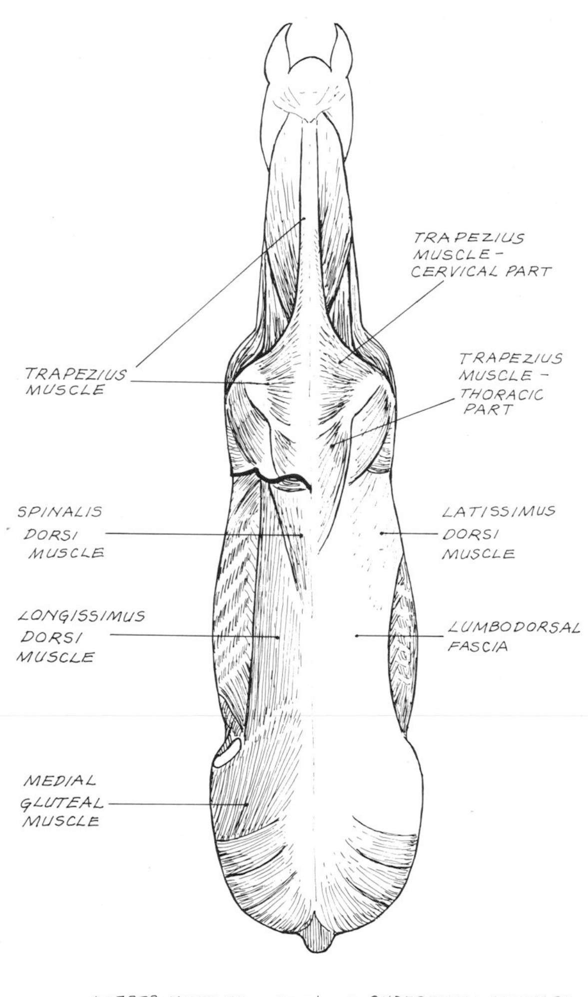

Diagram 16. The horse's back muscles shown from above. The right side of the horse shows the lumbo-dorsal fascia which lies under the skin, covering most of the horse's back. The thoracic part of the trapezius muscle extends backwards from the shoulder blade, ending at the tenth thoracic vertebra. The left-hand side of the diagram, from the shoulder blade backwards, shows the deeper muscles. I suspect that the end point of the trapezius muscle is the 'receptor' which the rider's seat bone must plug in to.

There are hassles and fights, or, at best, a loss of ease and smoothness. The rider's hands and legs work overtime, for her body senses that something is wrong and she instinctively uses *the wrong parts of her body to try to make things right*. Given that we are so much more facile with our hands than we are with our seat bones, it is hardly surprising that we should be as obtuse as we are about their connection with the horse's back – and also hardly surprising that the temptation to 'fiddle' should be as strong and pervasive as it undoubtedly is.

First-aid measures are often needed to help the rider to keep her hands still and to minimise the damage she does whilst she learns how to plug in with her seat bones. But the real correction lies here, with the *cause* and not the *symptom*. Gina is beginning to understand the connections between hand and seat bone, and between seat bone and horse's back. She also understands the enormous ramifications of these: in her learning, she has shown tremendous insight and she has often given me very interesting feedback. But when she gets more ambitious, this clarity disappears and her original desperation reasserts itself. For Gina can only think highly of herself when she is performing well, and she has a whole list of things which she 'ought to be able to do by now'. Her need to progress quickly makes her impatient, and although she is not an aggressive person, she has a rather short fuse. Like all of us, she is her own worst enemy, for through her hasty actions she dooms herself to fail, and then to think badly of herself.

In effect, Dante presses Gina's 'mad button' and Gina presses Dante's 'panic button'. Gina pays very highly for her mistakes, for after the heat of the moment she is inclined to torture herself with recriminations. Dante punishes her too, for he is so wary of her hand that he runs away from it as soon as it begins to dominate – and he continues to run away from it for the next week. This makes it harder for her to plug in and it sucks them both more and more deeply into 'the spiral of increasing tension'. Gina does not have an arena, so she does much of her schooling on the roads. Many a road ride has degenerated into a battle in which she is trying to stop Dante, who begins to run away from her in walk, using an incredibly fast and uneven tempo which goes 1, 2 . . . 3, 4 . . . 1, 2 . . . 3, 4 . . . . He also foils Gina by thinking up a new evasion every time she has learnt how to counteract the last one. At first he was horribly hollow, but when Gina learnt how to make him reach down into the rein, he soon took to working with his nose almost on the floor so that she could not bring it up again! In Figure 58 he is attempting to do this, and Gina has not quite fathomed out how to bring him back up into place. When she does, she still finds it hard to get him exactly right – he likes to add a subtle degree of overbending which can foil her yet again (Lesson 10 with Jill explains the cure for this). Figure 59 shows some quite nice work, although Dante is not truly in front of Gina and his neck is a little contracted. On the day we took these photographs, he surprised her by *not* trying to run away; in fact he was unprecedentedly lazy. Usually, Gina is struggling to keep up with him, so that she does not fall into the trap of water-skiing. She came out with the same expectation in this lesson, and despite all my efforts she was very slow to change her tactics and to think of coming behind him instead. It is always much easier to follow your old tramlines and ride the horse *as you think he will be*, rather than receiving the 'news of difference' which enables you to ride him *as he actually is*!

58. Dante wants to work long and low – his favourite party trick now that Gina has learnt to lift his back. The push out from her lower stomach is going too far up his neck, and correcting this will make a significant difference to his carriage.

59. Gina has Dante in a more upright carriage, although his neck is a little contracted and he is slightly overbent. She is not completely behind him because her backside has slipped back and her body has tipped forward.

Dante's temperament makes him something of a quick-change artist, which really tests Gina's ability to adapt. (Some horses – Queen, for instance – have one evasion which they perform to the ultimate, and they are very much slower to think up something new.) Riding Dante is rather like taking part in a tennis match, where as soon as you get to fifteen-love, your partner equalises to make it fifteen-all and starts thinking up a way to make it fifteen-thirty . . . When it comes to riding, Gina's brain has a hard time keeping up with Dante's, and in order to take the initiative she will have to become incredibly skilful. I tease her by saying that Dante is very thorough in his teaching and is obviously determined that anyone who graduates from his riding school is going to be extremely good! To be fair to Gina, however, many people would have made a worse job of riding him, and some would have given up by now. If Gina gives up, I am first in the queue to buy Dante, and I suspect that my faith in his ability fuels her determination to keep going!

When I think about Gina's learning process, and the comments that she has made to me along the way, it reaffirms my belief that learning inevitably happens in layers, rather like the layers of an onion. You *think* that you have learnt to pinch and bear down, and then you begin the more difficult work – extensions perhaps – and suddenly find that you are no longer pinching and bearing down *enough*. Then, of course, you find yourself riding from your hand,

and you have to learn about pinching and bearing down all over again. This may bring some new elements into these apparently simple ideas, adjusting exactly how you do them. (This has happened to me many times!) The same thing happens when you start using the school movements more, and find, for instance, that you instinctively grab the inside rein every time you come onto a circle. Again, you have to re-learn how to surrender the hand and advance the pelvis. Learning the lateral movements almost always brings this pattern to the fore again, peeling away another layer. So does competition, which is a good reason for not competing until your skill is well established. Several of my more advanced and sensible pupils have taken 'sabbaticals' from competition for at least six months when they started to do this work, but it is all too easy, in our modern day culture, to value results so highly that we lose interest in the purity of our work. Many people have insisted on undermining the growth of their skill by rushing off to compete or to work with trainers who asked them to run before they could walk.

One of Gina's major breakthroughs happened when we began paying greater attention to the movement of her seat bones in the walk. She had already begun to understand the idea of being 'still relative to the horse', but I sensed that she was still not quite plugged in. I also wanted to give Gina some ideas which would be helpful on her road rides, so I asked her to call 'left' to me every time her left seat bone moved forward. Then I asked her, 'Does this coincide with the time when his left hind leg is on the ground, or when it is in the air?' She thought that the hind leg was moving forward – which indeed it was. I then asked her about the right seat bone and the right hind leg: she now consistently called 'right' to me at the time when the right hind leg was on the ground – even though she thought that it was in the air. Something was obviously amiss.

When the hind leg on one side moves forward in walk or trot, the horse's rib cage is displaced towards the other side. This gives room for the forward swing of the hind leg, and displaces the horse's weight to the side where it can be supported by the hind leg which is on the ground. If you stand behind any four-legged creature and watch it moving, you will see the same effect. As the rib cage moves over to the weight-bearing side, the body is moving forward over this hind leg and the long back muscle on that side contracts one segment at a time, creating a ripple which travels from the croup to the lower part of the neck. The muscle fills out *automatically* raising the seat bone and drawing it out a little; the rider does not have to think about moving it. Meanwhile, the long back muscle on the side where the hind leg moves forward is lengthening, so that it becomes thinner as it elongates. (Put your fingers on your own long back muscles and feel the changes in them as you walk: the muscle on each side swells out whilst your foot is on the ground and again when it pushes off.) As the hind leg moves forward, the seat bone on that side moves forward too, following the seam-line of the saddle so that it comes forward, in and up. This keeps it plugged in. By the time it arrives at the top, it is ready to be lifted by the horse's long back muscle as it swells out in the weight-bearing phase of the stride, effectively acting as a pivot whilst the other seat bone advances and takes its turn in 'bottom walking'. *Many people have this movement back to front*, so that they move their seat bone forward over the back muscle which is filled out, thus discouraging the horse from using it to the full. Other people, like Gina, have one seat bone which moves in its turn and one which gets stuck and moves late, if at all.

When I was first shown this I did not know what had hit me! My seat bones were moving the opposite way to the way my trainer wanted them to, and it took me a very long time to come to terms with his demands. I had to make myself do the equivalent of changing diagonal in rising trot: instead of going left, right, left, right, left, right, I had to reverse the movement of my seat bones by going left, right, *right*, left, right . . . I could then carry on in the new pattern. But once I got the idea, my efforts were repaid by a phenomenal increase in my influence over the backs of the horses I was riding: I had at last plugged in to them correctly. To learn the detail of this, it is best to focus on one hind leg at a time. When the left hind leg is moving forward, the foreleg on the same side is about to begin its forward movement, and you can see the point of the shoulder advancing. This is the time to call to yourself 'left'. Then do whatever is needed to reverse your left/right pattern so that your left seat bone moves forward as you call. As this happens, feel the swelling out under the right seat bone as well as the thigh and calf. Once you have the left side organised, change to calling 'right'. Only when you have each side working well and are clear in body and mind should you attempt to put both sides together.

In trot, the horse's long back muscles and rib cage move in a similar way to walk, so there is still a left, right, left, right pattern. The issue here is not so much that riders move their seat bones the wrong way round, it is more that they do not separate their two sides, so they often feel them moving both together. Once the wobbles and bumps are out of the way, this side-to-side movement is not difficult to feel, and again moulding onto it is the only way to plug in to the horse's long back muscles. Then you know exactly what is happening underneath you and you become causal. Your control of the horse's tempo is increased and your timing when you want to give a canter aid, or to ask for a lateral movement, can become very much more precise. In trot, as one hind leg advances, the shoulder on the same side is moving *back*: this is what you must look for as you begin to call 'left' or 'right' to yourself. Again, only put the two sides together when you have worked on both of them one at a time.

In walk, Gina found it very easy to locate the correct timing and movement with her left seat bone and extremely tricky with her right. (In sitting trot, she is still struggling with this, and she manages it for short periods until something disturbs her sitting.) She had to *make* her right seat bone move – still with the idea, of course, that her outsides must remain still even though her insides are moving. She finished the lesson resolving to hack around Wiltshire using the movement of the horse's shoulder as a reference point and calling 'right' to herself at each stride. She gradually found that she had much more control over Dante's tempo: the late movement of her right seat bone had given him the opportunity to rush out from underneath her in every stride, but now that this was not possible *he* was foiled. It was also much easier for Gina not to resort to her hand, although she has admitted in later lessons that if I had not been there to hold her on the straight and narrow she would have given up and pulled him in the mouth. His laziness on the day we took these photographs was the result, I discovered later, of two weeks' work in a hackamore. With nothing to run away from, and good regulation from Gina's seat, he had begun to behave like a normal horse.

Gina had started to learn leg-yielding quite a few lessons before the one in which these photographs were taken. When we first began, I had asked her to show me what she had been doing at home, so she came down the threequarter line and moved Dante over towards the track. There was only one problem – she was not leg-yielding. Instead she was 'wandering vaguely sideways' in the direction of the track, with no lateral stepping of the horse's legs. Nine times out of ten, this is what riders show me, and, like most of the people I meet, Gina was surprised at my insistence that this was not leg-yielding. She was equally surprised when she experienced the feeling of a correct lateral step.

I like to begin leg-yielding in the walk, by placing the horse at an angle to the long side and having him move along it as if he was doing a large-angle shoulder-in with no bend. I also like to manoeuvre the horse into the movement from the ground, so that the rider is freed from the need to *make* the horse go sideways. (I have been influenced in this by my training in Portugal, where I learnt to work young horses in hand.) I might well not do this with a rider who was already practised in the lateral work, but I find that it is the best choice for a beginner. In doing this I am deliberately choosing to exaggerate the movement. I am not beginning in a very subtle way (for instance, with shoulder-fore, a very small-angle shoulder-in) and then gradually amplifying the movement. I think that asking for this degree of subtlety is rather like expecting the horse and rider to be grown-ups, with the ability to do joined-up writing without ever having learnt to do big letters first!

I have two major aims when I first start teaching the lateral movements. The first is to give the rider the feeling of a correct lateral step, so that she cannot wander about thinking that she is doing leg-yield or shoulder-in when she actually is not. The second is to do this *without* her setting up all sorts of contortions in her body: her major task is simply to stay plugged in. Most riders, however, do not think about their seat bones – they think only about their hands and their legs, and, in particular, they get carried away with the idea of *pushing the horse away from their active leg*. This makes them kick, shove, squeeze and lean over that leg in the process. Then, instead of remaining vertical, their upper body tilts away from the direction in which they are going and they unplug their leading seat bone. They act as if they think that force is required, and their experience seems to prove that it is – for the harder they try, and the more they collapse and shove, the less the horse responds . . . so the harder they have to try. (It amazes me that human beings are so slow to consider changing their tactics and so quick to resort to more force.) The problem arises because they forget entirely about the side of their body that lies *in the direction of motion*. If it were true to say that the rider's active seat bone pushes the horse across (an idea which I dislike), it would be equally true to say that the seat bone in the direction of motion also has to *push back*, otherwise the rider becomes completely lop-sided, losing the outside of her framework so that there is no barrier holding the outside of the horse in place. You can see the effects of this in Figure 60.

Imagine that you were carrying somebody piggy-back, and that she moved over to one side on your back. How would you have to move underneath her in order to stay in balance? You would need to move in the same direction as her, so that you effectively put her back above your centre again. (I have met many people who are convinced that they should move the other way. If you are in doubt about this, try it.) So if you put your body weight on the side of the horse *away* from the direction in which you want him to move, what will happen? Undoubtedly, he will not fulfil your expectations; in fact, he is likely to move in the opposite direction to the one you want! This is why the idea of 'pushing' him over is so ridiculous, and it is much more helpful to think of luring him over by positioning your centre of gravity in the direction of motion so that you tactfully give him *no choice* but to step under your body weight. One of my pupils likes to think of the arrows showing the horse's direction of motion which you often see in the diagrams of riding texts. She imagines that the arrows are pulling her and her horse along – a lovely way for the rider to counteract the tendency to 'push' and to move her centre of gravity over so that she effectively 'pulls' instead.

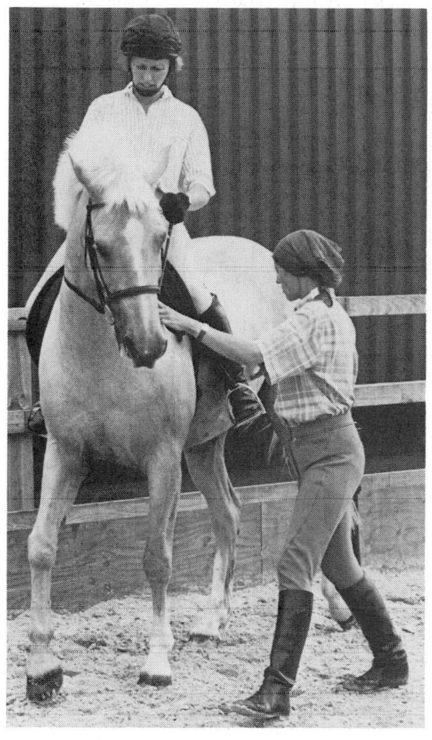

60. In this attempt at leg-yield in walk, Gina has lost control of Dante's outside shoulder. She has brought his forehand off the track by using her inside rein and, as a result, he has jack-knifed. Notice that the central axis of her body is misplaced – she has probably lifted her outside seat bone and weighted her inside one too much.

61. This is much better leg-yielding. Notice how the axis of Gina's body is much straighter: she has succeeded in advancing her outside seat bone and has kept equal weight on both, placing them correctly on top of his long back muscles. This has given her control of Dante's outside shoulder.

Moving your weight over correctly, is, however, not just a question of weighting one seat bone more than the other: as we have seen previously, bringing one of them *down* tends to cause the other one to come *up*. Instead, the pelvis has to move over in the horizontal plane. It is drawn across by changing the angle of each thigh, which in turn changes the placing of each seat bone (see Lesson 3 with Jan, and especially Figures 24 and 25). Unless the rider is absolutely precise in the way in which she does this, she will unplug one or both seat bones, allowing the horse to position himself according to his own whims and her lop-sidedness. In effect, the rider who is causal remains plugged in, so her seat bones remain connected to the 'sockets' in the horse's back and she *moulds the horse's body around these 'receptors' into the shape and position which she wants.*

If the rider was sitting in the middle of a clock face, with twelve o'clock being the direction of the horse's head and neck as it points straight ahead, symmetry would have her thighs point to about ten to and ten past the hour. Correct positioning on a circle brings the inside thigh closer to twelve o'clock, with the outside one remaining at about ten to or ten past. This brings the rider's backside over to the inside of the saddle, and positions her thighs correctly around his now asymmetrical rib cage, which bulges out more on the outside (see Lesson 7 with Margaret). In the lateral work, the thigh in the direction of motion – the outside in shoulder-in and the inside in travers and half-pass – comes *even closer* to twelve o'clock, moving the pelvis even more.

To understand precisely how the seat bones are involved in this as well, put a dressage whip on the ground and position your fists on each side of it as if the whip represented the horse's spine and your fists represented your seat bones. (This is the insight I spoke about in the Introduction which had me leaping out of bed with excitement that day in Portugal.) If the whip (horse) were going round on a circle, your fists would be positioned with the inside one in advance, so that they lay on the ten past eight axis (right rein) or the ten to four axis (left rein) (see Diagram 17). If you wanted to position the horse into travers, moving his quarters inwards on the circle, your outside seat bone would move back and your inside seat bone would move forward, bringing them onto the five past seven axis (right rein) or the five to five axis (left rein). With this extra narrowing, it feels almost as if the horse's spine were held in place between the two seat bones. Now imagine that you wanted to position the horse into shoulder-in on the circle. How must your fists (seat bones) move? The outer one now has to come forward, whilst the inside one comes back. This brings your seat bones onto the five to five axis (right rein) or the five past seven axis (left rein). With your seat bones in each of these positions, you have at least an approximate match for the new position of the horse's 'receptors' in each movement.

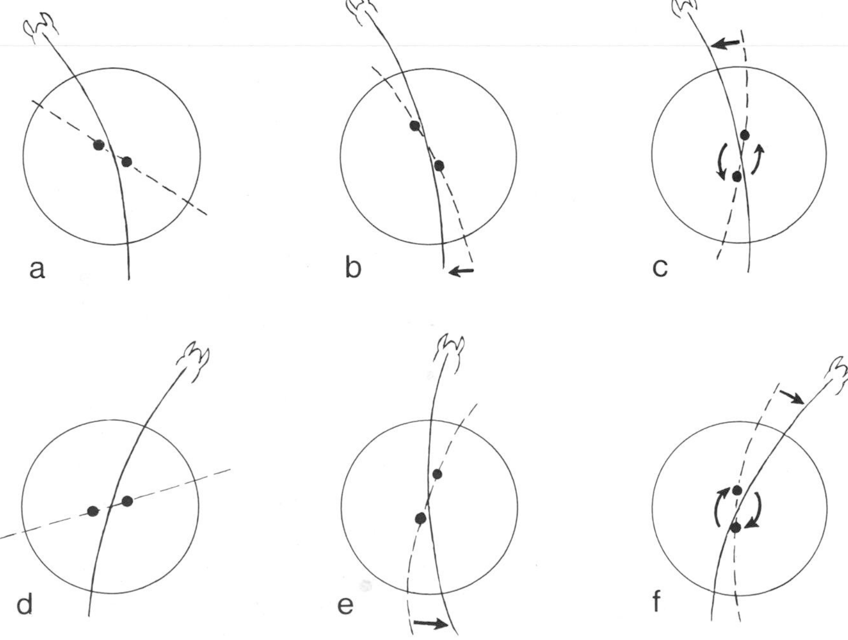

Diagram 17. On circle left, the rider's seat bones lie on the ten to four axis, as in (a). To position the horse into travers on the circle, they shift around to five to five, holding the horse's spine more closely between them, as in (b). To position him into shoulder-in on the circle, they almost reverse their placings, coming to five past seven, and again, it is as if they hold the horse's spine more firmly between them, as in (c). On circle right, the rider's seat bones lie on the ten past eight axis, as in (d). To position the horse into travers on the circle, they shift around to five past seven, holding the horse's spine more closely between them, as in (e). To position him into shoulder-in, they almost reverse their placings, coming to the five to five axis, as if (f).

Although this may sound complex when you read it, it is relatively easy to do when you have enough control of your basic positioning – but it is not worth trying until you do! The pinch feeling becomes particularly important in the lateral movements, as it helps to keep the space between the rider's seat bones *narrow* enough to keep her plugged in. As long as the rider still has both of her 'stabilisers' down (see Lesson 3 with Jan), there is no loss of stability. Inevitably, however, everyone has more difficulty on one rein than they do on the other, for very few riders can easily adjust the angles of their thighs and the positions of their seat bones on the clock face. Usually these are chosen for them by the horse and their own asymmetry; they have one pattern, which is extremely hard to get out of. If that pattern includes a tendency to fall off one of the horse's long back muscles, and/or to lean to one side as well (which it usually does), the rider 'misses' so grossly that her task becomes even more difficult. To add to the complications, anyone who succeeds in her attempts to adjust her own habitual pattern will probably be put off by the accompanying feeling of 'weirdness'. The proof of the pudding lies with the horse, whose body responds to the correct positioning of the rider by moulding itself into the shape of the movement as if of its own accord.

As I helped Gina to position Dante into the leg-yield, I reminded her to advance her outside seat bone as she came around the corner onto the long side where she was to begin the movement. Her first task was then to bring his outside shoulder away from the wall. In Figure 60 this has not happened well, and Dante has jack-knifed. Gina does not have control of his outside shoulder, and you can see how she has resorted to pulling on the inside rein – which, of course, can only make his jack-knife worse. She has also leant inwards in her attempts to push him over, and you can see that the axis of her body is not vertical. In Figure 61 we have remedied the situation: Dante is now much straighter and Gina has control of his outside shoulder.

The difficulty that Gina is having here is very similar to the problem with which I helped Margaret in Lesson 7 (see Figures 51 and 52), and is a common one for many riders who do not have control of the horse's outside shoulder in leg-yield or shoulder-in. Like Margaret, Gina has to be careful not to unplug either of her seat bones and to fall off Dante's long back muscles. As she positions into the movement, it helps her to ask, 'How must I sit so that, relative to me, his shoulders come more to the inside?' The answer is: more to the outside, and advancing her outside seat bone to create this shift. (As Margaret was positioning her horse onto a circle, she had to remedy her situation a little differently. Do not get confused between the two.) Essentially, the rider's inside aids – primarily her thigh and seat bone – move the horse more to the outside, and her outside aids move him more to the inside. So if she thinks of positioning his wither by sandwiching it between the two, she begins to know how to respond to any deviations the horse might make. She also creates a strong and stable framework which limits the deviations which are possible.

With Gina's pelvis in the correct position, moving Dante sideways requires minimal use of her inside leg – especially as I am there to help her. As I was walking with Dante, I reminded Gina to keep taking him, maintaining the pinch and the bearing down so that she retained control of the tempo and could not start water-skiing. She also needed to keep her seat bones walking along, following the seam-lines of the saddle, so that she could not seize up and unplug herself, forgetting about the one that lies in the direction of motion. In fact, Gina did her leg-yield on the left rein calling 'right, right, right', in time with the movement of his right hind leg, so that she could not over-emphasise the left seat bone and forget the all-important right seat bone – the tricky one for her.

It is very important for Gina not to do very much of this work on her own, because she is likely to create more problems than she cures. She wrote some notes to me after her holiday, when she was getting Dante fit again, and she said, 'I love doing this basic fittening work, and I can feel so many little changes in his back and in myself as well. It's really delightful, but I need to be so careful when I start doing more advanced stuff . . .'

Learning to ride the lateral movements will really test her, and I suspect that she will only succeed as she becomes able to separate her self-image from her performance. She will then know that she is a good and valuable person regardless of how she rides: she will not need to ride well in order to prove her worth to herself, nor will she disprove it by riding badly. Then, she will find that she has a much more even keel, and that she is able to enjoy the journey instead of longing to arrive. Without this added burden of significance, her riding will matter to her much less. When I think of this, I always remember the story told by a friend of mine who used to have help from Robert Hall. He once said to her, 'When I am riding, the result I want has to matter enough that I am willing to put myself out for it, but not so much that it matters if I don't get it.' I wish Gina this kind of equilibrium more than I wish her anything else, because I know that with it, the techniques she is lacking will simply fall into her lap, giving her the rewards that she undoubtedly deserves.

Lesson 10

Jill: The Rider's Framework

Before she came to me for lessons, Jill had participated in several of my dismounted workshop courses, so I had known her for over a year before I actually saw her ride. It was obvious from her comments and questions in the workshops that she had quite some degree of skill and experience. She also talked about her previous work with several trainers whose approach had, she felt in retrospect, been damaging to her horses. I suspected – and she later admitted – that she wanted to check me out very fully before committing herself to a lesson! She is a well-qualified professional rider and teacher who has done very well, running her own small business and competing her two horses in dressage and eventing. She has had fairly regular lessons with me over about two years and has made a great deal of progress over that time, although, like everyone, she has one or two idiosyncrasies which have been very pervasive and which we are only now really beginning to eradicate.

Jill has owned her horse, King, for about three years. He is a 17.2-hand Dutch warmblood and is twelve years old. He has over two hundred dressage points, mostly gained with his previous owner, and Jill bought him as a school-master. Many people expect this to be the easy answer to learning, dreaming of pushing button B and getting the right result. But as Jill has found, it can become difficult and frustrating when the horse discovers that you leave him many more loopholes than did his previous rider and that he has the freedom to add some poetic licence to his rendering of the movements. King is not an easy horse to ride: he is not very generous and is a long horse who is built very hollow. During her working day, Jill rides many different horses and one of her persistent problems has been her difficulty in flexing almost all of them to the left. Her own two, of course, are familiar with her weaknesses and may even have built their evasive patterns around them (I always find myself wondering, in these situations, who is the chicken and who is the egg); but a high proportion of horses who are stiff to the right for other riders miraculously become stiff to the left soon after Jill gets on them!

Fortunately, it has been obvious to Jill that the common denominator in all of this must be her way of sitting, and her experience only goes to prove that the horse can read his rider like a book. Jill initially had to correct her asymmetry in a similar way to Val, although the pattern in Jill's body was much more subtle and difficult to detect. However, whilst these changes always have immediate and dramatic effects, it is much more difficult than you might imagine to ingrain them. From that initial leap, it takes a very long time of dedicated practice before they begin to feel relatively easy, and even longer before they become second nature. Jill is close to this now, and when we spoke on the telephone soon after this course she was horrified to report that although she was riding well on the left rein, she had found it difficult to flex several horses to the right – something which she had always regarded as a fail-safe bet! Whilst *I* could define this as progress, she was not so sure. When a rider's standard asymmetry begins to break down, she usually experiences a reversal of her 'bad' side. In effect, she goes from habitually falling off one of the horse's long back muscles to habitually falling off the other one – and it can take quite some while for her to really understand the dynamics of how to position herself on both of them, regardless of which rein she is riding on.

Figure 62 shows Jill coming off the track onto a circle left, with a good positioning from both her and King. It is particularly interesting to notice the axes of both their bodies. Firstly, note that they are aligned. Secondly, notice that they are not vertical: both Jill and King are angled inwards, going around the turn just like a bicycle rider or an aeroplane. This is *not the same* as falling in, which would cause the horse to lose the bend in his body and to overburden his inside shoulder. Neither is Jill collapsing, which would make the axis of her body lie on a different angle from the axis of King's (you can see this happening to Margaret in Figure 51, page 143).

Many riders judge a correct bend by whether or not they can see the horse's inside eye: Val could see her horse's inside eye in Figure 31 (page 92), but China was jack-knifing, remaining upright and breaking at the wither instead of producing a correct bend. Used on its own, the idea of being able to see the horse's inside eye is not a sufficient gauge of correctness; in fact, I believe it causes many more problems than it cures. Think of it this way: the horse's shoulder blades are not attached to his rib cage by bone, as ours are; instead, they are only held in place by ligaments and muscles. When the horse's forehand lightens, the shoulder blades are drawn upwards, towards the point of an inverted 'V'. The wither and rib cage, which are shaped like a tear drop, are then drawn upwards between them. This whole mechanism then acts as one unit, tilting inwards to the appropriate degree and causing a corresponding change in the angle of the rib cage, which now bulges to the outside (see Diagram 18). The horse can only fall onto his inside or outside shoulder when the shoulder blade, instead of being drawn up, acts *independently* and drops away to the side. (This was happening to Val, Janet, Sarah and Margaret in Lessons 4, 5, 6 and 7, and it is a very common problem.)

Of course, this also stops the correct lifting of the wither, and many horses use an asymmetrical holding like this in order to save themselves from having to step through correctly so that the forehand lifts and lightens in the back/front plane.

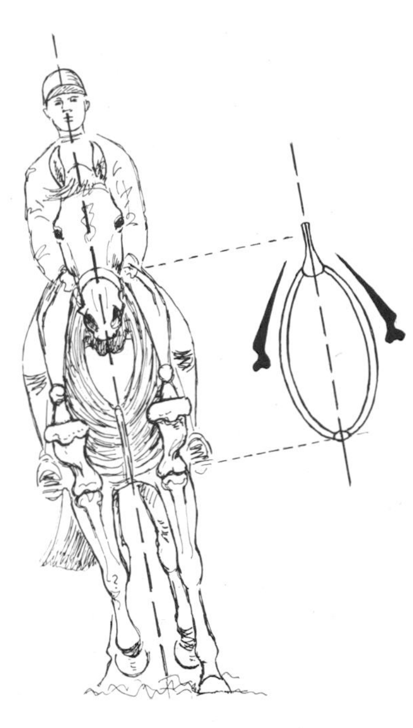

62. Jill and King are coming off the track onto circle left, and both of them are very well positioned. Notice particularly the axes of both their bodies.

Diagram 18. A cross-section through the horse's wither, showing the shoulder blades and rib cage. In a correct turn (here on circle right), they are all drawn up so that they act as one unit and are angled in the same way in which a bicycle rider or an aeroplane would go round a turn. If one or both shoulder blades do not lift up, this can no longer happen.

Jill was riding King very well on the day of this lesson, so I cannot show you a contrasting photograph of this turn done badly, but historically, her difficulty lay in a rather weak left thigh, which tended to lie less snugly on the saddle than the right, and to feel as if the thigh bone did not have the quality of a clear, solid iron bar. It turned 'rubbery' down towards Jill's left knee, which stopped the knee from being a stable pivot point in her rising trot. To change this, she had to think of her thigh muscles hugging the bone more firmly and also of her knee cap pointing more down and lying very snugly against the saddle, so that her thigh could function like the army barrier in Diagram 13 (page 148). This helped her body control enormously, and it also began to straighten her horses. All of the horses she sat on had instantly noticed this weakness in the framework which she had created around them: so they bulged their rib cage to the left, falling onto the left shoulder and foiling her attempts to create a bend. (Sarah's horse responded in the same way to her asymmetry as Jill's is doing here; Val's and Janet's horses responded in the opposite way. Almost certainly, they both had their inside seat bone lying closer to the midline of the saddle than either Sarah's or Jill's, which is responsible for the difference.)

If the horse were a thick, viscous liquid, and the rider were a container into which this liquid is put, the liquid would inevitably take up the space and shape which is available to it. Jill's left thigh was like a *bulge* in the container, and her hand attempted to compensate for its effects by creating a *constriction*. Like everyone else, Jill found herself drawing her left hand backwards in an attempt to create a bend and, as she did this, her right shoulder and hand advanced. This twist also made her right seat bone lighten and advance so that her left seat bone became more heavily weighted. This in turn undermined the strength of Jill's left knee and thigh so that they did not hold her out of the 'mantrap'. With her inside hip dropping backwards, she was caught like a lion in the pit, and was left powerless as the horse reacted to her asymmetry and used it to his own ends.

Although it has always helped Jill to think of bringing her left hip towards the horse's right ear, it is even more important for her to think of sitting on the tip of the left seat bone so that she does not allow herself to roll onto the back of it. This would make her 'flashlight' point too far forwards – towards King's front feet – so that she is then not correctly 'plugged in'. This balance over the seat bone is very delicate (rather like being on tiptoe), and it is a significant stress on the muscles in Jill's left thigh. But as soon as she loses it, Jill is always subtly behind the movement on the left rein and it becomes very difficult for her to advance her left hip. (This is always difficult if the rider's seat bone points forward instead of down, so it helps to think of having the point of hip *in front of* the seat bone.) Since she has understood all this, her left hand has become very much more light and still. She has also had to think of keeping her right shoulder back, aligning her body on the radius of the circle she is riding. She was initially quite resistant to this idea, as she had been taught to turn her shoulders as the horse turned. (On the right rein, however, her body remained on the radius and she did not obey her own rule.) An evening watching video tapes of the top riders convinced her that the way forward lay in aligning her shoulders with her pelvis, and her horses have responded with a resounding 'Yes!'

Whilst Jill's left side encourages the horse to drop his long back muscles and fall against her thigh, she finds it difficult to make her right side do its share of the work, drawing the horse's rib cage out to the right and holding it so that it presses into her right thigh instead of her left. It has helped her enormously to think of having suction pads on the inside of her right thigh, but she also needs to take great care with the positioning of her right seat bone and shoulder. The bottom line is that Jill finds it extremely difficult to get her seat bones and their 'plugs' to match with the horse's 'receptors' on the left rein: she cannot easily put them on the ten to four or the five to five axis. To make it worse, the left one not only 'misses', but also tends to fall off the horse's long back muscle. Both it and her thigh like to come away from the midline of her body, so when she does succeed in advancing her left hip, she has to be careful that her seat bone does not fly off the edge of the clock face! When she can find this correct positioning, and she 'plugs in', magic happens, and the whole picture on the left rein instantaneously changes. (Conversely, the ten past eight positioning of the right rein has always come naturally to her, and her horses have reflected this in their carriage.) She has encapsulated all these ideas in an image which has worked extremely well for her, by thinking of 'cooking the sausage' (putting it in the pan straight and bringing it out curved) as she holds the horse's spine between her two seat bones and wraps him around her inside leg.

It is very interesting to compare Figure 62, in which Jill is coming off the track onto a circle, with Figure 63, in which she is riding shoulder-in. Look at her and King's central axes in Figure 63: they are now both vertical. These photographs were taken from very similar angles, but whereas Figure 62 shows Jill's midline directly above King's, Figure 63 shows it displaced slightly to the right – their direction of motion. To position him into shoulder-in,

63. Horse and rider are shown from a very similar angle to that in Figure 62, but in shoulder-in. Notice how differently the axes of their bodies are positioned.

she has moved across the saddle, drawn over by her right thigh, which is now more parallel to King's side. This encourages him to step sideways under her centre of gravity. Positioning him into shoulder-in left is easy for her, since her stronger right thigh is now dominant and advancing her right point of hip is easy. She just has to be careful that she really does get a true bend and does not allow King to fall against her weak left thigh and take the easy option of leg-yielding.

Shoulder-in right is a little trickier, because to begin the movement, Jill must bring King's left shoulder away from the track. King, however, likes to lean on his left shoulder, and he would happily leave it on the wall and bring just his head and neck to the inside – our now familiar jack-knife. When this happens, his right long back muscle is likely to move in under the supraspinous ligament, just as Saffron's did in Lesson 7. To produce a correct shoulder-in, Jill must bring his shoulders to the right of his quarters, and must be careful to stay correctly positioned on this muscle. King, however, would much prefer to move with his shoulders to the *left* of his quarters. Again, Jill must position herself so that his forehand acts as one unit and his left shoulder cannot drop outwards (see Diagram 18). Her left thigh must pull her pelvis across the saddle as she comes around the corner into the movement, and all the while she must take care that her seat bones remain plugged

64 and 65. Both of these show right shoulder-in. Compare the amount of King's rib cage visible beneath Jill's left foot in each case. This difference is due partly to the different phase in the walk stride and partly to King's better bend in Figure 64.

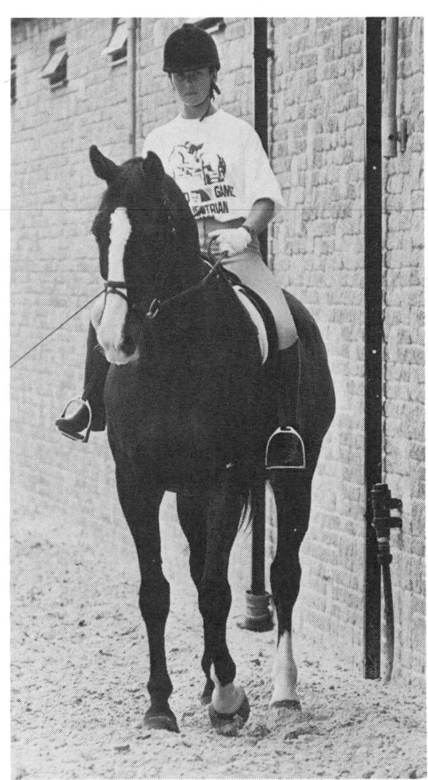

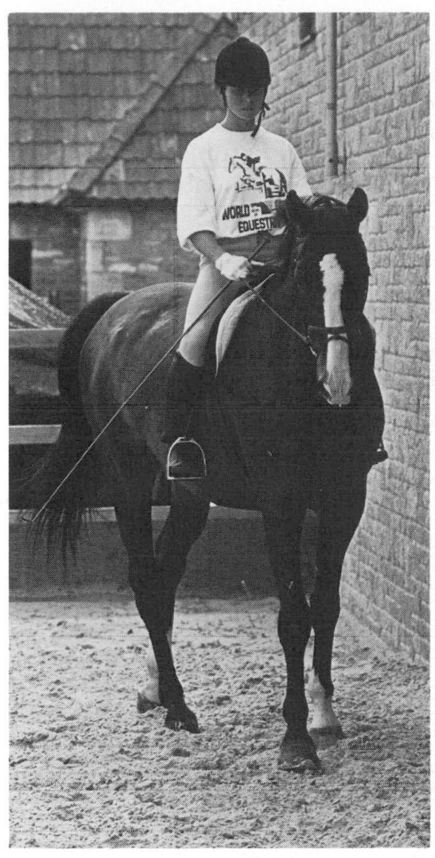

66 and 67. Both of these show travers right. In Figure 66 King's quarters have come too much to the inside – his favourite evasion on this rein. In Figure 67 Jill has placed him exactly on three tracks. Her body is very nicely straight.

in to their 'sockets' on top of each long back muscle. Figure 64 shows a good shoulder-in in walk, although Jill's body is slightly off axis. It is interesting to compare it with Figure 65, taken during a different phase of the stride. Notice how King's rib cage is much more over to the left (the direction of motion) in the first picture. This is partly because the right hind leg and foreleg are stepping rather than weight-bearing, but I suspect that it is also because Jill has him better positioned into the movement, with a truer bend. In Figure 65 she has determinedly brought his shoulder off the wall and has overdone it, going from one extreme to the other and losing the bend as a result.

Travers right is King's party piece, because the movement specifically demands that his shoulders are to the left of his quarters. This means that Jill has to be careful not to over-use the movement and give him ideas which he carries over into his work on one track! Figures 66 and 67 show her positioned into the movement in walk. Its companion movement, half-pass right, is also relatively easy (Figure 68), although Jill still rides the movement without a large degree of angle or bend. She had a 'bogey' about half-pass when I first met her. This largely dissolved when I drew a line in the surface of the arena and asked Jill to 'travers

68. Half-pass right. This is Jill's easier rein in half-pass, as her seat bones will quite easily go onto the five past seven axis.

along the line'. When I told her that she had just done half-pass she was stunned. ('Is that all? I thought it was supposed to be really complicated!')

Flying changes are Jill's current 'bogey'. They do not send her into quite that panic state which Gina gets into over leg-yield or Janet gets into over riding her horse 'on the bit', but she rates them as a nine out of ten in difficulty and importance. I change her perspective on them by reminding her of the time when half-pass was a nine: it is now about a five, and shoulder-in has dropped from five or six to only two or three. By the time Jill is desperate to ride tempo changes, canter pirouettes, piaffe and passage, all the other movements will probably be zero-rated!

Travers left, however, and half-pass left, will take longer to become zero-rated than their counterparts to the right. As King would love to fall onto his left shoulder and to keep it to the left of his quarters, a correct travers left is the most difficult position in which to place him. Since the left thigh and hip are now in the direction of motion, they become dominant – but this is Jill's weak side: it is extremely hard for her to position her pelvis on the five to five axis, and the position for travers or half-pass left stresses her more than any other. She is still rather hit-and-miss with it, but on this day she rode the travers really well (see Figure 69) and also made a good attempt at half-pass (Figure 70).

I placed a higher value, however, on the experience she had the following day. As the rider comes around the corner to position into travers, her outside seat bone moves further back and her inside seat bone advances, taking them both, on the left rein, from the ten to four axis to the five to five axis. The inside thigh acts as a barrier which stops the rib cage falling to the left, and the outside thigh keeps its suction pads, which hold it out to the right. As Jill positioned into the movement, I heard her yell, 'The rotten little . . . ! I just felt him do it – he thrust his rib cage over to the left and knocked me out of place!' Of course, this had been happening before, but somehow Jill had never noticed. I rate very highly the learning inherent in this moment: it is a similar experience, on a more subtle level, to the one Margaret had in Lesson 7 when she felt her horse fall out on a circle. This discovery of 'what is' is invaluable, and it is a one-way door – for neither Jill nor Margaret will ever be able to return to their original state of naivety.

69. Travers left is one of the movements which Jill finds most difficult. Here she has positioned King into it very well, with a good bend left.

70. Again, Jill has positioned King well into half-pass left, even though this is the most difficult movement for her to ride. He is spooking at something, hence his rather hollow carriage. Jill has maintained the bend well, although her outside shoulder has dropped, signifying that she has fallen into the trap of attempting to 'push' him over.

Of course, Jill's work has not all been focussed around the lateral movements, and, like everyone else, she has had her fair share of learning how to sit well and influence the horse's carriage. Jill's backside is definitely not 'spongy', and her biggest difficulty in trot has been a tendency deliberately to move too much in each stride, especially when she has to 'drive the horse forward'. When I met her, she thought that she had actively to push her backside underneath her as each hind leg moved. This is not the same as 'bottom walking', however, as it creates both an exaggerated jerk which affects the whole body and produces wobbles in the lower leg. Thinking of 'plugging in' to the horse's back has helped Jill enormously, since moving too much stops the 'plugs' from fitting into the 'sockets'. Since she does not have this problem in walk, it also helps her to think that she must 'trot like walking'. To keep her lower leg still, so that the ankle acts as the anchor point for the knee (see Lesson 2), she thinks of having a little gap in the ankle joint, and of having an imaginary iron bar which passes through the horse's belly and joins her ankles together. (This is similar to the bar which some of the other riders have imagined through their knees.) Jill finds it most difficult to sit 'still relative to the horse' on horses with powerful movement, and when she is struggling I get her to exaggerate the extraneous movements she is making. Asking the rider to exaggerate her mistakes in this way is extremely helpful, because the more Jill discovers about how she makes them, the easier it becomes for her to choose *not* to make them.

The idea of 'plugging in' becomes much richer and more pervasive when it is extended to include the muscles which lie deep in the rider's abdominal cavity on either side of the spine. At the level of the lumbar spine, the vertebrae are very thick, and they come almost half-way through the body. On each side of them lies a muscle called the psoas. Beginning by attaching into the bottom thoracic vertebra, it attaches into the sides of each of the lumbar vertebrae, forming an increasingly thick column as it passes down each side of the spine within the abdominal cavity itself (see Diagram 19). It also joins up with the iliacus muscle, which covers the inside of the ilia – the bony sides of the pelvic bowl, which you can feel most clearly at the points of the hip. The two then pass very close to the seat bones and over the front edge of the pelvis near to the pubic bone before attaching into the back of the thigh bones, on the lesser trochanters of the femur. This is the 'stabiliser' which we discussed in Lesson 3 with Jan. In *The Anatomy Colouring Book*, Wynn Kapit and Lawrence M. Elson describe the iliopsoas muscle as 'a principle flexor of the hip joint. It may play a role in balancing the torso during sitting. In standing there is evidence that the iliopsoas functions to counteract the tendency of the torso to fall back of the line of gravity, which passes somewhat behind the hip joints. It is certainly an important postural muscle in aligning the lower limb with the body trunk.'

If you think of the psoas muscles forming two columns coming down to the seat bones, the bottom line in correct riding becomes extremely simple: WHEN THE RIDER'S TWO PSOAS MUSCLES, HER SEAT BONES AND THEIR IMAGINARY EXTENSIONS CONNECT CORRECTLY WITH THE 'RECEPTORS' IN THE HORSE'S LONG BACK MUSCLES, MAGIC BEGINS TO HAPPEN. Firstly, both columns and seat bones must point vertically downwards. Often one or both of them does not naturally do this, and the rider needs to adjust its angle. (Jill's left seat bone, for instance, tends to point forward, and this is part of her difficulty on the left rein.) Secondly, both columns must be positioned so that they fit exactly into the 'receptors' on the horse's long back muscles, shifting their position to keep this connection throughout each step of each movement. I have suggested to Jill and to other riders that they visualise this, and organise the whole of the rest of their body around it. Doing this can save them from overkill and tell them exactly how much pinch and bearing down they need. This gives the torso not only its correct positioning and alignment, but also a wonderful elegance and resilience which I have not otherwise been able to create in myself or others. Using this image also helps the rider to assess whether her axis is correctly aligned or whether she is tipping off to one side.

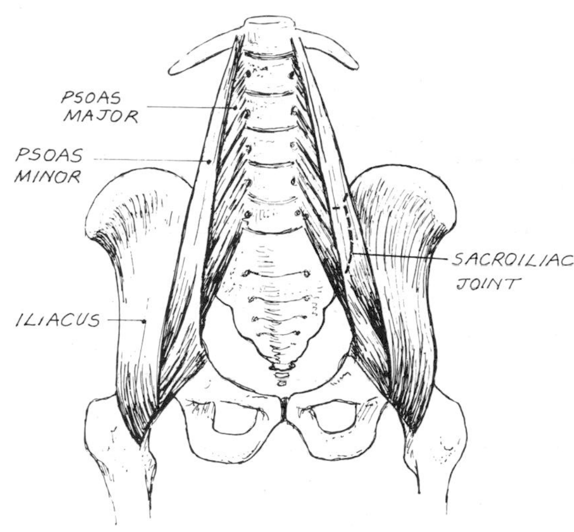

Diagram 19. The psoas muscles are the most important postural muscles in the body. Beginning from the bottom rib, they run down each side of the spine within the abdominal cavity, connecting with each of the lumbar vertebrae and forming a column of gradually increasing thickness. They join with the iliacus muscle, which covers the inside of the pelvic bones, and pass close to the seat bones before inserting into the lesser trochanter of the femur.

Some riders undoubtedly find that an imbalance in the development of their two psoas muscles lies at the core of their asymmetry. Jill has found it particularly helpful to think of these muscles when the horse does not want to angle his body correctly in a turn. Visualising the two columns and their connection into the horse's back muscles has suddenly made her realise that she is beginning to tilt without him!

Thinking of the columns also gives the rider a more precise way of identifying the correct placing for each seat bone and the exact position of the horse's 'receptors' – for if she can find these and plug into them, she can turn any evasive pattern into a correct bend. When she has exactly the correct positioning for the column which lies on the inside of a circle or a lateral movement, the result is unmistakable: it is as if the column were the central pole of a merry-go-round, the pivot around which the horse bends. With your pelvis in this correct positioning, and your outside seat bone also in place, you can literally *curl* the horse around your inside leg (or, as Jill would say, you can 'cook the sausage'). I am sure that the Great Masters were referring to this same phenomenon when they talked of bending the horse around the inside leg, or of having the inside leg like a door post. The problem is that none of them realised how their pelvic positioning was responsible for an effect which they attributed to their leg, and which most riders since have (rightly or wrongly) interpreted to mean their calf. This feeling of curling the horse around your inside leg is tremendously important and it is usually the end point of all the rider's hard work – her reward for absolutely correct positioning.

Jill's canter seat has changed dramatically in the time that I have known her, and Figure 71 shows her and King working quite well.

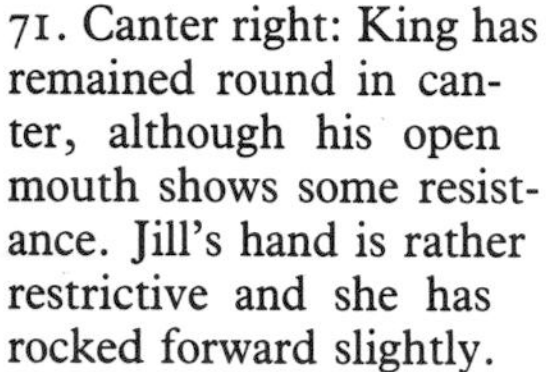

71. Canter right: King has remained round in canter, although his open mouth shows some resistance. Jill's hand is rather restrictive and she has rocked forward slightly.

Like most people, the back of her backside made a small bump at every stride, even though it looked as if she was making a great effort to sit. The breakthrough came when I likened the dynamics of the canter to bouncing a ball against the ground with your hand: when the ball comes up into your hand you move your hand *up with it*, and only when the ball reaches the top of its rise do you press it back down again. If you did not do this, there would be considerable shock as the ball hit against your hand. Jill was trying so hard to sit *down* that she was not allowing the horse to come *up* underneath her and to bring her up. The change when she thought of this was instantaneous: it helped her trot seat as well, and it also carried through into counter canter.

Jill has had to deal with many different types of horses, both in her work and in her lessons with me. King is naturally hollow, so it requires extremely good sitting really to bring his back up into a rounded carriage. Chester (who features in the Jumping section) is a very compact horse who likes to compress himself even more, contracting the whole of his forehand backwards into his wither. Jill's most difficult challenge is to lengthen him out in front of her so that he lifts his wither and stretches through his neck. She has also ridden other horses whose primary evasion is to overbend, and I am grateful to her for coming up with an extremely useful image. Once the rider has got the horse in front of her, with the push from her lower stomach landing by the breast-plate, the next stage (having stretched the horse out) is to imagine his wither being *drawn up* towards her navel as if on a winch. By thinking of a series of strings attaching to the lower part of the horse's crest and drawing the neck up towards her abdomen, Jill has had an immediate and profound effect on the horses. (I explain in *Ride With Your Mind* how overbending is a problem which originates near the base of the neck. I believe that it happens when there is insufficient tone in the front segments of the long back muscles as they attach into the vertebrae at the root of the neck – see Diagram 10, page 136). When we first came up with this image, she talked of feeling the change in her abdominal muscles, right up the midline of her body. Later that same day I worked a pupil's horse who was extremely keen to overbend. As I thought of this image, and the horse's carriage immediately changed, I felt exactly the same sensation in my own body. It is very exciting for me to know that we can communicate this precisely with each other – especially when the pupil starts to teach the teacher, and to contribute to our shared body of knowledge.

As Jill's sitting and her understanding of rider/horse dynamics have improved, she has also worked a good deal with the transitions, and with the variations within each gait. Figures 72 and 73 show very similar moments in the trot stride in medium and collected trot respectively, the difference in the stride lengths being obvious. King has a very powerful extension and, since he is a long horse with a hollow back, he is very reluctant to sit himself down and create true collection. In Figure 73 it looks as though there may be a loss of diagonal unison, since the foreleg appears to have lifted off the ground slightly higher than the hind leg. Jill's sitting is a little suspect too, and she has lost some of the wrapping around the horse that comes from having the pelvis angled correctly and the front of the body pushing forward. When the work we are doing stresses her, it helps her enormously to think of riding as if she were her hero, Carl Hester, whose body demonstrates this push superbly. She also gets much more 'suction' when she thinks of this, which lifts the horse underneath her and makes her body

72 and 73. These show very similar movements in medium and collected trot. The difference in the stride length is obvious. Jill's body is quite well in place in Figure 72 (and at last she is smiling!), but her front has 'caved in' in Figure 73. This happened as she was riding the transition between the two. King's front, however, is definitely more elevated in Figure 73. (Compare the positions of his nose relative to his chest, and the point of his buttock.)

more still – right down to her feet. The increase in her 'push' almost makes the front of her body become curved outwards like a 'D', instead of caving in towards the 'C' shape that you see here.

The challenge of the upward transitions is to stay with the horse as he accelerates, for which more push forward and a very stable body are required. The challenge of the downward transitions and half halts is, for most people, the harder one, and I rarely see them done well. A half halt is all but instantaneous. It is as if the horse pauses for a moment and sits himself down. If it becomes prolonged in any way, and particularly if it becomes a pulling match, then it is not a half halt. Except for the most novice riders, who tip forward, there seems to be a universal tendency to want to lean back, pull back, pull in the stomach and draw the ribs up away from the hips. This creates a situation in which the horse is bound to pull back (see Lesson 2 with Gail). Take the downward transition from canter to trot as an example: most riders pull and pray, but this 'unplugs' them, and as they begin to float above the horse's back they can no longer feel its movement. When they can keep bearing down and taking the horse, however, they feel the canter movement very clearly underneath them. In the moment of the transition, *they advance their outside seat bone*, which has always remained behind the inside one in canter (see Lesson 8 with Carol). This transforms the canter movement of their seat bones into the left, right, left, right, movement of the trot – and the horse has no choice but to transform his movement into trot underneath them.

Jill deliberately rides her downward transitions breathing out, since this helps her to keep pushing out and taking the horse. She also thinks of drawing her horse's wither even more up towards her navel, which helps her to keep her body angled correctly. Leaning back – which is advocated by most trainers – can only work if the horse 'sits down' so much that the rider is still 'plugged in', which can only happen when the horse's and rider's backs remain at ninety degrees to each other so that both the 'pins' and the 'receptors' are angled forward (see Diagram 20). Normally, however, the rider 'unplugs' herself in her attempt to lean back and stop the horse: the horse does not 'sit down', their backs are no longer at a ninety-degree angle to each other and the transition becomes a pulling match.

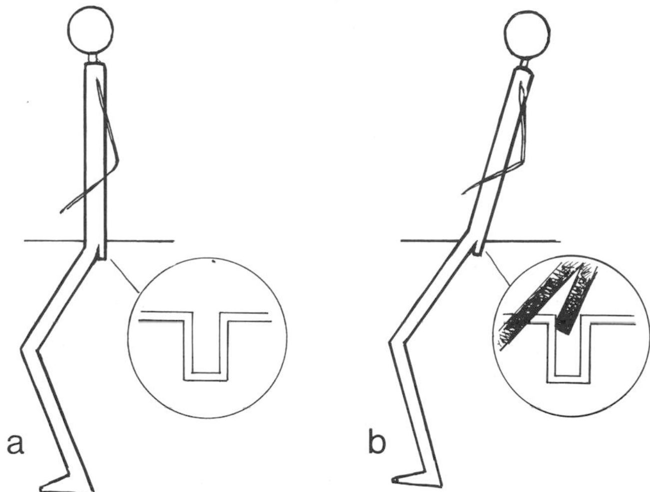

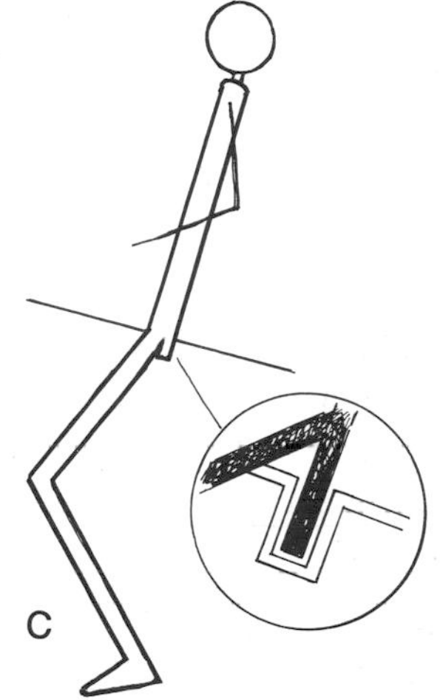

Diagram 20. The rider who is 'plugged in' to the 'receptors' in the horse's long back muscles sits with her spine at a ninety-degree angle to his, as in (a). If she leans back in a downward transition, she usually 'unplugs' herself, as in (b), but masterful riders can change the angle of the horse's spine through leaning back, so that they remain at ninety degrees to his back and are still 'plugged in', as in (c).

A pupil of mine devised a wonderful image, which drew on her experience of sailing, to describe her feeling of a correct half halt or downward transition. I can relate to it through my experience of surfing, and I hope that you can make sense of it too. If you are riding on the crest of a wave, either on a boat or a surf board, you cannot make the wave slow down for you. Instead, you have to keep up with the wave – and if it leaves you behind, it is an extremely frustrating experience! In their transitions down, nine riders out of ten have the illusion that they can make the wave (horse) slow down by pulling, and in the process they *pull themselves backwards off the top of the wave*. They then lose their dynamic connection with the horse's energy and are left behind. The secret of the transition lies in bringing yourself *right up onto the uppermost point of the wave* and holding yourself there, since only this enables it to swell up more fully underneath you.

Jill has practised this a great deal, thinking of holding her body up on the crest of the wave so that she can keep the horse's back lifting up underneath her within the transition. She also thinks of keeping herself 'plugged in' so that there is always a ninety-degree angle between her body and the horse's back. She has found it particularly helpful to practise this using small variations within each gait and these have provided the 'blueprint' which has then helped her to ride the half halts and the transitions between the gaits: she gets her best results when she rides these transitions 'as if' they were transitions between lengthening and shortening rather than from one gait to another. Whilst her skill is still somewhat hit-and-miss, the majority of Jill's downward transitions are now good. I regard good downward transitions as the proof of the pudding, a sign that our basic work has been correct. As well as doing these specific exercises, Jill has benefited enormously in her learning by having to ride a great many different horses, which gives her an overview which one cannot gain by riding one horse alone. She understands how her sitting must change with horses which either run off or want to come behind her, and with horses who have various different asymmetries. Discovering the differences between individual horses helps one to realise how different each horse can be, both from moment to moment and from day to day. There are basic rules underlying the rider/horse interaction which never change, but the concept of 'one correct position' is an erroneous one. When the rider discovers this, and learns how to use her body as a tool which functions well in every situation, the majority of our work is done.

Lesson 11

Jumping

The riders in the jumping lesson presented here have a wide variety of backgrounds and differing degrees of competence and enthusiasm. Some would have preferred not to jump at all, whilst others regarded it as the high point of their riding, their *raison d'être* for everything else. Katie and Carol are dressage enthusiasts who tolerated the jumping lessons on their course at West Wilts Equestrian Centre by convincing themselves that jumping was 'good for them'. Clare originally bought her horse to event, but a soundness problem has relegated him to occasional gymnastic jumping, and his flatwork has improved so much that dressage has become her first love. Janet is extremely enthusiastic about eventing; she is actively competing and desperate to leave the ground at every possible opportunity. Herbert, too, is very keen, and he hopes to event his horse, who is only five, when they have both gained more experience. Jill evented Chester a great deal several years ago, but now that she is not jumping regularly she feels that she has to 'psyche herself up' for it, and she has been through a phase of feeling much less confident and enthusiastic than she used to be. I had previously taught Jill quite a bit over fences, Herbert a few times and Carol just once. I had seen Clare jump but only taught her on the flat, and had only taught Janet on the flat. Katie and I met each other for the first time on this day.

As experience and many textbooks will tell you, many of the principles of flatwork pass over into jumping. In both, good external results are underpinned by the subtle internal components which are the secrets of success: not surprisingly, the same coordinations which stabilise the rider on the flat underpin the ability to set up a good approach in jumping, to be in balance over a fence, to recover after it and even to 'see a stride'. When the rider can do these consistently, she has every reason to feel confident, secure and to enjoy jumping. When her balance and her striding cause problems, she has every reason to feel apprehensive – especially if she has the kind of sensitivity which will not tolerate very much 'not rightness'.

When I am teaching jumping to a group of riders I do not know, I usually like to begin by asking them, 'What is big?' and 'What is small?' This information tells me the limits of their comfort, stretch and panic zones, and helps me to gear the lesson to their needs. I take no delight in making them go over fences which frighten them silly – in fact, I definitely want to avoid this, since it signals danger. But neither do I want to bore them with tiny little grids which are insufficiently challenging. Initially, I need to create a situation in which the rider can change her jumping technique, if necessary, this, rather than the height of the jumps, becoming the primary challenge of the lesson. A change in technique can only be made safely when the height of the jumps is well within the rider's comfort zone and that of her horse. She needs to have some leeway for error, as concentration on one specific point may well cause other facets of her riding to go wrong – and the mistakes this could create must not be costly. Once the rider has begun to ingrain the change, she requires sheer repetition, probably over gradually increasing height. The new co-ordination can then be tested more by working in her stretch zone, using higher fences and different gymnastic exercises which take the horse into his stretch zone too. Over time, horse and rider reach the stage of 'unconscious competence' wherein the work they have been doing is relegated to their comfort zone. This allows them to tackle some more challenging learning – and challenging jumps!

In teaching jumping, it is important to realise just how much security people get from working through a grid. Some riders immediately pass from their comfort zone to their stretch zone when faced with a course (or possibly a single jump) – even if it is only half the size of the fences they have just been jumping in gymnastic exercises. Others go from their stretch zone to their panic zone as soon as the placing poles are gone. The issue here is obviously their fear about whether they will arrive at each fence 'right': this is alleviated within the grid itself, making it an extremely good environment to learn about basic balance over the fence. Whether fears arise on the flat or in jumping, will-power alone is rarely enough to overcome them. Usually the rider needs to make several key changes in her technique which will offer her the same sense of safety that they offer to the naturally bold riders who stumbled across them by accident. To cement the change, the rider also needs to develop faith in these techniques, which can only come when she has proved their effectiveness through repeated successful performance.

I began this lesson by working the horses in trot over poles on the ground, which were spaced at 4 feet 6 inches apart. These served to settle the horses down, to make the riders order and space themselves sensibly as a ride and to gear them towards jumping. They all had their stirrups at jumping length and rode with the idea of going through the poles as if they were not there, with no change in the mechanism of their rise or the balance of their body weight over their feet. Through their rise and sit, the riders were to regulate their horses' tempi, but they were not to attempt to 'place' them (so that they met the first pole at the right point in their step) by altering the length of their strides. The poles are intended to encourage the horses to lower their heads, stretch through their top-lines and make a more lively, regular step. However, they do not necessarily have this effect unless the horses are extremely well ridden. Already we are facing the key issues of riding: does the rider take the horse or does the horse take the rider? Is the rider's push forward bigger than the horse's push back (allowing her to encourage the correct carriage), or does the horse contract his front end backwards and push *her* back? Is she squashing the horse's back or encouraging it to lift and stay rounded? Can the rider maintain her body balance as she frees her hand, and is she sensitive enough to do this at exactly the moment when the horse stretches his top-line? Does she regulate the tempo so well that the horse dances to her tune or is the horse the one who is causal, so that the rider is reactive and is thrown around to his tune?

Very often, when I watch even this early stage in a jumping lesson, I find myself longing to get my hands on the riders on the flat! That is the place to teach them to pinch, bear down and breathe, to keep their thighs pulling forward out of their hip joints, and to keep their internal columns (the psoas muscles and seat bones) connecting correctly with the 'receptors' in the horse's long back muscles. All these ideas can be strengthened and tested, but preferably not learnt from scratch, in a jumping lesson. These basic co-ordinations require only two major changes for jumping. These concern the length of the stirrup and the balance over it.

In Figure 74 I am demonstrating the folding down action of the rider as the horse takes off, and proving that she can remain in balance over her feet throughout his jump. This fold requires a sudden change in the angle of her hip joint, and it also closes the angle behind her knee. This is impossible with long stirrups, which is why jumping riders shorten anything from two to six holes from their flatwork length. The exact number varies according to the length they ride on the flat and whether they change their saddle for jumping, but the two holes which are normally prescribed are rarely enough, I think – certainly for adult riders. (Interestingly, the Italian cavalry officer Caprilli, who first developed the jumping seat, had very short legs. Using the longer stirrup and upright body which were the standard teaching of his day, he kept falling off. The forward seat was his solution to the problem!)

The balance of the rider's body over her feet also changes from flatwork to jumping. If you make the fold-down in Figure 74 (try it), you will find that you can be in balance in this position with your toes lifted up and only your heels on the floor. This is very much harder if you stand in the more upright position of flatwork.

To a degree, you push the heel *down and forward against the stirrup in jumping*; if you do not do this, you tend to find that the lower leg flies backwards over the fence. You may get away with this in show jumping, but it is inherently unstable, and it becomes dangerous in cross-country riding where you may suddenly have to contend with drops, banks and steep slopes.

74. The folding down action of the rider as she goes over the fence. I can balance over my feet throughout this manoeuvre, which proves that it keeps the rider's centre of gravity over her base of support. It is even possible to balance in this position with the weight of the body taken just on the heels.

In flatwork lessons, I spend a great deal of my time correcting riders who veer towards using a jumping-style lower leg. Everyone knows that you should 'push your heels down', and in our everyday riding, they are very often pushed *down and forward* when they should be *down and back* (see Lesson 1). Somehow the difference between the jumping and the flatwork lower leg has never been fully acknowledged, and the distinction is not made clearly enough in our teaching. (This may be a particularly British trait, since so many riders have come to flatwork through hunting and jumping. We lack the heritage of dressage which is passed on to every European rider before she even contemplates going outdoors or leaving the ground.) The heel which is pushed down and forward in jumping keeps the rider in balance over her feet as she folds down over the fence: the weight in the heel is counter-balanced by the amount of her body and thigh which have come in front of the line of gravity (see Figures 82, 88 and 89, and 103). The approach to the fence is the only time during which you might doubt whether the rider would balance on a diving board (see Figures 87 and 96). Only here is this permissible, as a safety measure in preparation for the jump. Paradoxically, many riders who demonstrate a jumping lower leg on the flat seem to show a flatwork lower leg over jumps: their legs fly backwards just after take-off and, inevitably, their bodies topple forward. They are then forced to rest their hands on the horses' necks in order to stay on board.

This difference in the lower leg also extends down to the foot:

in flatwork the rider spreads her weight across the ball of the foot from the big toe to the little toe. This brings the foot almost parallel to the horse's side. Many people over-weight the outside of the foot in an attempt to achieve this, rolling their ankle outwards, which can be damaging to the ankle joint. The problem usually has its origins in the way in which the thigh comes out of the hip joint. A greater inward rotation is required in the *hip*, rather than in the ankle: it helps to think of holding the thighs snugly in against the saddle, with the bulk of the hamstring muscle rolled right around to the back (see Lesson 2). In jumping, an outward rotation of the ankle joint is even more dangerous than it is on the flat, and the rider's weight is best taken more on the inside of the foot towards the big toe, which is placed on the inside of the stirrup. If anything, this rolls the ankle *inwards*, which helps to give the rider a more stable base and to draw the thigh and lower leg even more snugly in against the horse.

Many teachers of flatwork – and some of jumping – frown on the idea of contact with the thigh, and frown even more on the idea of grip. However, grip is often required, and the adductor muscles of the inner thigh have a very important part to play. It is vital, however, that they are used correctly; when the knee serves as an anchor point for the pelvis, the thigh muscles draw the rider *down around* the horse, at the same time drawing the horse's rib cage *upwards* to 'fill her seat' (see Lessons 2 and 8). When used the wrong way round, so that the pelvis is the anchor point and the knee the mobile point, the thigh muscles have no positive effect on the horse. The rider's knee may become very loose – making the rider loose along with it – or if the thigh muscles are firmly placed on the saddle, they squeeze the rider up off the top of the horse like a clothes peg. The objection to grip is, I think, normally voiced by people who do not realise that the thigh muscles can work in two ways: but when I watch top-class eventers and show jumpers, it is obvious to me that the firmness and security of their thigh is one of the major components of their skill. This is increased even more by having thigh bones which pull forward out of the hip joints and act like iron bars (see Lesson 8).

After working the riders through trotting poles, and correcting some of their imbalances, I asked them all to jump a small cross pole placed 9 feet from three trotting poles. We then graduated to just one placing pole at 9 feet from the cross pole and added a small fence 18 feet further on, so that with a trot approach this gave space for one canter stride. We gradually built up the height of this fence, making it into a parallel. Some of the more experienced riders jumped this at about 3 foot 6 inches. We then finished our session by cantering over a parallel fence on a circle which was about 3 foot 3 inches. The exercises used were absolutely basic, as it was not my intention to demonstrate all the fascinating possibilities of grid work. Early on in the lesson – after I had seen all the riders go several times through the small double – I asked them what they wanted to achieve from the session, and learnt about their hopes, fears and failings. I also compared their ideas about jumping with my own and offered them the demonstration you see in Figure 74.

The greatest argument in the theory of jumping concerns whether the rider should approach the fence in a forward position, with her upper body inclined forward and her backside slightly out of the saddle, or whether she should approach in a more upright position with her weight and backside *in* the saddle. The argument also extends to how the horse should be ridden between fences, with some riders preferring to be more forward and others more upright. (In cross-country riding, everyone is agreed that the rider should remain out of the saddle between fences and should not bump against it at all. It is in show jumping that styles vary.) The argument for the forward seat emphasises that it puts the novice rider in the best position to 'go with' the horse over the fence, so that should he stand off unexpectedly she is less likely to be left behind. However, she is also more vulnerable should he suddenly stop, since she could fall off, and if he hesitates on the approach to the fence she cannot take strong preventative action. To do this, she pulls her thigh bones forward out of her hip sockets and makes them feel like iron bars, using them like buffers so that she can hold her upper body back in place behind them. This is the mechanism which holds the horse out in front of her, and it is so effective that it becomes extremely difficult for him to stop!

Advocates of the forward seat worry that a rider who is actually *sitting* in the saddle might interfere with the correct functioning of the horse's back so that he cannot lift and use it well. The opposite problem occurs, however, if the rider is leaning too far forward, especially at the moment when the horse's forelegs are leaving the ground. Her weight is then so much over his forehand that it becomes extremely difficult for him to lift it up off the ground. The rider has to position her centre of gravity very carefully so that it is neither behind nor in front of the horse's, otherwise she inhibits his use of either his back end or his front end. If she sits in the saddle, in balance with the horse, she becomes a minimal encumbrance – and to assume that sitting in the saddle *necessarily* inhibits the lifting of the horse's back is also to assume a very low level of competence. The perpetrators of this argument are either unaware of the very positive effects which the rider's seat can have on the horse's back, or they assume that these are beyond the scope of the average rider, who is therefore best advised to leave her horse's back alone.

It is also interesting to speculate on the effect that a rider has on the horse's back when she brings her backside into the saddle just a few strides away from the fence. Could this disturb the horse more than having it in the saddle all the time? If she thumps down heavily, it certainly could – especially in comparison with the rider who sits all the time and 'uses her seat' well, so that it does not flatten and hollow the horse's back. Advocates of the more upright seat also argue that it is easier for the rider to use her leg effectively when she sits in the saddle, since more of her weight is supported on the backside and thigh. In the forward seat, more of her body weight is out of the saddle and is supported by the stirrup. This makes the lower leg less available.

Everyone acknowledges that unless the rider is well balanced and experienced, there is a danger of her being 'left behind' when the horse stands off too far, but many riders, even novices, deal better than one might expect with this situation. Little damage is done to the horse if the rider can free her hand and give the horse enough rein to get himself out of trouble. Advocates of the upright seat argue that more damage would be done if the rider came in front of the horse, making the opposite mistake and leaving the saddle a fraction too early. It seems to me that this is much more common and that more horses have their confidence undermined by this than by its opposite. In time, the horse's fears undermine the rider's confidence too, so that their performance spirals downward, creating a vicious circle in which the fearful rider becomes ever more likely to tip forward just before take-off and to 'drop' him.

Another important argument concerns the need for there to be a sudden and dramatic change in the rider's position in the moment of take-off. As the horse suddenly straightens his hock and his stifle, he creates the enormous thrust which catapults him into the air: at the same time, the rider suddenly closes her hip joint. But if her hip joint is *already* closed, there is nothing she can do to absorb this thrust. Small children are often taught to approach a jump in a very forward position, so as the pony takes off they have no way to adapt, inevitably falling forward onto his neck. By the time he lands, they are practically draped around his neck – and they inevitably feel insecure. It would have been less traumatic if the teacher had *trusted their ability to learn to fold down* as the pony took off.

I propose that EACH OF THESE TWO SCHOOLS EXPRESSES ONE-HALF OF THE TRUTH, and that both halves only come together when the pelvis and thigh are used correctly. If the rider has the correct relationship between 'down' and 'up', she will not flatten the horse by sitting: on the contrary, using her thighs well enables her to stay out of the 'mantrap' so that she lifts

75 and 76. In Figure 75, Chester has surprised Jill by standing off this small fence, but she has still folded down well. She has not freed her hand enough, however. In some cases, being allowed this extra reach would make all the difference to the horse's ability to clear the fence. In Figure 76, the dangers of a jump like this become obvious. Chester has cleared it with his front legs, but will inevitably demolish it with his hind legs.

rather than hollows the horse's back. So much weight is taken down her thigh that she is much less of a burden to the horse than she would be if she sat as if in an armchair. This, along with a slight forward incline of the body and the very forward angle of the thigh, helps to counter-balance the effects of her lowered heel. This weight distribution enables her to react very quickly should the horse stand off too far (see Figures 75 and 76). If she thinks of her thighs pulling forward out of her hip joint, with thigh bones which have the solidity of iron bars, she also gains the ability to stay behind the horse. This attitude of the body (rather than any other version of 'driving with the seat') creates impulsion in and of itself, and it puts the rider in a powerful position from which all her other aids work. Her lower leg in particular becomes very effective, and she is also held in a safe position should the horse stop. The advantages of both seats are gained in one, and with them comes the style which the American show jumpers, for example, demonstrate so superbly.

Figures 75 and 76 show one of Jill's first jumps with Chester, who has demonstrated his wish to jump more often than usual by making a 'Let me at them!' approach. He maintained trot through the trotting poles but stood off a step too early. Jill was surprised by this, but she has folded down well and has remained in balance with him. Her only mistake lies in not freeing her hand sufficiently. Figure 76 shows the dangers of this stand-off and, inevitably, Chester hit the poles with his hind legs. If this had been a solid cross-country obstacle they would both have been in trouble, and we will talk more later about the dangers of a riding style which encourages these kamikaze leaps.

Figures 77 to 79 show an early jump from Herbert. In Figure 77 all is well, with good impulsion and balance over the trotting poles, although the lifting of Herbert's shoulders may well be the small beginning of what is about to go wrong, for in Figure 78 he has tipped forward, resting his hands on Jolly's neck. This is the all-important moment where the rider has to stay behind the horse; but Herbert has 'dropped' him. This puts Jolly in an extremely difficult position, since Herbert is overburdening his forehand at just the moment when he is about to bring it up off the ground. Herbert has also made the classic mistake of straightening his knee to propel his body forward up the horse's neck over the jump. Compare his body position with Jill's in Figures 75 and 103, and with mine in Figure 74. The secret of staying in balance over the fence lies in bringing your backside *backwards* as you fold down; the angle behind the knee then closes rather than opens. Trainer Pat Burgess suggests that the rider thinks of 'folding down like an ironing board', which is a wonderful image. This brings her belly button very close to the front of the saddle – one of my pupils has added the idea of squashing a grape with it as she goes over the jump!

In jumping, everything happens so fast that it is much harder to feel in charge of one's body than it is on the flat, and as a teacher I find it more difficult to make corrections with the riders. Over fences, most riders feel that *things happen to them* rather than that *they make things happen*: they are reactive rather than causal. Some riders will even go through a line of jumps without really knowing what happened – their minds blank out, almost as if they lose consciousness. For most people, this is an extremely unpleasant experience – and *until they overcome it nothing else can change* – so it is the first problem we must tackle. To counteract it, I have found it helpful to ask riders to rate the clarity of their perceptions out of ten each time they have been through a grid. This is not the same as asking them to rate how well they rode: if somebody said, 'I felt my toes curl up and my lower leg come backwards,' their perceptions might well have been close to ten, even though their jumping style was only a three. Another rider might show much better style through the grid, whilst missing the more subtle mistakes she made. Her perceptions would rate much lower.

This exercise is extremely helpful because the rider must first become conscious of her incompetence before she can make any adjustments. However, becoming causal requires one more step; for with her perceptions down at a two or a three, time seems to flash by so fast that it is hard for the rider to intervene and make improvements. However, once her perceptions come up towards seven or eight, time seems to slow down, giving her the time to direct her own actions. This knowledge alone has helped many

77, 78 and 79. Herbert rides through trotting poles on the approach to a small cross pole. In Figure 77 all is well, but in Figure 78 he has 'dropped' Jolly and in Figure 79 he has straightened his knee over the fence. This brings his backside forwards rather than backwards.

riders: Katie, for instance, was unaware that it was humanly possible to perceive jumping any differently from the whirlwind experience in which she did not know what had hit her. (Not surprisingly, she had always wondered how it was that some people managed to enjoy it!) As her perceptions gradually increased over the four days of the course, she had the experience of having more control and more time, as if everything was happening more slowly. As a result, she became much more happy and confident about her jumping. In my most profound experiences of jumping I have felt as if everything was happening in slow motion: in the stride between two elements of a double I have felt each hoof beat, and felt the gap in between each hoof beat, and then I have felt the gap before the horse's hind legs beat against the ground to propel him into take-off – a delightful experience, which I am sure that top-class riders have almost all of the time (with very little awareness, no doubt, that other riders perceive it differently!).

But even when riders have a clearer sense of time, it is extremely difficult to persuade them that standing in their stirrups and catapulting themselves up the horse's neck is not a necessary part of jumping. Tense, worried riders also tend to brace into the stirrups (as they do on the flat), which makes it *impossible* for the knee and hip joints to close (see Figure 85). Herbert, I am sure, would not like me to describe him as tense and worried; at a superficial glance, it appears that his confidence outweighs his competence. However, as he admitted to me later, this is a game of 'inner bluff', which he uses to con himself, for he knows that if he succumbs to feelings of trepidation, his body control will be diminished – and this worries him more than anything else. Underneath his apparent confidence, he does not completely trust himself to know when his horse is going to take off, and he is so scared of being left behind that he reacts by throwing himself forward. But this too makes it difficult for Jolly to jump well, and it is not surprising to see in Figure 79 that he has not taken off with both hind legs together, and that he is scrabbling with his forelegs, even though the shape of the cross pole encourages a neat, symmetrical jump. Jolly is an extremely generous young horse who consistently gives Herbert the benefit of the doubt, and despite the odds he usually jumps clean. But his task is far harder than it would be if Herbert could find the middle ground which lies between the fear of under-compensating and the action of over-compensating, which between them throw him off balance before and during the moment of take-off.

It is interesting to make a comparison between Figure 79 and the good shape in which horses usually jump when they are at liberty. (Although not at liberty, Mayday and Chester are demonstrating this shape well in Figures 100 and 103.) Here, they very rarely scrabble or hit a jump, and it could well benefit Jolly – as it does all young horses – to be loose-schooled over fences and to establish his jump without the added burden of a rider. My emphasis on good style is *not* intended to create something which is merely pleasing to the eye: my major concern is that we, as riders, do not hamper our horses and make their jobs more difficult. By being correctly balanced and freeing the hand well, we can actively help our horses to produce neat, round, clean jumps. Riders tend to forget that horses do not like to hit fences, and whilst it is all too easy to blame the horse, I suspect that the vast majority of knock-downs are caused by rider imbalance. I have some concern for Jolly's future honesty and generosity, for even though Herbert often rides into fences quite well (see Figures 77 and 96), his last-minute tendency to 'drop' the horse and straighten his knee could well generate problems from which Jolly cannot extract him.

80. Herbert and Jolly jump a parallel later in the lesson. Although in better balance, Herbert is still in front of his horse, and his knee has almost come off the front of the saddle. It is not surprising that he likes to rest his hands on his horse's neck – this gives him extra security but restricts the amount of rein which he can give his horse over the fence.

Fairly early on in each lesson, I like to do an exercise which helps each rider to establish her balance away from the heat of the moment. With the horses in trot, the riders alternate five strides of rising trot with five strides folded down in jumping position. This is particularly useful for riders who tend to stand up in their stirrups rather than fold down. It helps the rider to use the stirrup correctly and to establish her balance without resting her hands on the horse's neck; but it is still quite difficult to carry the improvement through to the jumps themselves. Figure 80 shows Herbert later in the lesson, slightly improved, and in a later phase of the jump so that his imbalance does not show up quite so strongly. But he is still in front of his horse. By the fourth day of the course he had dispensed with his pelham and was riding Jolly quite happily in a snaffle bit, with no spurs; his approaches were much more fluent, especially when riding a course, and he was amazed to discover that he did not need such strong measures to help him to start and stop. But he was still not folding down to my satisfaction. This is not an easy change to make: when it happens for Herbert, it will happen suddenly – from one jump to the next – although ingraining it will take time, and in the early stages this will inevitably be a hit-and-miss affair. The secret lies in being able to close the hip and knee joints; but perhaps more important is trust in

81 and 82. Carol and Queen are jumping the second element of a small double. Compare Carol's body position with Herbert's in Figures 77 to 79. Her body is much better placed than his, but is still not as strong and secure as it could be. (In Figure 91 she has this extra strength.) As she folds down, she tends to round her back, and she is not secure enough over her lower leg, which tends to come backwards.

one's ability to respond appropriately to the jump. This only comes when the rider discovers for herself that the apparently strange manoeuvre of bringing the backside *backwards* does indeed keep her in balance with the horse.

It is interesting to compare Figures 78 and 79 with Figures 81 and 82, which show Carol working through a small double. In Figure 81 Queen is in almost exactly the same point just before take-off as Jolly was in Figure 78; but Carol's body position is very different from Herbert's. She has not toppled forward onto the horse's neck; in fact, she has stayed quite well behind her. The secret of the last trot stride, or the second and third beats of the last canter stride, is *to lighten the hand* – since the horse needs to stretch his head and neck down in order to assess the fence – *but not to topple forward with the body*. This is not as easy as it sounds, and Carol could be slightly more upright, with a stronger push out through the front of her body, pressing it against imaginary iron bars. (Figure 91 shows her in a much stronger position.) In Figure 82 she has folded down over the jump well, although her back is a little rounded and her lower leg shows signs of coming too far back. She has, however, given with her hand, which she had not been doing well in previous jumps.

Figures 83 and 84 show Katie at almost the same moment, also at the second element of a double. Compare the angles of her upper body and the attitude of her hand in each case. Figure 83 is really quite good, but in Figure 84 she has taken off slightly in advance of George: at this point he could still stop, and she would be in an extremely vulnerable position if he did. In fact, he made the jump you see in Figure 85, which is very big and very round, and Katie has 'pinged' up off the top of his back, looking rather precarious (as I look at this I imagine that she was saying, 'Eeek!' to herself as it was happening!). Although George usually jumps very round, it was not usual for him to give the jump so much clearance – notice that he has not dangled his front legs down, which is the reason why many horses consistently jump too big. In Figure 83 it looks as if Katie is lifting him up slightly with her hand on take-off. This may have played a part in producing the big jump you see here, but it is a potentially dangerous intervention, usually made by riders who do not trust that the horse can lift *himself* up off the ground and jump without their assistance! In time, the horse either becomes nervous of the rider's hand, or he leans more on it, creating a rider/horse interaction which must eventually lead to problems. Carol, in Figure 81, is demonstrating the best contact we have seen in this moment (compare it with Figures 78, 83 and 84). Her hand is light, and it has neither dropped down onto Queen's neck nor attempted to lift her up.

Looking at Figures 84 and 85, I suspect from Katie's body pos-

83 and 84. Katie is also jumping the second element of a small double. Figures 83 and 84 show almost exactly the same moment, but in Figure 84 she has taken off before her horse and is tending to lift him over the fence with her hand. In both cases her thigh is less strong than Carol's is in Figures 81 and 91. (This is *not* inherently to do with their different body shapes. Katie's thigh would look the same as Carol's if she were pulling the thigh bone forward out of her hip joint and keeping it like an iron bar.)

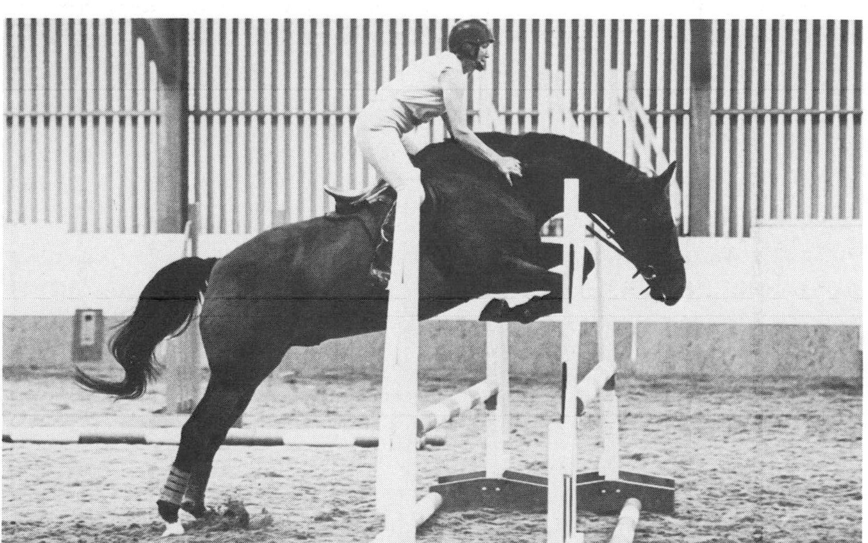

85. This follows on from the take-off in Figure 84. George has jumped very well, but Katie has come very much up off the top of his back into a position which looks rather insecure. To her credit, however, she has not hung onto the rein for support.

ition that she breathed in a stride or two away from the fence and then never breathed out again! Holding one's breath like this draws the body upward and makes bearing down impossible; so to force her to keep breathing I made her recite her name and address to me each time she went through the grid. Given that there is so much daylight between her body and the horse's back over the fence, I am not surprised that she feels unstable and does not much like jumping. It took her some time to stop bracing into the stirrup and to bend her knee so that her upper body could come much closer to the horse – and it helped her to think of 'folding down like an ironing board'. Towards the end of the lesson, Katie's fold-down was still not consistent, but it was much improved, as you can see in Figure 86.

86. A much better fold-down from Katie, whose body is a great deal closer to her horse's back (although from the expression on her face, I suspect that she is still not entirely happy!). It would be better if she were more securely balanced over her stirrup, with the heel more down and forward, and if she had given George a little more rein.

On the flat, I reckon that most riders can cope with about three pieces of input, cycling through them one after the other. This is already a rather frustrating limitation – and it usually does not take very long for at least one of the points to escape the memory! But in jumping, *one* piece of input is all that most people can manage. As on the flat, it takes some time for the rider to become specific enough in the way she directs her body: the classic example of this occurs when the teacher tells a pupil to free her hand over the fence, and in the next jump, she frees not only her hand but her whole body as well, sending her thighs and knees flying away from the saddle! The need for the rider to gain independence of all her various body parts can make learning rather slow – although the more sophisticated she is on the flat, the more easily she will attain this same sophistication in jumping. (I worked on my riding on the flat, and did not jump, for a period of about eight years. When I returned to jumping, I was immediately aware of problems I had not even sensed before. I could diagnose exactly what was needed to solve them and make the necessary corrections very easily. What is more, I could work out how my body position on the approach was influencing the horse's jump, which opened the door to subtleties that I had never even dreamt of in my jumping previously.)

As we have seen by looking at Jill, Herbert, Carol and Katie, one of the most difficult moments for the rider is just on and before take-off. If the rider is anxious, and if she under- or – as is much more likely – over-compensates for the horse's jump, she creates problems. But even without this added problem of anxiety, many riders are not sophisticated enough to be able to keep their upper body stable whilst softening their hand: either nothing gives or everything does. Getting the rider's brain to function well is the first prerequisite in developing this subtlety – and this can take her far further, to the point where she discovers how the precise positioning of her upper body, her thighs and her seat bones influences the horse's striding as well as his jump. (There is more on this later.) But most riders spend their jumping lessons repeating gymnastic exercises in which they practise their limitations and their bad habits. It takes skilful work from both teacher and pupils to develop their awareness, and 'slow down time', to the degree that the lesson can take them into the realm of learning new skills and co-ordinations.

Another major stumbling block concerns vision. Quite early in a jumping lesson I like to bring each rider, in turn, onto the approach line for the grid. I then stand beside her and say, 'Look at the first jump. What you do in your approach is not this. Now look at the last jump. What you do in your approach is not this. Now look right down to the end wall of the school. What you do in your approach is not this. Now look all along the line of jumps, right to the end of the school, without focussing on any of them, but looking in the way that you would if you were looking down a tunnel or driving a car.' When jumping a horse or driving a car, you cannot afford to focus on one specific point for very long: if you look specifically at the top of the fence, this has to be done momentarily, within the context of the overview. It courts danger to look only in the far distance – so that you virtually ignore the fences – or to look only at the next fence. (Imagine looking just in front of the car bonnet or staring at an approaching drain cover as you were driving along the road!) Learner riders, like learner drivers, tend

87, 88 and 89. Clare approaches and jumps a small cross pole. In Figure 87 she is well behind her horse, with a nice, light rein contact. Her thigh, and the push out from her lower stomach, are both helping to hold her body in place. She maintains her strong position throughout, her backside goes backwards as she folds down and she is more stable over her lower leg than any of the riders we have seen so far.

to be restricted in their vision: novices often look no further than the next jump, which seems so important that it fills the whole of their consciousness – as if the world ends after it. This leads to some very jagged performances, and fluency will only come when the status of the fence is relegated to that of something to be gone over whilst on the way to the next. In a similar way, bold riders reduce the buck of a fresh or nappy horse to the same status: more nervous riders cannot think beyond it, which can be their downfall!

When riders perceive their track through a line of fences in the way in which they perceive the road ahead of them when driving, it becomes much easier for them to stay behind the horse. The quality of their vision is directly linked with their control of their upper body. If the rider's eyes 'pop out of her head', her body strains to go forward after them. This both puts her in front of the horse and tends to take her out of the calmness of her comfort or stretch zone and into her panic zone. The correct way of looking helps her to hold her body back whilst pushing forward: she aims the push from her lower stomach out to the horse's breast-plate, pushes the whole of the front of her body forward against iron bars and pulls her thigh forward out of her hip joint. The more the rider pushes out, the more securely her body is held in place and the less easily she topples forward before take-off. This in turn helps her to develop an attitude of *waiting* rather than 'going for it', almost as if the fence were coming towards her rather than her going towards the fence.

Figures 87, 88 and 89 show Clare very early in the lesson. In Figure 87 she is very well behind Charlie, and the push out from her lower stomach does indeed land at the breast-plate. Charlie would find it extremely difficult to stop, and Clare's strong position follows through over the jump. She has given with her hands to the extreme, but has done this without losing her fold-down or throwing her body forward. She was so determined to give enough rein that in Figure 88 she has given too much too soon; but by Figure 89 Charlie has taken all the rein offered. Clare has moved her hands forward along the horse's crest, which means that the line from her elbow to the horse's mouth is not direct: some trainers advocate this, whilst others do not like it. I would much rather see this than a very low hand, which tends to drop the rider's body weight right down onto the horse's neck. This encourages her to round her back and look down, and it may be a factor in the way that Carol has rounded her back in Figure 82. Taking the hand up the crest has an added advantage for nervous riders, who can hold the mane if they start to feel insecure!

Compare Clare's approach in Figure 87 with Janet's in Figure 90. Janet's thigh looks 'mushy' in comparison to Clare's, and the front of her body is crumpled instead of firm: Mayday could prob-

90. This photograph is taken in exactly the same moment as Figure 87. However, Janet's position is much less secure than Clare's. More of her weight is taken in her stirrups, so the underneath of her thigh and backside are not so well placed in the saddle. The front of her body is weak and she has tipped forward.

ably stop if she wanted to. In fact, she made an uncharacteristically bad jump, probably because she rushed the trotting poles and her hind foot came onto the wrong side of this last one. Although Janet's body position is rather weak, she does not make the mistake of over-compensating for the jump, and she does not interfere with her horse either on the approach to the fence or on take-off and in the air. Many people who *looked* like her would not feel secure; but Janet trusts herself, and she also trusts Mayday – who is an unusually talented horse over fences. Clare and Carol are more secure and correct in their jumping than either Janet, Herbert (see Figure 78) or Katie (see Figures 83 and 84). (Jill, too, usually *looks* secure, but she is not as trusting as Janet, and she has an Achilles heel which we will come to later.) Look at Carol's body in Figure 91. Both she and Clare are much more firmly placed than any of

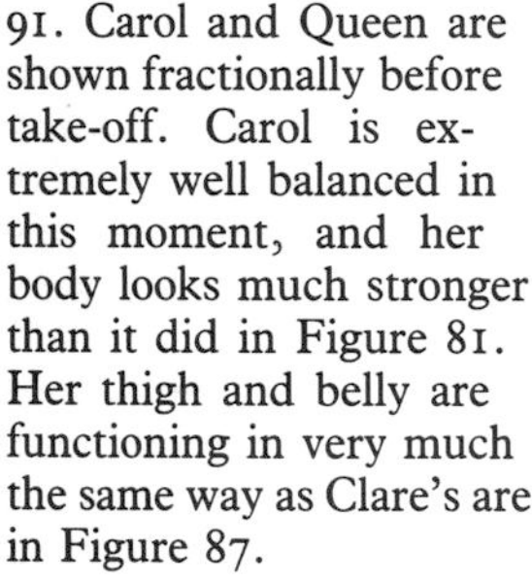

91. Carol and Queen are shown fractionally before take-off. Carol is extremely well balanced in this moment, and her body looks much stronger than it did in Figure 81. Her thigh and belly are functioning in very much the same way as Clare's are in Figure 87.

the other riders and Carol, like Clare, is well behind her horse, with a strong thigh and a firmly placed upper body, which is now much more secure than it was in Figure 81.

Figures 92 and 93 show Clare in the landing and get-away stages, and Figures 94 and 95 show Katie at almost the same moments. The landing stages of the jump never make very flattering photographs, but in Figures 92 and 94 both riders are doing well, although Katie has straightened her knee, sending her foot forward and bringing her backside into the saddle a little too soon. This often happens when the rider's stirrups are too long or when she does not trust how her horse will behave after landing from the fence. In the early part of the first stride after landing, riders always come slightly forward again: however, Katie has done this so much that she is almost resting on George's neck in Figure 95. If she were about to face another jump, a turn or a downhill slope, she would be in trouble. (She might, however, make a good gallop to the finish!) Charlie, in his more rounded carriage, is much more malleable than George would be.

The ability to recover quickly after a fence is tremendously important, and course builders deliberately test it, both in show jumping and cross-country. It is always difficult for the rider when she knows that her horse will gain speed very soon after landing, for she must not preempt his desire to rush off by restricting him with her hand or her body whilst he is in the air. If she does this, he becomes much more likely to hit the fence. The more highly trained a jumping horse is, the less his canter rhythm is disturbed by the jump. A friend of mine recently told me the story of her attempt to buy a Grade A show jumper when she was still a teenager: she tried eighteen different horses and learnt a tremendous amount from the experience. What impressed her particularly was the way in which most of them landed after a fence and cantered away as if nothing had happened. This showed her the importance of training the horse to do this. The time to rebalance a green or a strong horse is in the first two strides after landing, for it is here that he may begin (metaphorically speaking) to pull the rug out from under the rider's feet, so that he takes her. To leave this rebalancing any later puts the rider at a great disadvantage, for prevention is much more effective than cure. She is only causal when she is taking the horse, and once she is reactive, it is almost impossible to stop him from gaining speed and becoming even more unbalanced before the next question is asked.

Figures 96, 97 and 98 show three riders in the non-jumping stride of a small double. All of them are shown in the second beat of the canter stride (following on from the first beat which is shown in Figures 93 and 95). Herbert in Figure 96 is riding rather well: when he feels insecure about his horse's striding, his balance before

92, 93, 94 and 95. Clare and Katie are shown at almost exactly the same moments as they land after a fence. Clare has maintained a good knee and lower leg position, whilst Katie's knee has straightened slightly, throwing her upper body back into the saddle. As a result, she has come a little too upright too soon – notice how she has had to extend her arm fully to give George enough rein. Notice also that Charlie has a slightly bent knee on the foreleg that is about to hit the ground. This will give him better shock-absorption than George will have with his rather straight knee, caused by the constriction in his back resulting from Katie's imbalance. Charlie's freer back, along with Clare's better balance over the fence contribute to his rounder shape in the get-away stride.

FIRE EXIT
B

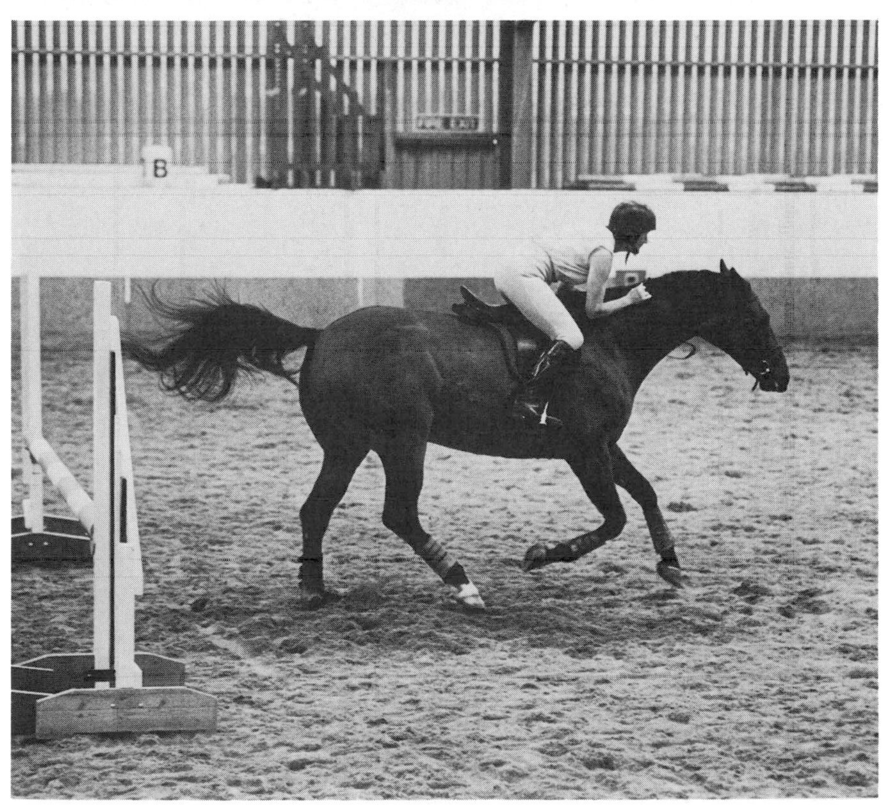

FIRE EXIT
B

96, 97 and 98. The non-jumping stride in a small double: Herbert is quite well positioned here, although he has weighted his backside slightly too much. It would be better if more of his weight were carried down his thigh, so that his knee pointed more down, and his lower leg were a little more underneath him. Clare has a better balance over her thigh and foot, but her upper body has come forward too much. Compare her position with that in Figure 87, in which she is more behind her horse. Katie's backside has bounced out of the saddle, putting her in front of her horse in a rather weak position.

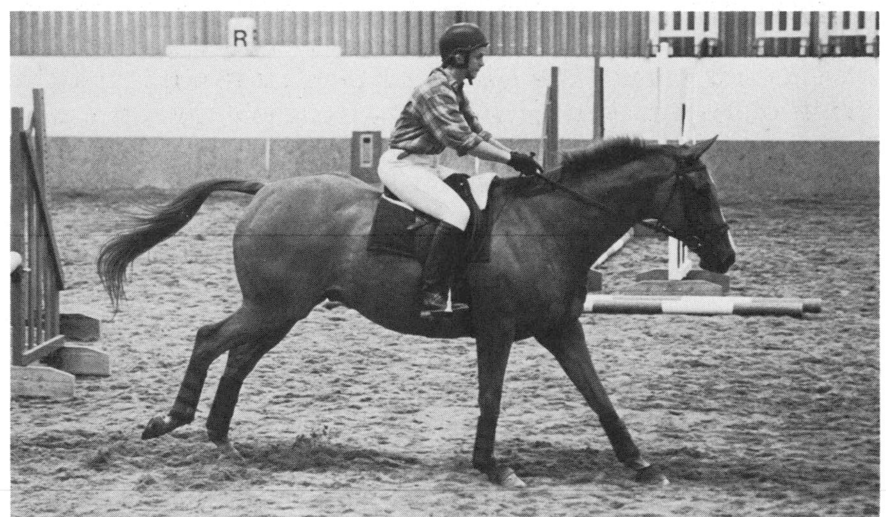

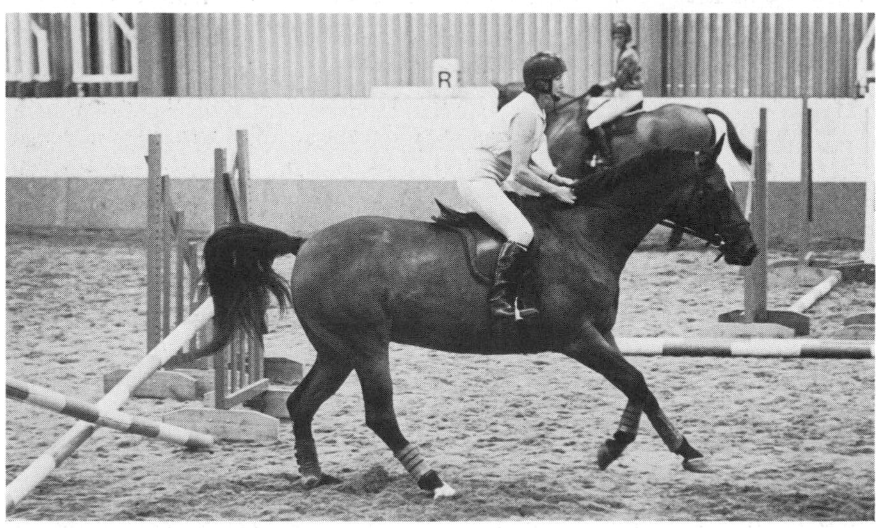

and during take-off becomes suspect, but here in the double he can predict exactly what will happen. So far, his body position is giving Jolly a good chance of jumping well. He has allowed the horse enough rein to reach down and assess the fence, but his fingers and arms are rather tight – compare them to Clare's in Figure 97. Herbert's body is held well in place: his backside makes a clear contact with the saddle but it is weighted slightly too much, squashing the horse very slightly. His lower leg looks secure, but if anything it has come too far forward, which plays a part in tipping his weight back.

Clare looks quite good in Figure 97, but if you compare her body position with Figure 87, you realise that her backside has come rather far back in the saddle, causing her to lean more forward and to close the angle of her hip joint. A better placing of the upper body could make all the difference in her ability to rebalance Charlie before his next jump, particularly if the distance in the combination is rather short. Katie in Figure 98 has landed in the saddle after the first jump and then bounced, as riders so often do in the middle of combinations. Her lack of contact with the horse puts her in a position where she has very little influence – and it contributes to her sense of having no time and no control. It is easy to see that she is in front of George, who has very little stuffing: notice how much more horse the other two riders have in front of them.

One of the things I find so impressive in top-class riders is their ability to bring their thigh and backside down into the saddle so precisely that they 'plug in' to the horse's long back muscles even in the very short space of time between the two elements of a combination. Less experienced riders usually struggle to become quick enough in their reactions: initially it is difficult for them to sit up into the first fence, fold down over it, sit up in the non-jumping stride, fold down over the second fence and then sit up again for the get-away. A tremendous amount happens very quickly, and some riders make every move slightly late – which of course has a knock-on effect. Others find it difficult because of their tendency to bounce when they land after the first fence. I am convinced that the ability to 'plug in' to the horse's long back muscles between fences is a major factor in the superior performance of the talented 5 per cent. But this can be learnt, and riders usually understand this idea remarkably quickly in their work on the flat (see Lesson 7). Learning to 'plug in' consistently, and in more taxing situations, is only a matter of time and practice.

Janet too had difficulty in the non-jumping stride, her body crumpling in just the same way as it has in Figure 90. Figure 99, taken during our last exercise – a parallel ridden off a circle – shows this to an even greater extreme. Janet tended to collapse her front slightly on the flat (see Lesson 5), so, given the added stress of

99. Janet and Mayday approach a fence in canter. Although the quality of the muscles in Janet's thigh is better, her knee and foot have come up, and it looks as though this might have been caused, at least partially, by the way in which she is using her leg. Her upper body has crumpled, tipping her forward too much and weakening the push out from her lower stomach.

jumping, it is no surprise to see her doing it even more here. By the end of the four days there was a great improvement, which lasted only as long as she kept reminding herself to push the front of her body against imaginary iron bars. This in itself began to have a slowing effect on Mayday's canter, which leaves a lot to be desired and is the weakest link in their jumping. (In fact, one of my helpers commented that they were just the kind of combination which causes the audience to hold their breath at the local show!) Janet needs to improve the canter in her *flatwork* before she will carry that improvement into jumping. As always, her bodily use must be her starting point, and her most important priorities are to learn how to use her lower leg independently so that her thigh and knee stay in place and to position her upper body so that she does not topple forward.

When it comes to the actual jump, however, she and Mayday both do extremely well. Janet folds down and frees her hand in

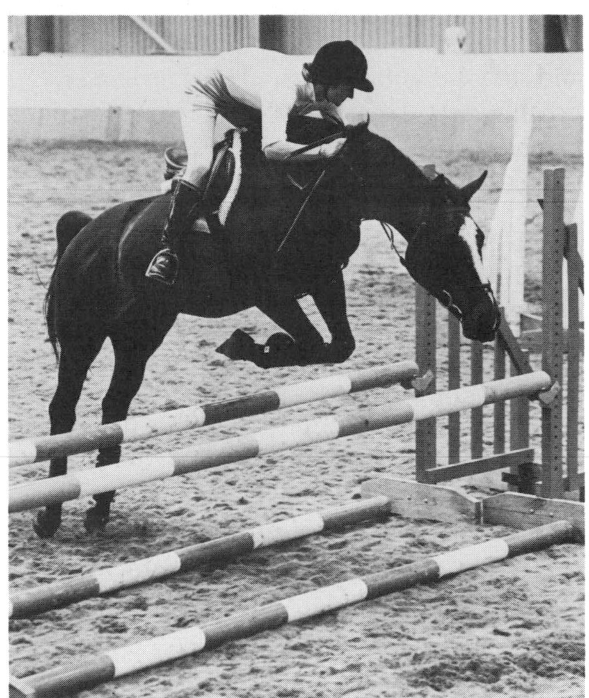

100. Janet and Mayday over a parallel. Mayday has made a particularly good jump, in which she has used her head and neck to the extreme. Janet's body position is slightly weak, and given how much she crouches forward on the approach, it is not surprising that she should tend to come in front of her horse over the fence itself.

good style, although she tends to come in front of Mayday. Figure 100 shows her fairly well placed on a very athletic jump, which demonstrates the degree to which a talented horse will stretch his head and neck down, using it as a balancing pole over a fence. (Compare Mayday's jump with George's in Figure 86. George is already jumping quite round, but he does not use his neck in the same way.) Only this allows him to get his hind end *up*, so when the rider restricts him with her hand, she usually pays the price with knocked poles. Mayday makes even big jumps look extremely easy; she appears to just step over them, and when Janet has more control of her canter they could do very well. Meanwhile, their verve and enthusiasm make up for the technique and discipline which they lack.

Carol's approach in Figure 101 shows a much stronger, open, more upright upper body, even though Queen has lost the good canter of our flatwork lesson and come above the bit. Figure 102 shows her most athletic jump of the day; for even as the fences went up she kept offering the rather flat jump which you see in Figure 82. She likes to give herself plenty of room so that she does not have to bascule and snap her forelegs up quickly: compare the degree to which she has brought them up and stretched her neck down in each case. Knowing her work on the flat, it is no surprise to me to find that it does not come easily to her to round herself over a jump. I have known several horses with an exceptionally good bascule, all of whom have had an equally good free walk on a long rein, in which they reached forward and down to an unusual degree (see Lesson 3, and especially Figure 28). This lifts the wither and the long back muscles to an unusual degree, bringing the horse's nose right down to the floor and mirroring the jumping mechanism. Even though Queen is a talented horse on the flat, this is just what she does *not* want to do, and her long back muscles rarely offer more than the acceptable minimum (see Lesson 8). They are equally economical in jumping, and although good riding and gymnastic exercises will no doubt help, I suspect that she will never become generous in the way she bascules.

101. Carol and Queen approach a fence in canter. Compare Carol's more open, upright upper body with Janet's body in Figure 99.

102. Queen has jumped well. Compare this with Figure 82, where the jump is flatter and her forelegs are much less well tucked-up. Carol is showing the same faults in her jumping position, however, and she is not really giving Queen enough rein.

In Figure 102 Carol shows the same faults as she shows in Figure 82, except that they are possibly more exaggerated. (So much for my good teaching!) This time her lower leg definitely has come back, and she needs to consciously feel her heel lowering and her feet pressing against the stirrups as she jumps. Her back is still slightly rounded, and her hand, which is not as low as it was in Figure 82, could free more. Carol quite likes jumping but is much more committed to her flatwork, so I suspect that she is unlikely to give herself the dedicated practice which would be required to ingrain the changes she needs to make. However, she told me recently that she could clearly feel the difference between the times when Queen jumped flat and the times when she used a more rounded bascule, and that she had jumped her several times at home to good effect.

103. Chester shows a very neat, symmetrical jump with a good bascule. Jill's backside has possibly come too far out of the saddle, but she looks very secure.

104. A later stage in the jump. Notice how close Jill's backside is to the saddle and how well she is balanced over her lower leg. Compare her position with Herbert's in Figure 80.

The last two pictures, Figures 103 and 104, show some of the best jumps of the day, with Chester making up for his previous display over the smaller fences! Figure 103 shows a particularly good bascule, although Jill's backside has come rather too far out of the saddle. Chester has positioned himself for take-off very well, and has snapped up quickly. Both hind legs and both forelegs are together, which makes the jump powerful and streamlined. It is interesting to compare Jill's body in Figure 104 with Herbert's in Figure 80. Jill's style is typical of event riders, offering much more security than Herbert's more loose and forward body, which would be more typical of show jumpers. There are times when Jill does not free her hand enough, and she could still be more secure over her lower leg, but recently her learning has focussed on how she rides the approach. For although her body position is good and she trusts it once she is airborne she has not trusted herself – or her horse – on the approach.

Chester has quite often surprised Jill with the kind of big stand-off that you see in Figure 75, and on a couple of occasions he has stopped with her. Together, these have created a situation in which they both became insecure about the approach, which has had a 'will s/he? . . . won't s/he?' feel to it. We cannot know which of them was the chicken and which of them was the egg, but regardless of who started it, Jill has since panicked when she has been on the approach to a fence and has realised that they were going to arrive wrong. As a result she has either frozen – denying Chester the help that he needs at this critical moment – or 'gone for a big one', pushing him on so that he rushes into the jump on a long, flat stride. Should he then arrive wrong (which is likely, since Jill's judgement in that moment could well be suspect), he has little chance to manoeuvre. As his canter becomes more flat and sprawling, it is increasingly difficult for him to adjust his striding by sitting himself down and putting in a short extra stride. If he does, he knows that Jill could possibly jump a stride before him, and that she might 'drop' him at the last moment. So Chester is quite likely to make the kamikaze leap that Jill has, in effect, asked him for; or, if he does not fancy his chances, he might stop.

Next time, the 'will s/he? . . . won't s/he?' question could become even more urgent. Either of them might dither, or panic, and neither of them trusts the other. To make it worse, Jill is the kind of person who only needs one mishap to convince her that she will never get it right; unfortunately, though, it takes many more correct, fluent approaches to convince her that she could never get it wrong! Once the rider has chased the horse into the fence a few times, he begins to expect to be asked to suddenly accelerate, so he may beat the rider to it and speed up of his own accord. This is how horses learn to rush. Since he too is fired by panic, he may not have the confidence to follow through on his judgement. Horse and rider are in a situation which has become a frightening vicious circle which acts as a self-fulfilling prophecy confirming all their worst fears. As with all riders in this situation, it is not enough to say to Jill, 'Don't panic,' as she rides into a fence; her only chance of stopping herself lies in having *something else to do in its place*.

A few years ago I began to realise that I, as an observer, could watch a rider approach a fence and know that she was going to arrive correctly at it even when she was still a very long way away. I had no idea how many strides the horse would take, but my judgement always proved to be correct; and when I did not have this sense, the striding invariably became a problem. I began to ask myself, 'What am I seeing that lets me know this?' I also had the same sense as a rider. Counting strides into a fence had never helped me, and neither had it helped anyone else I knew who was worried about their striding; in fact I think it encouraged us all to ride 'three . . . two . . . ONE!' approaches in which we overrode the horse and pushed him out of his stride, creating either a big stand-off or a small extra stride put in at the last minute. Although placing poles etc. can ease the rider's fears, they never provide a lasting answer. Like many riders, I have been left wondering, 'What is the secret?'

Jill is one of the people who has served as an experimental guinea pig for me in finding the answer. She too has sometimes had the sense that there will be no problem, but in its absence she soon becomes insecure, so our quest has been to discover how we can create this feeling for her all the time, bringing the ball back into her court instead of leaving her fate in the lap of the gods. Philosophically, I have worked from two premises: the first is that we all have the right equipment to jump horses well, and that individual differences lie not in what we have got but in what we *do* with what we have got. This has always been borne out for me on the flat. The second premise is that it is the *horse's* job, and not the rider's job, to sort his legs out on the way into a fence. Without consciously directing your body, you can run down steps, cross a road and jump up the kerb at the other side; the horse is equally, if not more, capable. The rider's job is to put the horse's body and brain in the best possible mode for doing this. The only time that you or he are likely to make a mistake is if you are in a panic, half asleep or thinking about something else. This means that the horse, on his approach, must be held in a state of focussed attention which is centred on the jump, and that you as rider must not distract him.

Look at Janet's horse in Figure 99. It is obvious that this is no ordinary canter stride. Mayday is looking at the fence and backing off it, arranging her striding in relation to it. This gives the horse much more scope than simply lengthening and bounding into it – which is what anxious riders like Jill tend to force their horses to do. Where Chester sometimes rushes into the fence and loses athleticism, Mayday chooses to bring her hocks increasingly underneath her as the fence approaches. Although her canter itself is very unbalanced, this is her natural response when she sees a jump. Provided that Janet does not interfere with this, she will do it even better when her athleticism improves on the flat. Show-jumping riders lay great store on the horse's ability to back off a fence, and they cultivate it, since it becomes increasingly important as the fences get higher. Few event riders, whose horses jump across country from a much longer stride, change their tactics for show jumping; in fact, many of the event riders I know regard show jumping as their Achilles heel.

The idea of putting the horse in the best state from which to jump suggests that the rider should create a well-balanced canter on a medium-length stride with plenty of impulsion. The worst thing that can possibly happen is that the horse arrives at the fence half a stride wrong; but from a canter stride of medium length, he has the athleticism to lengthen or shorten. He also has the power to stand off the fence or to right himself by putting in a short stride. This is denied him if the stride is already rather long or rather short. However, this is downside planning – the way out of the worst possible scenario – and we need a policy which goes one stage further than this, so that adjustments are made much earlier and in such a subtle, fluid way that everything seems to turn out right of its own accord.

The horse's rhythm in canter is like a 'carrier frequency', the background 'hum' which carries all other signals along with it. It helps the rider to put her attention *here*, rather than worrying where the horse's legs are in relation to the fence. Most people find that consciously thinking about striding only creates problems of the 'will s/he . . . won't s/he . . .' variety – and any rider who thinks that she can arrange the horse's legs better than he can assumes tremendous supremacy! To put their attention on rhythm rather than on placing the horse, some riders count 'one' to themselves with each canter stride, so that they do not vary their count as they approach the fence. (In contrast, counting 'three . . . two . . . one . . .' or 'one . . . two . . . three . . .' encourages the rider to anticipate.) Paying attention to this count, to the position of the upper body and to vision have helped Jill but have not actually cured the problem. My work with her and other riders has led me part way to the solution, but (as usual) it was my own experiences jumping which added the most important piece to the puzzle.

As you ride in jumping position, think of the lines of your inside thighs making a 'V' shape and imagine that those lines could extend backwards into your body. If you have snug thighs and a good pinch feeling, each of your seat bones will lie on the 'V', and if you focus on the internal columns formed by the psoas muscles, you will also have a connection down through each seat bone into the horse's long back muscles. As the rider approaches the fence, one of two things tends to happen: if she panics and tips forwards, she closes the angle at the front of her body so that her seat bones now point *backwards*, so she 'unplugs' herself from the 'receptors' in the horse's long back muscles. At the same time, her seat bones come off the 'V'. But if she leans back, either in sending the horse forward or in holding him rather strongly, her seat bones begin to point *forwards*, and again they come 'unplugged' and off the 'V' (this is similar to Diagram 20, page 185). Think of keeping the seat bones pointing straight down, so that they stay on the 'V' and remain 'plugged in' to the 'receptors' in the horse's long back muscles. To maintain this connection, you may have *deliberately to bring the seat bones back and in, following the line of the 'V' back towards its point*. You may also need to keep your thigh bones pulling forward out of the hip joints: both of these increase the gap in each hip joint and play a vital part in keeping the horse in front of you.

It is also very helpful to think of this during downward transitions, where most riders have exactly the same tendency to tip forward or back, so that the seat bones point in a different direction and no longer 'plug in' (see Lesson 10). One rarely sees downward transitions well ridden, primarily because it is so easy to lose this connection (even when you realise that it is an important point on which to focus). In my experience, it is the link-pin which changes everything else, since it maintains the correct connection between the rider's seat and the horse's back. The loss of this is tremendously disturbing to the horse – he loses his natural ability to make a 'clean' transition, and, equally, he loses his natural ability to make a fluent, rhythmic approach to a fence. When Jill has 'plugged in' by accident, Chester has approached the fences very happily, Jill has sensed that all was well, and as a result she has felt secure; in contrast, losing it has always left her (and Chester) feeling much less safe. Herbert, too, has occasionally experienced the feeling of being 'plugged in', which has enabled him to make some much better approaches. But he has much less body control than Jill, so he cannot home in on this feeling so easily. Jill now knows what to do, and she has the subtlety to be able to do it: the vital piece is in the puzzle and the problem is basically solved. Seeing a stride, it seems, is only partially to do with vision. It is equally dependent on the quality of the rider's contact with the horse's back.

Our last exercise, cantering over a parallel fence on a circle, gave everybody the chance to test this out. The exercise poses exactly the same problems as jumping a course, and the rider's success is dependent on creating a balanced canter which is rhythmic, impulsive and has a medium-length stride. This gives the horse the power and the flexibility to adjust his striding if required, but if the rider is correctly 'plugged in', last-minute adjustments are never necessary. The rider's control of the canter is tested even more as she turns and rebalances the horse after the jump. The riders have no security blanket, as they do in the placing poles or the first small jump which establishes a good approach into the bigger fences of a grid. All the difficulties in the canter itself – and in the rider's sitting – immediately show up, and have their inevitable influence over the horse's jump. All of the riders have their successes and failures – they hit-and-miss as they attempt to make changes in their body position and to understand the cause-and-effect principles which underlie their interaction with the horse. But when they know *where to focus their attention*, they know the secret of good performance, and it is only a matter of time before this becomes second nature to them, giving them the skill which has seemed, so far, to be reserved for the talented few.

PART THREE

Solving the Riddle

Any sufficiently developed technology is indistinguishable from magic.

Arthur C. Clarke

Solving the Riddle

In terms of the time they took, the lessons you have just witnessed in the Masterclass section of this book were incredibly insignificant – a drop in the ocean that is created during the course of each rider's learning process. But in terms of their *effect*, I hope they were very much more – and I hope that the riders in these pages will look back over their learning process and find that their initial lessons with me were a significant turning point which shifted it to a completely new level. In each person's learning, there are always significant turning points and moments of particularly profound insight which will stand out in her memory. These moments are like quantum leaps, and after each one, many hours of quiet work are usually needed to ingrain and integrate the change that has been made.

In a self-motivated, cybernetic learning process (in which the rider homes in on her goal like a self-guided torpedo), most of this work is done by the rider between lessons. (Learning comes a good deal cheaper this way, and although our forefathers always had their students under constant observation, I am not convinced that this is indeed the best way.) Working on her own encourages the rider to become more self-reliant, and once she has a good baseline of knowledge she begins to create these transformative moments on her own. Then, she visits her teacher for confirmation that she is indeed on the right track. But in the early stages of her learning, these moments usually happen within the lessons themselves.

When a rider takes responsibility for her own learning, this encompasses almost all of the hours that she spends in the saddle: she uses this time to clarify the difference between right and wrong, to reinforce the correct neurological patterns and to strengthen her muscles. (And as she does this, she automatically helps her horse to do the same.) But most people, in their everyday riding, either give up or 'switch off', and few remain motivated and focussed in the way that the vast majority of my pupils – and all top performers – do. Undoubtedly, it is easier for a rider to maintain her faith and endurance when she has a clear understanding of what she is supposed to do and how she is supposed to do it – without this, boredom and frustration are all too often the order of the day. As the rider improves the way in which she uses her body, she concurrently learns *how* to concentrate and *what to concentrate on*. People whose brains naturally tend to be either sluggish or busy elsewhere can find that this process is rather like getting a snowball rolling; but in time, it always gathers its own momentum, and learning to concentrate must go hand-in-hand with learning to ride. (This is something which Katie, whom you met in Lesson 1, really began to appreciate during her stay with me, and with which Janet in Lesson 5 is grappling as well.)

In my work, I am helping the rider to home in on the straight and narrow path of riding – the classical ideal, in which the circuit is complete and the horse's movement shows the correct mechanism. When I first meet them, most riders are careering off in the wrong direction, unaware of the way in which their bodily use is creating problems which can so easily be blamed on their horse. Very often, their attempts to solve these problems on their own have taken them even further away from the straight and narrow. Riding would be a great deal easier if the solutions to the problems it presents were as obvious as most of the problems themselves! The solutions are cleverly hidden, yet they do exist, and by using the right key one can always open the door. But as in other spheres of life, the attempt to solve the problem can all too often *become* the problem. (Lesson 5 with Janet gives a particularly good example of this, for her efforts to bring Mayday 'onto the bit' created a whole new range of difficulties.) My aim, in presenting more intricate but effective solutions, is to make learning easier for all concerned, and to streamline a process in which it is all too easy to get stuck, lost and frustrated.

In the early stages of our work together, as I bring the rider 'on course', it is easy to make dramatic, profound changes with her. Then, as she progresses, we usually find that there are one or two more insidious problems which hold her away from the classical ideal: some of these have always been obvious to her and her teachers, but some are so subtle, and so ingrained and familiar to the rider, that she has been blissfully unaware of them. (She is rather like a goldfish, who is so completely immersed in water that she would never discover it alone!) Sometimes problems which have appeared to be enormous can be shifted remarkably easily – I routinely make changes with riders which have previously seemed to them to be beyond the realms of possibility – and sometimes those which look minor turn out to be huge. Jill's difficulty in sitting to the canter, for instance, looked a huge and insurmountable problem, but two sentences from me eradicated it so completely that the change fell into her lap, with minimal need to work on it (see Lesson 10). Her asymmetry, however, looks subtle compared to many, but it has been very pervasive – and I suspect that there may never be a time when she does not have to think about it.

Although some of the changes I make with riders could be seen as miracles, this work is not a miracle cure. It *would be*, perhaps, if the rider were guaranteed to arrive for the next lesson sitting and performing as she was at the end of the last one. I do all that I can to increase the likelihood of this, by going right to the core of each problem and by making my corrections as clear and precise as possible. I frequently ask the rider, 'How will you recognise this again? What will you have to do to reproduce it?' And sometimes, I will not let her go home until I am sure that she knows! I like her to go right through the stages of overload and disorientation while she is still in my presence, so that her mind is clear when she leaves the session. I also encourage her to write down the salient points of each lesson, and to keep a journal about her learnings. But between lessons the ball is in her court, and she has a lot of homework to do. All too easily she can forget one important point and lose the correct balance between all the pieces of input she has been given (Carol did this between her first lesson and the one you have read about when she over-emphasised bearing down and forgot to think of the horse coming up underneath her). Riding is like a recipe in which it is not easy to combine all the right ingredients in the correct proportions, especially at first. Throughout the rider's learning, she is gradually homing in on an ideal which is rarely reached.

Not every lesson brings new discoveries and insights, but most do: after the initial major changes, some of our subsequent sessions together simply consolidate these. Riders often drift off course when I have not seen them for a while. They may lose the correction we made, or they may over-correct – but this is an inevitable part of 'groping' their way along. Each time, they have to be brought back onto the straight and narrow before I can take them any further, and most people have to re-learn the same thing several times before it 'sticks'. But if I find that I am continually giving a rider the same lesson over and over again, I have to ask her, 'What are you doing in your work at home? How committed are you to these ideas?' Some repetition is inevitable (after all, we are essentially only dealing with walk, trot and canter – there is nothing else!), and as I said in Lesson 9 with Gina, learning typically happens in *layers*. These return the rider again and again to the basics of her bodily use and her interaction with the horse, and each time she gains a fuller appreciation of their scope and importance. Most lessons review old ground, make the rider and the horse as 'right' as they have been in the past, and then add several new ideas which take them a stage further.

When the rider does enough of this work, there comes a time when she understands the laws of cause and effect which underlie the rider/horse interaction and can use them to her advantage. Essentially, she knows *how* to ride. The rider who has reached this stage is not perfect – her body still has its idiosyncrasies, which she may still have a good deal of work to do to iron out; but she has become causal. Riders then *choose* the correct path for themselves, and it is no longer a list of 'oughts' which are imposed by teachers or books. They are much less tempted to deviate – either actively or passively – from the classical ideal. In this stage of the rider's development, it is more a question of refinement than of learning.

Jill is reaching the stage, and it is not far away for Carol, too. (This is as much by virtue of her natural ability as it is by virtue of my good teaching!) Margaret and Gina will both get there in time: Margaret is learning incredibly fast, especially considering her starting point. Gina's progress is much less slow than she thinks it is, although she easily loses faith in herself and allows Dante to call the tune. Janet is probably running about average in her learning, but she will go very much faster if she can shift her focus from the *product* of her interaction with the horse to the *process* of that interaction. I cannot vouch for any of the other riders who met me for the first time in these lessons. A great deal depends on their dedication in working with the input they already have, as well as on how often they come to me (or to another competent trainer), so that I can bring them back on course and then give them their next steps.

I estimate that it takes most riders between sixteen and twenty-four lessons fully to understand the system I am teaching, and to be able to monitor themselves so that they do not wander far off the straight and narrow path during the time they spend alone. They then have the essentials in place. Most riders take these lessons over a period of about two years, and although I have seen people consolidate their learning very much faster, this amount of time is usually needed to ingrain the changes they are making.

Like many good riders, the pupils who have been through this process are unlikely completely to have conquered their asymmetry, and they may well still look down and use their hand too much on occasion. These habits seem to be almost universal: but despite that, I like to instill in my pupils the belief that with enough faith and commitment, the problems *will* melt away in time. In the absence of someone like myself who can offer this assurance, however, most people decide to live with them. But I really appreciate people who attempt to find creative, ethical solutions to these old demons: my favourite example of this came from an unusually talented and committed young friend of mine who is training with one of Germany's highly respected riders. She became extremely fed up with her tendency to look down whilst she was riding, so when no one was looking she fixed a piece of sticky tape onto her pony tail and then stuck it down onto her back. This worked well until she began to warm up, but as her skin became moist the tape came unstuck! So then she tried taping a little prickle onto her neck just under her chin: this worked well too until the tape again came unstuck and the prickle began to slip down. To add embarrassment to her failure, her teacher happened to see her, and to ask, 'Vaz iz zat you 'ave zere?' This stumped her for a while – although I am sure that it does not represent the limit of either her ingenuity or her determination. When I last saw her, she kept asking me, 'Why can't I do it? It ought to be so easy . . .' Rather than repeatedly bashing her head against the same brick wall, she was at least asking the right question. For is it the case that only a very few extremely talented riders are able to conquer these habits, or is it that they are the latter stages of a process which very few people complete?

Very often, the rider does not find the cure for these really pervasive problems until she becomes unwilling to live with them any longer. Most riding teachers realise this, and it explains why their traditional tactic of terrorising the pupil has always worked to a degree! But whilst riding is a very disciplined, exacting tradition, this does not imply that it should become 'serious'. Becoming *thorough* is much more productive. I have the idea that with a thorough enough approach, all problems become solved in their own time. Attempts to keep the hands still, for instance, tend to fail until the rider realises that it is not her hands but her *seat bones* which need adjusting (see Lesson 9 with Gina). My young friend with the pony tail will look up, I am sure, when she has her head 'above water', and she can process so much information unconsciously that her conscious mind is much freer. Like most people, her ability with parallel processing ends before she gets to her head; but when her riding is based more on unconscious competence she will be able to disengage her eyes from the task. Neither will-power nor sticky tape can produce this prematurely; both body and mind must be ready.

As I have been developing my approach over the last twelve years, my primary aim has been to understand exactly how the rider/horse interaction works, and exactly what sequences a rider must go through in learning. (I have, thank God, matured beyond the stage of attempting to teach my pupils everything all at once!) I began my quest from the premise that there must be some hidden 'keys' which unlock the secrets of riding, making the rider's and the horse's bodies behave in exactly the way which textbooks have repeatedly told us they should. As I was uncovering these, my parallel quest was to find ways of communicating them which worked quickly, efficiently and easily for as many riders as possible.

Over recent years, this has led me to search for images which are as streamlined and effective as possible, and which cut down the amount of 'groping' that the rider has to do as she homes in on the correct feeling. For instance, if I say to a rider, 'You need to lean back more,' one of two things is likely to happen. I may see her in a few weeks' or months' time and find that her own sense of 'rightness' overrode my words of wisdom, and that they effectively went in one ear and out of the other. Or I may find that she has taken my words to heart and has leant back for all she is worth, using the strange sensations she had in her body as her guide. The problem is that over time, her body will have adapted to them – so in order to feel just as strange now as she felt then, she will have to lean much further back than I ever intended! Of course, when I see her next and suggest that she needs to lean forward more she will be both perplexed and disappointed!

In my experience, about 70 per cent of people tend to under-do the corrections I suggest and are not rigorous enough in their attempts to reproduce them. From my own experience, I find this absolutely understandable. This is particularly true when the rider is correcting a very gross pattern (for example, the tendency to lean forward, back or off to one side) or a very subtle one. In contrast, about 25 per cent of people *over-do* a correction. I feel much happier when the rider does this, since it is obvious that she has at least applied herself: she is taking the feelings in her body seriously, which is a necessary first step. The remaining 5 per cent of people hit it just right: they work both from their own body sensations and from the feedback they get from their horse. They use him as their ultimate guide, so when he says, 'Too much!' they back off a bit. But to sense this, they need a very refined understanding of horse language. Their sensitivity to cause and effect is already so precise that they barely need a teacher!

Except in the realm of asymmetries – where most people struggle long and hard to obtain a large enough change – riders do not usually ingrain a correction until they have been through a stage where they over-shoot the mark. It is as if they have to swing the pendulum *too far* in order to recognise enough. (I always think that this is rather like eating: it is very difficult to recognise enough at exactly the right mouthful . . . and one is much more likely to diagnose one's over-indulgence about two slices of cake too late!) If we can cut down the number and the extent of the swings which are necessary before the person *really knows* how much is enough, we can streamline the learning process considerably, making it far less tedious and confusing.

This is why I am so fond of the question, 'Would you balance on a diving board?' This image has built into it the idea of 'How much is enough?', and the rider is much less likely to over-correct than she is if I ask her to 'bring her lower leg back'. Similarly, if I suggest that she thinks of the columns of her psoas muscles, and of aligning them so that they are vertical, she has a much clearer image than if I tell her to lean forward or to lean back. Learning about the positions of the seat bones on the clock face, and about the function of the 'merry-go-round', makes the rider far more likely to position herself correctly on the horse's back, so that she hits the nail straight on the head. Precision is also built into these images, and they are no more difficult to understand because of that – in fact, they become much easier to comprehend and to work with. Some of my other favourites – the idea of not deadening the trampoline, for instance – express concepts which are very hard to communicate through any other means.

In effect, we are searching for *the highest organising principles of riding* – the few hinge points which, when they are in place, bring everything else with them. This saves us from having to deal with a large number of small, intricate pieces, which make it dangerously likely that the rider will confuse herself. In this state, she becomes unable to see the wood for the trees. Modern-day teaching has tried to avoid this by keeping riding very simple and reducing it down to a few 'golden rules' (like 'sit up straight and keep your heels down'). But unfortunately, these are not universally applicable, and they are not the highest organising principles. If they were, there would not be such a devastatingly huge gap between theory and practice, and we would all be demonstrating their validity by riding very much better than we are!

There is a very strange paradox between the simplicity and the complexity of riding. The highest organising principles which underlie it are indeed very simple – once you know them. But when no one has let you into the secret, riding seems incredibly complicated and mysterious (even though our conventional theory seems to imply that it ought to be easy!). As you can tell from reading the lessons in this book, the riders who have found these principles demonstrate them in exactly the same way – they do the same, look the same and get the same results – consistently. But when they lose them, they all become totally unique, with individual idiosyncrasies which add spice to the challenge of teaching. It is the same with horses: in correct movement, they all essentially look and feel the same. I proved this to myself in practice long before I realised that if it were not the case, how could the rider ever know what correct movement was? But in his evasive movement patterns, each horse is unique. Evasions and problems come in families, but one can 'mix and match' them in endless different ways.

It is as if the correct way of sitting and interacting with the horse were like a pot of gold in the centre of a maze, each rider coming into the maze from a different entrance. She has to turn different corners, and go in different directions, and the path she has to follow is unique to her. Furthermore, neither she nor the horse enters the maze from exactly the same point on each day (a fact that Gina is just learning to appreciate). This is a complex situation – and whilst the searchers sweat and sigh, the pot of gold sits there, undisturbed by the efforts and the wrong turnings of all those who are questing after it. So does the person who has already found it.

For me, it belittles riding to reduce it to 'sit up straight and push your heels down', 'put your inside leg on the girth and your outside leg behind the girth'. But even if the twenty-first century saw riding teachers replacing these maxims by 'bear down and hold the pinch', 'keep each of your seat bones on the horse's long back muscles', I would not be sure if I had done riding a great favour. For the artistry lies in the subtle combinations – the nuances which trainer Erik Herbermann describes so beautifully when he talks about 'The Symphony of Aids'. Complexity and simplicity must go hand-in-hand. As soon as we lose one or the other, we are teaching a debauched version of the real thing. What is more, it cannot work.

Very few people, however, appreciate this paradox, and most take either one side or the other. It follows that some people will criticise me for being too simple and others for being too complicated. Some may say, 'It can't be that easy!' whilst others proclaim, 'Ah yes, it's all so obvious. *Of course* one has to keep one's seat bones on top of the horse's long back muscles.' Riders who have already found the pot of gold may well dismiss my attempts to communicate in words the complexities which they understand, but have no language for. Both to good riders, and to people who are looking for simple solutions, the intricacy of this work could seem quite unnecessary.

Inevitably, my approach is most appreciated by people who have spent years attempting to overcome certain problems, and who therefore value their solutions. But my aim is to go wider than this, and to reach people who have far more to gain than they currently realise. When our culture values learning higher than trying, and when people discover the potential that lies in using even 1 per cent more of the dormant 90 per cent of our brain power, the effects will be phenomenal. Our expectations, our teaching methods and our value systems will undoubtedly change. To me, riding is just the thin end of the wedge – a wonderful example of what the human body-mind is capable of learning, and of how sensitive a highly tuned human being (and a highly tuned horse) can become.

I particularly appreciate the scope of riding: it begins with the nitty-gritty pieces (seat bones, thigh muscles, knees and feet), and as the rider comes to terms with a seemingly endless list of these, she progresses into the stage of conscious competence. Here she learns about the laws of mechanics which underlie the rider/horse interaction. (She discovers the dangers of water-skiing and falling down the 'mantrap', and about the advantages of balancing her body weight over her base of support.) Knowledge of these laws – which are apparently so technical and mundane – ultimately refines riding to the degree that it takes on the subtlety and beauty of an art form. At this level, the attempt to keep track of all those nitty-gritty pieces gradually gives way to a sense of 'oneness' with the horse. This is the gateway to the seemingly mystical experiences which good riders regularly have with horses. Many riders glimpse these occasionally – and the longing for them spurs us on during times when the going gets tough. For whether we realise it or not, I believe that all of us crave these moments.

They become a possibility at the point when the rider and the horse both give up the 'agendas' that they brought to the session. (The horse's agenda might be, 'Oh no, not again. Where's my dinner?' or 'I'm so full of beans that I want to jump in the air!' The rider's might be, 'I mustn't let him get away with it!' or, 'I've got to get it right this time.') These imply that riding could well be a battle of wills, and perhaps also a battle of bodies. But in good work, both rider and horse *transcend* the conflicts inherent in their separate agendas. In effect, they both become so absorbed in what they are doing that they forget about dinner, and about the petty concerns of their personalities. This only becomes possible when the rider has cultivated the art of focussing and 'tuning' herself, so that she becomes 'centred'. Having done that, she is in a position to centre or 'tune' her horse. The rewards when she can do this are enormous, because the horse offers himself to her in what Erik Herbermann calls 'the blank cheque state'. The rider can 'write' on him whatever she will, and she has the magical experience that when she thinks something, it happens. If we could all reach the point where this was our norm, the ramifications for each individual, each horse – and even for society, and our future as a species – would be huge.

It seems paradoxical that understanding the laws of mechanics should develop the rider's sensitivity and intuition, allowing riding to become an art form. This is rather like music, and in both, a few underlying principles can be expressed subtly and uniquely in each moment, creating 'The Symphony of Aids'. But if riders attempt to over-simplify the theory and the practice of riding, they fall into the trap of 'obeying the rules'. (The effects of this are so enormous that it almost does not matter which rules these are!) Their riding becomes mechanistic: it is governed by *left-brain* logic, which is completely divorced from the body's ability to feel its way along. Only this tells the rider how to position herself, and how and when to make interventions. It also tells her whether her tactics are working, when each stage is complete and where she can go from there. This is a *right-brain* understanding of the whole – the basis of intuition.

When the rider has whole-brain knowing, she can both ride intuitively and break her skill down into pieces. She can then justify her actions in terms both of the laws of rider/horse interaction and the laws of physics. The laws of rider/horse interaction are to do with the detailed positioning of bones and muscles – the effects of the rider's framework on the horse's carriage. The laws of physics are primarily to do with centres of gravity. To understand their importance, consider the following: if you fix a metal ring around a javelin, the presence of that ring will alter the javelin's flight unless it is placed precisely at the javelin's centre of gravity. Then, it will fly as if the ring were not there. Or if you were to sit astride a tree trunk which was floating in a lake, you would need to sit precisely at its centre of gravity; for if you sat in advance of it, the front end would begin to sink, and if you sat behind it, the back end would begin to sink.* (It is this that makes climbing onto a lilo unbelievably difficult. In some ways, it is a pity that one's influence on the horse's stability is not equally obvious!)

In a similar way, the rider who does not sit above the horse's centre of gravity either overburdens his forehand or his hindquarters. When she sits in balance with him, *she burdens each of his limbs in exactly the same proportions as he does*: this means that if the horse naturally carries two-thirds of his weight on his fore limbs, then two-thirds of the rider's weight must be carried there too. There are two criteria for a 'balanced seat': the first is that the rider's centre of gravity is over her base of support. The second is that the rider's weight is supported by the horse's limbs in exactly the same proportions as his own. This may be a surprising definition to many people; but if we attempt to distribute our weight so that more of it is carried by the hindquarters – which many people think they should do – we only succeed in *overburdening* them.

The issue is complicated by a common misconception: many people will tell you that a horse is only in balance if all four of his limbs carry equal weight. Others have done research which suggests that it is extremely rare for the horse's hindquarters to carry equal weight to his forehand, even in the most collected work. Changes in the position of the horse's centre of gravity determine the movements produced; but these occur in the side-to-side plane

* These ideas, and the arguments that follow from them, were first put forward by Gregor de Romaszkan in his book *Riding Problems* (1968). Although I do not agree with all of his conclusions – and those I present here differ from his at times – I am very impressed by his work, and saddened that he never received the acknowledgement and respect which I feel he deserved. I am also indebted to Peter Wakeham in Melbourne, Australia, who introduced me to his work.

as well as the back-to-front plane. When the horse falls outwards on a circle, the outer legs are weighted more, and when he falls inwards, the inner legs are weighted more. I believe that all of the horse's legs are weighted differently in most movements, *even when they are performed correctly*. I do not deny that it is possible for all four legs to be weighted equally, but I am sure that it is rare.

During the course of the horse's training, the rider's task is to persuade him to burden his hindquarters more and his forehand less. As he does this, he increases the weight-bearing capacity of his quarters, which naturally decreases their propulsive force. As a result, his hind legs take the shorter, higher steps of collection. When he burdens them *less*, they have much more propulsive force, propelling him forward into the larger steps of extension, in which he lowers his head and neck and lengthens his frame. (This in turn moves his centre of gravity forward – as indeed it must in order to weight his fore limbs more and his hind limbs less.) But – and this is a big 'but' – the weight-bearing capacity of the quarters will only be increased when the horse *agrees* to this change: unlike the javelin or the tree trunk, he has some choice in the matter. When the horse's hindquarters are *overburdened* by the rider's way of sitting, he usually attempts to reduce the strain on them. Often, it is as if he says, 'Oh no you don't! I'm not falling for that one!' So what does he do? He decreases the load on them by increasing their propulsive force, and as a result, he plays the role of the motor boat. This is his natural response to the rider who overburdens his hindquarters by water-skiing; and her only hope is to change her body position so that she brings herself into balance with him, overburdening neither his forehand nor his quarters.

We are all taught to be concerned about the amount of weight naturally carried by the horse's forehand (and God forbid that we should add to it!). But our initial aim is not to *unburden* the forehand – it is to avoid *overburdening* it. This is subtly different. It may surprise you to discover that most naive riders overburden the horse's *hindquarters*, and in the early stages of our work together, many of them find that they have to sit much further forward in the saddle than they are used to. They also need to bring their body into the correct shoulder/hip/heel alignment, and to distribute their body weight down their thighs so that it is not concentrated in the 'mantrap'. Many riders are water-skiing to a degree, and the horse is towing them along; but when he becomes heavy in the rider's hand, she wrongly concludes that she must be overburdening his forehand. Miraculously, when her centre of gravity has 'caught up with' the horse's, she suddenly finds that her rein contact becomes lighter. Then she can begin to influence the centre of gravity of the *combined rider/horse system*, subtly bringing it back by changing her position and carriage, so that the horse changes his carriage too. But any attempts to do this *before* she has initially come into balance with him are doomed.

When riders *deliberately* lean back to ride an extension, they are bringing their centre of gravity back, and they utilise the mechanics of off-balance to produce the water-skiing effect as a temporary measure. However, as they increase the propulsive force of the horse's hind legs, their own and the horse's centres of gravity become maximally out of line with each other. The most classical trainers will tell you that this cannot be classed as a 'balanced seat', and that the rider should, if anything, lean *forward* slightly during an extension, so that her centre of gravity is still aligned with the horse's. A further difficulty arises because it is much harder to sit well if you lean forward, since the angle of the pelvis reduces shock absorption. In many cases, classical riders escape this dilemma by not riding extensions, or by riding them only in rising trot, and it is easy to understand why rising trot (in which one utilises the laws of balance instead of the laws of off-balance) is the easiest way to begin developing the extended gaits of a young horse.

A badly ridden half halt or downward transition, where the rider leans back and the horse continues to fall forward, pulling against her hand, is also a demonstration of off-balance (see Lessons 2 and 10 with Gail and Jill). I teach riders how to stay in balance during this time – 'plugged in', and out of the 'mantrap', with the push from their lower belly landing at the breast-plate. To help them maintain this, I suggest that they sit as if they were holding themselves up on the crest of a wave (see Lesson 10). They can only afford to lean back when they can keep themselves 'plugged in'; then, as the horse sits down their body is still at a ninety-degree angle to his back. For only this maintains their influence over the centre of gravity of the combined rider/horse system; if they 'unplug' themselves, they separate their own centre of gravity from the horse's – with disastrous consequences (see Diagram 20, page 185). In the downward transitions, the utilisation of the laws of balance is extremely important; but the utilisation of *off-balance* in the extensions is somewhat controversial, since it is against the rules of classical riding.

In the long term, the horse with overburdened hindquarters is often not willing to use extension as an option – it requires a great deal of adrenalin to keep pulling the rider along. Some horses are reluctant to do this at all, so their overburdened hindquarters may express the way they are hampered through making constricted, sluggish movements. This is extremely common – and the evasive patterns of many horses are built around their experience of having overburdened hindquarters. It is not valid to think – as many riders have done over the years – that the hind legs are like springs, so that the more you push them down, the more they bounce back up. When the rider pushes *down* in an attempt to liven up the hindquarters (and to compensate for the imposition of her weight), she does the equivalent of 'stopping the trampoline'. (Sarah was doing this with Swizzle in Lesson 6, although she thought that she was 'driving' or 'pushing' him forward.) 'Stopping the trampoline' can give the rider control of a rather 'fizzy' horse, but his impulsion and power are inevitably diminished, and she will all but stop a less forward-going horse. Riders very commonly *deaden* the horse's energy, either through misunderstanding or because it makes them feel safer; but they must instead learn to *channel* it, moulding its direction and form through the way in which they 'complete the circuit'.

It is this need to maintain the purity of the horse's impulse which leads some trainers to conclude that there is no such thing as 'the driving seat'. In its original use, this term might simply have referred to skilful use of the water-skiing effect. Leaning back and bearing down, both at the same time, constitute the action which Wilhelm Müseler discusses in *Riding Logic* when he draws an analogy between 'bracing the back' and pushing a swing. But he implies that this constitutes a half halt or stopping aid, and not a 'driving' aid – even though this action makes the swing move rather than stop! The term 'bracing the back' is not, I think, a good one. I talked with Carol in Lesson 8 about my understanding of 'using the back', and with Gail and Jill in Lessons 2 and 10 about the half halt and the stopping aid, emphasising the importance of *not* leaning back. (Müseler, perhaps, was one of the few riders who are capable of keeping themselves 'plugged in', sitting the horse down as they do this!)

'Driving' is a confusing term, which people use in different ways, thus complicating arguments about the existence of 'the driving seat'. When people tell me that they are 'driving the horse forward' or 'using their seat', they are usually shoving their seat about in the saddle and pressing strongly down with it – as Gail was doing in Lesson 2 or as Sarah was doing in Lesson 6. I often call these people 'down' riders. (Rarely are they leaning back, sitting still and bearing down, which we might accept as 'driving' – although I would rather not use this term at all.) If we define 'driving' according to this popular understanding of the term, then perhaps there really *is* no such thing as the 'driving seat', for (as we saw in Lessons 2 and 6) this does not work, regardless of whether the rider shoves her seat about or presses down hard with it.

At the opposite end of the scale, 'up' riders who 'ping' up off the horse's back and are thrown around by his impulse, are equally disadvantaged (see Lesson 7 with Margaret). Either way the rider breaks the circuit, and she can only hold it complete when she balances 'up' and 'down' correctly so that she becomes a very still, organised presence on the horse's back. She then takes responsibility for her own weight and transmits the impulse of the horse's step cleanly. She generates impulsion with very little movement of her body – for if it did move, she would interfere with her framework and the horse's carriage, and she would also compromise her way of transmitting his impulse. Instead of shoving, 'pushing' or 'driving' with her seat, she keeps her body from her knee upwards in place, so that it is 'still relative to the horse' (see Lesson 6 with Sarah and Lesson 9 with Gina). Then she sends the horse forward by using her lower leg, or the stick, and/or by utilising balance or off-balance to her advantage.

'Pushing', however (as I define it, and as I think it was originally meant), is a different thing entirely. It refers to the push from the back to the front of the rider's body as if she had no thickness. This culminates in her bearing down, which then becomes a push outwards towards the point on the horse's neck where a breast-plate would sit (see particularly Lesson 1 with Katie and Lesson 8 with Carol). This is *required* if the rider is to remain sitting at exactly the right point on the horse's back without bumping off it. Contrary to common opinion, 'pushing' does not involve any movement of the rider's backside in the saddle, or any 'push' downwards. (If we take 'driving' to mean the slight lean back which sends the horse forward, then neither does this.) These terms have become confused over the years, to the extent that they are now interchangeable, but it is much better to keep them separate and to define them carefully. I would suggest that you question any teacher who talks to you about them, and that you take care in the way you set about translating into action either their or my ideas. (Bear in mind, however, that people who cannot easily define or explain their terms tend to get very cross when asked!)

The critical factor is how the rider exchanges energy with the horse, so that she neither deadens his impulse nor is thrown about by it. She then has 'up' and 'down' in perfect balance: she both bears down and allows the horse to come up underneath her – as if he were a big balloon which she must not burst (see Lesson 8 with Carol). To achieve this, it is also helpful to think of bouncing a ball against the ground with your hand (this image transformed Jill's canter seat in Lesson 10), which is much more useful than the idea of pushing down springs. The first analogy encourages the rider to let the horse come fully *up* underneath her before she drops down with him, but the second emphasises the 'down' instead of the 'up'. When the horse's spring 'up' meets the rider's push 'down' at the wrong time (whether that stems from deliberate intervention or from bumping) her shock absorption becomes non-existent! When one is bouncing a ball, or bouncing on a trampoline, one does not make the mistake of deadening or hitting against the energy one is given. But when riding a horse the body does not have the same instinctive understanding of the dynamics that are operating.

When a rider overburdens the horse's forehand by sitting or leaning too far forward, he is usually more accepting of her weight than if she overburdens his hindquarters: he is unlikely to go, 'Oh no you don't!' and to sit himself down more. (Although, as we noted in Lesson 5 with Janet, the horse often does lift his head and neck in this situation, and despite the hollowness of his back and his trailing quarters, this does transfer his weight backwards.) When he has trouble 'keeping up with' the rider, he can easily escape the problem by lengthening his frame to move his centre of gravity forward and bring it underneath hers. Since his hindquarters are already unburdened, they should have enough propulsive power – and they are aided by the tendency of a weighted forehand to pull the horse along. Going fast also encourages the horse to lengthen his frame and transfer his centre of gravity forward – so he is likely to respond to the rider's overburdening of his forehand by running.

However, in this situation too, the horse can choose the evasive pattern which takes less energy, and then, the movement of his forehand becomes stuffy and restricted. Horses of this type are extremely reluctant to go forward, and it is difficult to get them to lengthen their stride – even to the degree that they produce the working gaits. The horse's back is usually so difficult to sit well on that it can be better to work him in rising trot: but the rider has to be extremely careful not to lean too far forward, for when she overburdens the forehand by *just a fraction*, the horse becomes even more stuffy. Horses with this pattern are so sensitive that looking down can be enough to make them fall into a restricted canter instead of lengthening their frame in trot!

None of the horses in these lessons showed this pattern developed to such a degree, but it is not uncommon, and such horses are very difficult for most riders to work with. They know that if they can keep the rider's centre of gravity in front of theirs, they can keep her powerless. Their determination can extend to nappiness – it is almost as if they are trying to crawl out backwards from underneath the rider! Like horses who expect or want the rider to water-ski, their evasive pattern sets up a self-fulfilling prophecy. When the horse is not going forward and the movement of his forehand is restricted, it is extremely difficult for the rider *not* to end up with her centre of gravity in front of his. It is equally difficult for her not to have her centre of gravity *behind* that of the horse who shoots out from underneath her like a bullet out of a gun, and who wants to play the role of the motor boat. Since the horse, of himself, will not volunteer to change this dynamic, it has to be the *rider* who makes adjustments, altering her body position to bring their centres of gravity into line.

Some of the riders in these lessons had to deal with a lesser degree of the evasive pattern which is produced by an overburdened forehand. They had to move *back* slightly in the saddle in order that the push out from their lower belly could land at the breastplate (see Lessons 5, 6 and 8 with Janet, Sarah and Carol). *This is an important diagnostic tool, which tells the rider when she has her centre of gravity in exactly the right place.* It also signifies that she is 'plugged in' to the 'receptors', which I speculate are at the end points of the horse's trapezius muscles.

These points, on a level with the tenth thoracic vertebra, are certainly very close to the centre of gravity, which lies a little behind the horse's wither. (If the horse carries 60 per cent of his weight on his forelegs and 40 per cent on his hind legs, then the centre of gravity divides the distance between them in the ratio 40:60.) Although we cannot know for sure, this suggests that the centre of gravity may lie on the same axis as the 'receptors'. The biophysicist, Dr Averil Cox, estimates that its position cannot move more than 2 inches (5 cm) from novice to collected work, so this is a tremendously refined system in which there is only a very small margin for error.

Janet, Sarah and Carol had already made corrections which brought their centre of gravity over their base of support, so they were not overburdening the horse's hindquarters by water-skiing (although they might well have been at the beginning of the lesson!). Neither was their weight concentrated down the 'mantrap', which again would put their centre of gravity too far back.

Stopping the rider from overburdening her horse's hindquarters is usually the first level of change to be made. Then, in the next level, the rider who is correctly aligned – and whose thighs are weight-bearing – suddenly finds that she is sitting too far forward and overburdening her horse's forehand: *because of her good weight distribution she can afford to move back in the saddle.* Interestingly, the evasive pattern which her horse produces in response to his overburdened forehand rarely makes him heavy in her hand – he just appears rather short-necked and stuffy. The horse which is heavy in the hand is usually either 'motor boating' or advancing his centre of gravity in a more subtle way. Instead of engaging his muscle ring and ligament system – which lifts and lightens the forehand (see Lesson 8 and Diagrams 14 and 15, pages 151 and 152) – he *lowers* his forehand and runs on, putting his centre of gravity fractionally in front of the rider's. Again, the horse is heavy in her hand, but she is overburdening his *hindquarters*. Her first task is to 'catch up with' him.

The rider who is overburdening the horse's forehand must make a two-pronged approach. Firstly, she moves herself back in the saddle (bringing her centre of gravity over that of the horse) and at the same time she puts more 'stuffing' out in front of her (which brings the centre of gravity of the combined rider/horse system back). To achieve these two, her movement backwards must be combined with the muscle use which aims the push from her lower stomach out to the horse's breast-plate. She must also be 'plugged in' and out of the 'mantrap', with her body weight aligned over her feet, otherwise she risks this manoeuvre returning her to the position where she overburdens the horse's hindquarters.

Put together, all of these are the rider's trump card, for the presence of the stuffing tells us that she has brought the horse's ring of muscles and his ligament system into play (see Lessons 7 and 8 to understand the detail of this). The stuffing fills out the horse's rib cage and back and makes his neck reach and arch out of his wither as if he were a brand new stuffed toy. He comes into the seeking reflexes and, metaphorically speaking, it becomes much harder for him to crawl out backwards from underneath the rider. (This does not mean, however, that his centre of gravity has come forward. The horse's forehand has *lifted and lightened* as a result of this muscle use. To understand this, think of a stallion prancing about in the presence of a mare and compare this with a rather old lumbering horse whose wither is dropped, whose quarters are trailing and whose neck hangs lower – much more like 'dead weight'.) By playing her trump card, the rider sits the horse down, and she does this without risking the dangers inherent in leaning back, where she so easily 'unplugs' herself and separates her centre of gravity from his.

When you think about the comparison with the javelin or the floating tree trunk, it is not surprising to realise that the sensitivity of the horse to the rider's weight and body positioning is as great as it undoubtedly is. I am convinced that there is always *one* right place, and right way, for the rider to sit – otherwise her centre of gravity is misaligned. The great classical Masters of riding knew this (but not in so many words) – hence their insistence on the rider's correct position. But given that the horse changes the proportions of the weight that he carries on each leg *with each step of each movement*, the implications of 'the balanced seat' are vast. The rider has to be unbelievably subtle and adaptable if she is to change the proportions of her weight accordingly so that she never overburdens any of his legs. At the same time, she has to keep her 'plugs' in contact with the 'receptors' at the end points of his trapezius muscles; but these two demands go hand-in-hand, and by satisfying one of them, she satisfies both of them. In fact, she has to go one stage further, and to *lead* the dance instead of following it, bringing the horse's 'receptors' and his centre of gravity with her every time she makes an adjustment. The limitation on her ability to do this is the limitation on her skill – and this is where her asymmetry and her lack of body control can really let her down.

Let me summarise all this (see also Diagram 21): the secret of good riding lies in gaining control of the centre of gravity of the combined rider/horse system, for only this makes the horse malleable and to gain this influence over him, the rider must firstly align her centre of gravity with his. If hers is too far forward he may well make an adjustment himself, lengthening his frame to bring his centre of gravity underneath it. Alternatively, he may decide to live with her overburdening, and as a result, the movement of his forehand becomes stuffy and restricted: he is behind the rider. If the rider is overburdening his quarters, he will *not* adapt by sitting himself down and moving his centre of gravity back: he is much more likely to resist this overburdening by increasing the propulsive force of his hind legs, so that he becomes the motor boat. Or again he may just live with the imposition of her weight, becoming restricted and stuffy in his movement behind.

The rider who has control of the positioning of both of their centres of gravity influences the horse on the back-to-front plane by utilising balance and off-balance to her advantage. By bringing her centre of gravity back a little, she can ride extensions. In her half halts – which bring the horse back to working and collected paces – she realigns her centre of gravity with his. This makes them become instantaneous and precise (unlike the half haul that one so often sees!). She can also stretch the horse out, lengthening his frame so that he reaches forward and down (see Lesson 3 with Jan), and she can bring him back up again into a more normal carriage. (Unlike changes between extension and collection, these changes can happen without affecting the speed at which the horse covers the ground, and this makes the mechanics of them slightly different.) One of the most important factors in creating them lies in thinking *either* of pushing out from the lower stomach to the breast-plate – as if you could push the horse's neck out and down, lengthening it away from you – *or* of imagining that his wither and the base of his neck could be hoisted up towards your navel, as if on a winch.

The rider who is truly causal can also influence the horse on the side-to-side plane. To understand how, remember the idea I used in Lesson 7 with Margaret: if the rider goes up to the top of her rise, and the horse falls onto his outside shoulder, the rider lands back in the saddle towards the inside, thus putting her centre of gravity towards the inside (see Figures 48 to 50 and Diagram 22). The horse then has a bigger bulge to the outside of his rib cage,

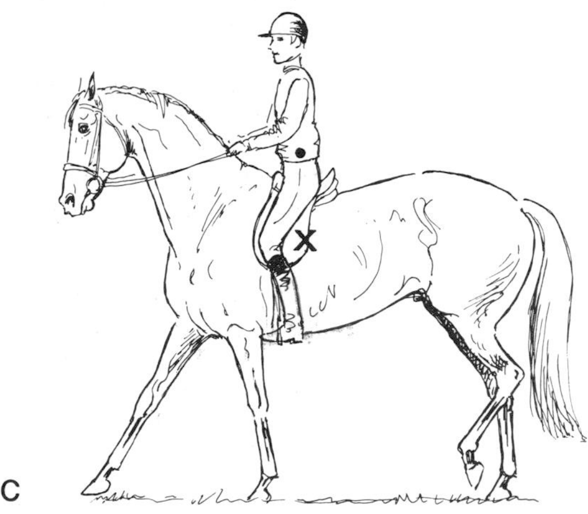

Diagram 21 (a). The rider's centre of gravity is behind that of the horse. To align them there are, in theory, two choices: the rider must advance her centre of gravity and/or the horse must bring his back. The rider can advance hers by sitting with a shoulder/hip/heel vertical line, by making sure that her body weight is carried all the way down the thigh to the knee and by thinking of sitting so that she does not fall into the 'mantrap'. This positions her as in (b).

When her centre of gravity is behind the horse's he may respond by saying (in effect):
1. 'I will not match you.' Then, his centre of gravity stays in front of the rider's, and he tows her along, acting like the motor boat and becoming heavy in her hand.
2. 'I will match you.' All the evidence suggests that the horse in this situation does not make this choice, which would move his centre of gravity back under the rider's, transferring weight to his hind legs.
3. 'I will endure this.' The horse then moves with restricted, hampered movement behind.
(c). The rider's centre of gravity is in front of that of the horse. To align them there are in theory two choices: the rider must move her centre of gravity back and/or the horse must bring his forward. The rider can bring hers back by moving back in the saddle, taking care to keep the correct shoulder/hip/heel line, with her weight taken down her thighs so that she stays out of the 'mantrap', as in (b).

When her centre of gravity is in front of the horse's, he may respond by saying (in effect):
1. 'I will not match you.' The horse in this situation contrives to keep the rider's centre of gravity in front of his, almost as if he is attempting to crawl out backwards from underneath her. He can become nappy and difficult to ride in this situation. He can also raise his head, which keeps his centre of gravity back behind the rider's.
2. 'I will match you.' The horse does this very easily, by lengthening his frame to bring his centre of gravity forward and underneath the rider's.
3. 'I will endure this.' The horse then has restricted, hampered movement in front.

The rider's task is to align her centre of gravity with the horse's, then she can gain control of the centre of gravity of the combined rider/horse system. Only this enables her to adjust the horse's carriage so that he 'sits down' and bears more weight on his hind legs.

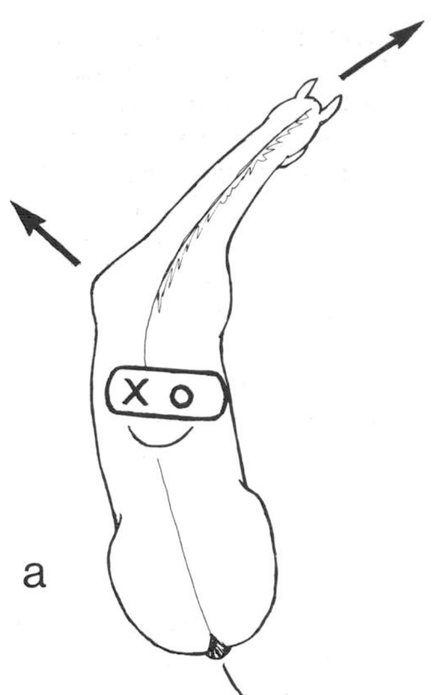

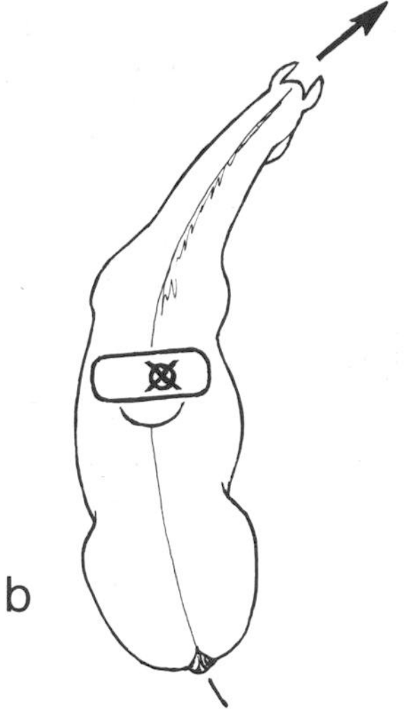

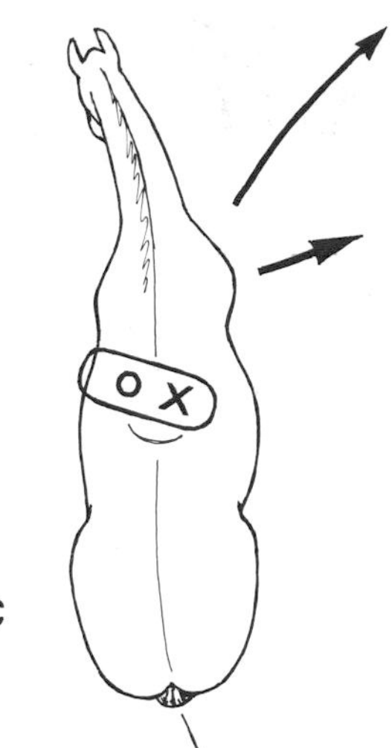

X HORSE'S CENTRE OF GRAVITY
O RIDER'S CENTRE OF GRAVITY

Diagram 22 (a). The horse falls onto his outside shoulder, leaving the rider sitting to the inside. Relative to her, the horse is bulging outwards, and she has to adjust her sitting so that, relative to her, he has more bulge to the inside. This gives her a correct bend rather than a 'jack-knife'. In effect, she is placing her centre of gravity directly over his, so that she gains control of the centre of gravity of the combined rider/horse system. Primarily, she brings her inside seat bone closer to his spine, and then thinks of drawing his inside long back muscle outwards. This helps her to find the right points for her 'plugs' to fit in to.

(c). The horse falls onto his inside shoulder, leaving the rider sitting to the outside. Relative to her, there is too much bulge to the inside, and she has to adjust her sitting so that, relative to her, there is more bulge on the outside. This will create a correct bend. In effect, she is placing her centre of gravity directly over his, so that she gains control of the centre of gravity of the combined rider/horse system. She also aligns her 'plugs' with the 'receptors' at the end points of the horse's trapezius muscles, finding the correct position for the 'merry-go-round'. Then, when the rider is causal, movement of her seat bones causes the equivalent movement in the horse's 'receptors', and they remain united in a way which makes them move as one.

and his centre of gravity is displaced that way. (The fact that he falls in that direction is a demonstration of this.) When the rider thinks of sitting so that, *relative to her, there is more bulge of horse on the inside*, she is actually bringing her centre of gravity to the outside, *over that of the horse*. This also puts her seat bones back on top of his long back muscles (see Diagram 11, page 137), lining them up with his 'receptors'. By gaining control of the centre of gravity of the combined rider/horse system, the rider gains control of the bend and the steering. This happens purely from her pelvic positioning, without the need to pull the horse about with her hand.

The converse is equally true, so when the horse falls onto his inside shoulder, the rider tends to land in the saddle towards the outside. Since the horse will not volunteer to change the positioning of his centre of gravity, the rider must change the placing of hers: this time she must match him by sitting more to the inside. Then, relative to her, there will be a bigger bulge of horse to the outside, and she will have succeeded in changing his bend. She is only completely successful when her inside seat bone finds the exact placing of the 'merry-go-round' (see Lesson 10 with Jill), for then her seat bones are positioned over the 'receptors' in the end points of the horse's trapezius muscles. In actual fact, her centre of gravity must be slightly to the inside of his, because the central axes of both their bodies are angled inwards, like a bicycle rider going around a turn (see Figure 62). This precise positioning of the rider's body gives her control of the placing of her own centre of gravity, and through this, she gains control of the combined rider/horse centre of gravity. She also becomes able to use her body as a framework around the horse, holding him in shape. This makes the horse malleable, and with this fine control she becomes all powerful, yet totally gentle. She becomes, in the words of T. S. Eliot, 'the still centre of the turning world'.

I once read an article by the Hungarian trainer Charles de Kunffy in the American magazine *Dressage and Combined Training*. In it, he talked about the rider's two tool kits: the first is her body, which she uses as a tool to influence the horse's carriage and movement. In theory, de Kunffy states, this is all that she needs. But in addition to this she also has the school movements, which can be worked in various configurations to help her glean the best movement from her horse and to bring him into self-carriage. It must be apparent by now that I am primarily a teacher of the first tool kit, and I am a great believer in its potency. I also believe, given my experiences with trainers from different schools, that this is what the Masters were attempting to teach – even though they often lacked the skills to pass on their knowledge to all but the most talented of pupils.

Long before I had a detailed understanding of the influence of the rider's centre of gravity on the horse's evasive patterns, I based my work around the first tool kit and the concept of completing the circuit. When a trainer does not acknowledge the importance of these, she frequently dooms her pupil to fail. In my own lessons, I have often felt tortured by the teacher's insistence that I should ride complicated movements when I was not sitting well, and my horse was not moving well, or correctly flexed – signs that my centre of gravity was not correctly positioned and that the circuit was not complete. This has happened particularly in my work with competition-based trainers. Since I rarely felt that I learnt anything or improved in this situation, I began to ask myself, 'Is riding about making the best of a bad job, or is it about developing the tools to do a good job?'

I have absolutely no wish to inflict this kind of torture on anybody else, and I also have no wish to watch horses and riders going round and round the school continually repeating the same mistakes – even when they have the honour of repeating them in the more advanced movements! So I usually begin with what looks, superficially, like very simple work – so simple that it could appear boring to someone who did not realise the importance of the correct rider/horse interaction and of setting a correct 'blueprint' within the body's neurology.

I think of these two tool kits as being rather like pure and applied mathematics. Firstly you have to learn the tools of pure mathematics, so that you understand algebra, trigonometry and calculus, etc. Then you can use them to solve the problems of applied mathematics (e.g., how much weight is required to balance a lever which has a 5 kg load at a distance of 3.5 m from the fulcrum?). Having taught the rider the elements of pure mathematics (or 'pure riding'), we can then apply her knowledge, riding the school movements as tests: in effect they challenge the rider, asking, 'Can she remain causal as she moves onto a circle, or rides a transition? Can she keep her correct positioning through a change of bend, or a lengthening of the stride, or into a lateral movement? Where are the limits of her knowledge and skill?'

I think few trainers would argue with the idea that the rider ideally chooses to work herself and her horse in their stretch zones, building outwards from a base of simple work that they can both do well. (Of course, their stretch zones may well not match up – for instance when an inexperienced rider is working a trained horse, or when a more experienced rider is performing very straightforward work on a green horse. But both of their performances improve enormously through finding the 'stretch' that is inherent in any situation.) The edges of the rider's and the horse's stretch zones may vary from day to day, and from moment to moment, the skilled rider noticing and respecting these differences – so she does not plummet herself and her horse into the frenzy and conflict that are inevitable once they enter their panic zones. She also limits the debilitating effects of fatigue by resting herself and her horse in their comfort zones. Her work is structured very carefully, and she has no difficulty knowing what she should do and how she should do it.

But which approach achieves this more easily? The trainer who primarily utilises the first tool kit, and the trainer who primarily utilises the second, each perceive cause and effect as working in opposite ways. The question is, 'Does riding the school movements cause the horse to move well, or does the horse who is moving well perform good movements?' In my work, I choose the gait, movement and positioning for the horse which will most support the rider in her learning. (In the early stages this can mean that we often go large in walk!) I may choose to work the horse on a certain rein, on a circle, or using the whole arena – either because this will make the rider's task easier or because it will set her a certain challenge. But I do not choose movements just because they come next in the progression which one would usually expect to ride. (Typically, this happens when the teacher falls into the trap of basing her instructions on what *she* would do next on this horse if *she* were riding him.) I believe that any movement which makes the rider reactive is not worth repeating – not unless the rider is breaking new ground and making discoveries which will, in time, make her causal in this situation too.

'Pure riding' is primarily the ability to gain control of the positioning of the centre of gravity of the combined rider/horse system. This – when it is coupled with the ability to transmit the horse's impulse cleanly – enables the rider to complete the circuit. The horse becomes *malleable* and the rider becomes able to mould his body into shapes and movements, rather as a potter moulds a form out of clay. Superficially, she may appear to work and learn very slowly, but the power of what she is learning is phenomenal – and by being willing to go slowly she ultimately finds that she is progressing unusually fast. But there is much more kudos in being seen to teach and ride complicated school movements, and it looks much more exciting. But who will have more kudos in the end: the rider whose advanced work is marred by some fundamental flaws, or the rider who can reproduce the classical ideal?

I think of the process of learning to ride as being rather like putting pieces into a puzzle. I begin with what I consider to be the most important pieces – although to an untrained eye they are barely visible. I then work outwards to the large, obvious, external pieces – the movements themselves. Beginning like this with 'pure riding' is very different from beginning with the movements – the outer and visible pieces – in the hope that the horse and rider will 'gel', finding the inner, invisible pieces as they go along. Most movements/competition-based trainers value *performance* more highly than *learning*, which increases the danger that even if the rider does find them (and produce good work), she will go away from the session without the ability to reproduce the gains she has made. This, to me, has limited value (and in Lesson 10 with Jill there is an example of the way in which I value learning more highly than performance). I would rather see the rider create a smaller but more far-reaching change, knowing that she has every chance of reproducing it on her own.

Once the rider is ready, however, 'applied riding' obviously has its place – just like applied mathematics – and she learns how to position her body and remain causal in the more complicated school movements. In time her influence extends even into situations which tend to compound the horse's evasions (as travers left does for King in Lesson 10). Then I can interact with the rider much more like a movements-based trainer. During our lesson, I offer her little reminders which she knows exactly how to implement ('Keep your inside hip to his opposite ear,' 'Remember the diving board,' 'Are you still on ten to four?'), which are enough to keep her on the straight and narrow path. The reminders given to the rider in a traditional lesson, however, often have the disadvantage that she does not know how to implement them! In effect, she has not learnt enough 'pure riding', and the extent of this knowledge within each individual determines how well the 'applied' approach will work for her. For me, it only becomes the medium of choice once the rider is causal and the circuit is complete. Working the horse through the movements is an interesting challenge, but it does not excite me as much as doing transformative work with the rider. When I give a movements-based session (perhaps in helping a rider to prepare for a dressage test), I walk away from it feeling rather unfulfilled, even if the horse has worked well. Because I have not taught the rider anything, it can feel to me – when I collect my fee – like receiving money for old rope.

The major argument used against my approach is that it can be 'boring' for the horse: inevitably, the focus of my work is initially on the rider, and the horse may have to go round and round for a while as she sorts herself out and establishes her influence over him. With some rather cunning horses who are reluctant to come into the correct carriage, this can set up a Catch 22 situation, for the only way to complete the circuit is to bamboozle them by riding plenty of different movements. But this is not often the case. (It pays to know what kind of brain your horse has between his ears before you ever start learning on him, as this has such a huge influence on the enormity of your task!) At the other end of the scale, I do not let the horses go to sleep: I demand, as you saw in Lesson 2 with Gail, that their brains are 'switched on', and that they are interacting with the rider. One often does not see this in riding schools, where most of the horses go round and round like zombies. Many club-level riders do not demand this of their horses either, which creates a severe limitation on their learning and performance.

Whatever the horse's evasive pattern, we need to put him in the state where his body and mind become available to the rider: he may need to be slowed down, woken up or positioned in a certain way. This is where the two schools of thought which utilise the first and second tool kits can meet – but all too often in a movements-based lesson, the horse is not challenged on this level, so he performs all his movements half asleep or running too fast. Teaching the rider about cause and effect in simple situations challenges the horse much more than one might expect – and even if it does not, is his plight worse than having the rider pull him about as she attempts to ride the movements? Which of these furthers his training more, and which one will ultimately make his work more correct?

Whichever way we go about our learning, the horse inevitably has to suffer to a degree. I attempt to minimise this, but I also accept that it is how he earns his keep on our planet. If he wants to be worked (and not eaten), he will have to live with our failings. But in the work I do, he can suddenly find that life is not so easy as he thought it was – not because of the demands of complicated school movements etc., but purely because of the change created by the rider in the way that he carries his body and moves his legs. I often tease riders by saying that they, at least, paid their money to come; they came voluntarily, and they had some idea of what they were letting themselves in for. But the horse did *not* volunteer, neither has he an intellectual framework for understanding the changes that are taking place in his body – and which must feel just as strange and taxing to him as they do to the rider! Because of this, my work is not the simple alternative it might appear to be initially.

I often hear people talking in a very simplistic way about the horse's movement patterns, and it seems to me that they do not understand the changes involved. It is true that horses usually move (and jump) much better at liberty than they do when they are ridden, and it can be both exciting and devastating to see what they can produce without our hindrance. But this is still not the horse's *very best* movement, for he will naturally carry his rib cage to one side, weight one hind leg more than the other and turn – whenever possible – in one preferred direction. Only on rare occasions will he activate his muscle ring and his ligament system. Like people walking down the street, horses all have their own idiosyncratic 'kinks'; and like people, some are much more 'kinked' than others.

To complicate the issue, they naturally turn by leaning on their inside shoulder, counter-balancing this by carrying their head and neck to the outside: this is much less stable than a turn with the correct bend, but this instability does not matter when there is no added load on their backs. (If you have ever ridden a horse who leans in like this, you will know just how unstable it becomes when there is!) So the rider's job is to influence the horse's natural carriage and movement – for better, not worse – and when it comes to turning, she has to persuade him to choose a mechanism which is completely different from his natural inclination.

I like to think that I do body work with horses, working on them in much the same way that an Alexander teacher might work on me. This is the skill that I love, and it is what I endeavour to teach. But if you have ever learnt riding using my techniques, or if you have ever been to a body worker, you will realise just what is involved in the changes that you (and also the horse) are asked to make. I do everything I can to maximise the rider's chances of reproducing at home the new patterns she has learnt – but I still leave her with a difficult task. My own most profound example of ingraining a change in my neurology happened when I first began, with the help of my Feldenkrais teacher, to get to the bottom of a pattern which had affected my left leg. The first time she shifted it I did not really realise what had happened until I got up from her table and walked around the room. The difference in my walk was enormous, and although it seemed strange, there was an accompanying feeling of rightness. I sat down on a chair to pay her, and to consult my diary: but when I got up, it was almost as if the change had never happened. I had been given a glimpse of the promised land, but there was nothing I could do to get it back. To make it worse, my old walk – familiar and comfortable for over thirty-five years – now felt ghastly!

After my next lesson, I held the new pattern as I walked out of her consulting room (I had realised meanwhile that it was important not to sit down!), but by the time I reached the bottom of the stairs it was gone. Again, my neurological wires had hooked themselves back up in their old familiar way, and my conscious mind lacked the tools to rearrange them. Over time I began to hold the new pattern as I travelled home, and then for the next few hours and days. But I remember very clearly, some months later when I was getting much better at it, rushing around Knightsbridge in the January sales, with my left leg feeling like a hunk of wood . . . and to my despair, none of the tricks which I had successfully used to influence it had any effect at all. Now, about three years later, the new pattern is still vulnerable: I often think about it, and I sometimes lose the good walk, but now I can easily find my way back to it.

With this particular pattern, I went through an unusually long and arduous process, getting it and losing it over and over again, as I gradually ingrained it in my neurology. (Do not be put off by this, please – many patterns are much easier to shift, and even here, the rewards for me have been well worth the effort!) At times when I could not shift the pattern walking, I found that I could do it riding, and that this then helped my walk. I practise my walk as I stomp around riding arenas – and it feels wonderful to get off a pupil's horse and find that I am walking very much better! At other times, my walking has helped my riding – which has improved enormously as a result of this change.

There are two important underlying issues here: I am extremely motivated in this kind of work, but any body worker will tell you how reluctant people usually are to change their habitual patterns – even when they are offered extremely good tools to help them. I have learnt to welcome the new and unfamiliar, but some people are scared off by it, particularly when they have not yet discovered the rewards waiting for them just around the corner. There is also the inevitable inertia: when you remember to sit up straight, how long do you usually remain in that posture before the desire to slouch takes over? (Bear in mind, though, that you may well, like Val in Lesson 4, be attempting to do this in a way that can never really work!) The next problem – even when you welcome the change, and you have made the *right* change, is the difficulty that I had here – the difficulty of reproducing it.

Fortunately, as I am a person and not a horse, no one threatened to beat me when I failed in this – and, thank God, I am well past the stage of metaphorically beating myself! I recognise that this process takes time, and this is why I expect most riders to take about two years to reach a basic stage of correctness in their riding. But supposing I had been a horse with a similar problem. How would my rider have responded to my predicament? Even the horse who is doing really well might react to the atmosphere of a competition just as I reacted to the January sales . . . and this is bound to cause displeasure. The horse's experience is, I am sure, at least as difficult as ours – and he did not choose it.

Firstly, he may not welcome the new and unfamiliar, so he may be happier in his cramped, asymmetrical movement pattern than he is when we straighten him out. Cries of, 'But surely it must be easier and nicer for him!' are both true and not true. A friend told me recently about her Grand Prix dressage horse who is absolutely reliable in the flying changes even at one-time, except when he has just been manipulated by a body worker who pays particular attention to the asymmetrical carriage of his rib cage. With his posture corrected, he often leaves a leg behind in the flying changes for the next few days, and then he returns to normal. I wish this were not true, because it undermines my arguments about correctness – and perhaps the story would be different if my friend had been able to straighten him by riding him more effectively in the early stages of his training. His old pattern might or might not be comfortable, but at least it is 'home', and horses undoubtedly vary in the relief, or the reluctance, that they show when asked to change their carriage. At times, we like the beauty and efficiency of straight movement in the 'seeking reflexes' very much better than they do!

As my experience shows, it is not easy to 'press the button in your brain' which goes to the muscles you want. Even when you are highly motivated and you concentrate well, it is difficult to reproduce this feeling even some of the time, and to live with the 'weirdness' and the weakness of it. If any horse I am working has half the trouble weighting his left hind leg that I have weighting mine, he has my sympathy! I delight in these changes, but horses have no inherent desire for them, no motivation and little concentration. The difficulty of reproducing them within the school movements is gradually increased by situations which are emotionally more taxing and gymnastically more demanding. If the rider is not careful, and she tries to do too much too soon, the horse starts to look for new ways to escape the 'weirdness' and the weakness. (This can happen too, even if she has not attempted to change his basic movement patterns.) New evasions are very easily born.

The horse who is involved in this work does not get bored: his brain is 'switched on', he is held in his stretch zone, and his movement patterns are being continually but carefully challenged. The rider makes it extremely difficult for him to move badly and to maintain his habitual breaks in the circuit; and by placing herself so that she does not overburden either his forehand or his quarters, she makes it as easy and natural as possible for him to move well, and to mend those breaks. The school movements then become an added challenge which strengthen his new movement patterns. Without this approach, there is a danger that he will perform all the school movements 'after a fashion', with his own idiosyncratic 'kinks'. These are highly likely to hamper his athleticism and provide the major limitations on the correctness of his work.

Some time ago I decided to start interviewing very successful riders who were not familiar with my work, to find out how they dealt with the problems that most riders are faced with in learning and competing. In particular, I wanted to contrast their experience with the average club- or novice-level competitor. (I am very familiar with the struggles of these people, since so many of them have talked in detail during the courses and workshops they have come to.) In general, what I found was no surprise: in fact, it was very validating for me to discover that almost all of the successful competitors owned up to the kinds of difficulties that have perplexed me and many others – they were not immune. At the same time, they had not fallen into the traps which beset riders who remain stuck at the lower levels.

It was very gratifying for me to find an attitude of great humility and commitment amongst these riders: I hope it is not too precious to call them 'seekers after truth'. They were obviously doing all they could to bring themselves closer to the ideal of the straight and narrow path. In my experience this is a significant contrast to the many riders who have had just a little success. When the world appears to validate their work, they can all too easily remain in the dangerous position where they do not know what they do not know.

One superb example of the difference in the way that club-level and highly skilled riders operate was brought home to me when I interviewed a successful event rider from Australia. I had previously been talking to a club-level rider, and I had asked her, 'Do you talk to yourself very much as you ride, and, if so, what do you say?'

'Oh yes,' she said. 'I talk to myself all the time. There's this critical voice in my head, and it keeps telling me what I've just done wrong, and what I ought to be doing. It berates me for not getting it right, and asks, "Are you ever going to be any good?" '

When I asked the event rider the same question, she said, 'No, never. I don't talk to myself at all.' I began to chuckle, and when she asked me what I was laughing about, I told her about this other rider, whose experience is, I believe, very common. She looked at me in amazement: 'Do people really do that?' she asked. 'That's amazing!'

Some while ago, I gave what I felt was an extremely good lesson to a young rider whom I only see occasionally. At times, she has ridden very well, but she always seems to pass through these phases and come out the other side into much less inspiring work. So I asked her, 'What happens?' She too had a voice in her head. Whilst she was riding, she continually rated herself on a scale of perfection, and in order to feel satisfied she had to reach at least a seven out of ten. As soon as her riding rated less than seven, one of two things happened: either she heard her own voice inside her head, firing her up and saying, 'Come on! You've got to do it. You're not going to give up. You're going to get this horse going whatever . . .' Or she heard a much more depressed voice saying,

'You'll never be able to do it, you might as well give up now. All these years of trying and you still can't get it right . . .' At times, when she began to get exhausted from her efforts, the first voice would give way to the second. Inevitably, her riding went through patches of determined trying, and patches where she felt like giving up – and only rarely did she find some middle ground.

To help her, we did several things: firstly, she took time to actually *listen* to the voices – she had only been half aware of them before – and she was shocked to realise just how much influence they had on her. We also found that the voices came from the right side of her head, and that if she shifted them over to the left they became much less believable. (This girl is not crazy – almost everybody talks to themselves, and the voices always have a location. Changing this can often dramatically change the influence the voices have on the feelings and behaviour of their owner.) We then found that when she talked to herself in the most helpful and inspiring way, the voice came from the front of her head, and it talked to her far more gently: 'It's OK if you can't do it now,' it said, 'you *will* do it in time. Just think things through: what's missing?' She could now stop the tyranny of the old voices and reassure herself with this new one. As a result, she no longer felt that she had to either reach a seven out of ten or give up, and with much more leeway for error she can live more comfortably with herself regardless of how she rides. Not surprisingly, she rides better too, and she talks to herself much less. She tells me that she now feels very much happier about her riding and her learning, and that her new strategy has also made a difference in other areas of her life.

The tell-tale signs of poor mental functioning – and the biggest killers when it comes to learning – are internal dialogue, focussed vision and excess tension. (This tension is not to be confused with the high muscle tone required in the working muscles of the body. One most often sees excess tension in shoulders, hands and arms, necks and jaws.) None of the good riders I talked to used much internal dialogue, although they often talked to their horses. I sometimes talk to myself in 'shorthand'; I might say, 'Whoops!' to myself, where once upon a time I would have given myself a lengthy talking to, along the lines of, 'Oh dear, that was very silly and I really ought to know better, and I must remember to put my outside leg behind the girth . . .' This is all wasted energy, and as I said earlier, it stops the rider from feeling what is happening. It also happens far too slowly for her to be able to keep up with her horse's bright ideas and to make the corrections which so quickly become necessary.

Some of the good riders I interviewed found that they tended to talk to themselves whenever they were worried about something external to their riding. Typically this concerned staff or horse owners, feed merchants or blacksmiths. The nitty-gritty problems of life, they felt, stole energy from their riding, and were the biggest threat to their consistency and performance. I taught one of them how to hum to herself when she began to work a horse and found that other thoughts were intruding. I learnt this trick from one of my teachers, whom I think did not even realise what she was doing! If you try it, you will find that it is extremely difficult to hum (anything will do, it can be absolutely tuneless) *and* have an internal dialogue at the same time. Once you have begun to concentrate, however, the humming will stop of its own accord – and so will the worries.

It is a joke between sports psychologists that if you approach a club-level competitor and say, 'Tell me about a good day,' and also, 'Tell me about a bad day,' you get very different answers from the ones you get from a successful rider. The club-level rider will tell you, 'Well, sometimes I have a good day and it's all so wonderful!' The detail of what happens is unknown to her. But when it comes to the bad day she will say, 'Well, I can feel my heart pounding, and then I begin to bump, and my left leg starts to wobble about, and then the horse begins to . . .' all in much greater detail. The successful rider, on the other hand, can tell you very much more about the good day: 'I can always tell when it's going to be good because of this feeling I get inside. And everything is so clear that it seems to happen in slow motion. My sitting is particularly good and . . .'. But when it comes to the bad day, she says, 'Well, sometimes it does go wrong,' with none of the accompanying detail.

From this, we can draw the agonising conclusion that the club-level rider knows much more about how to do it *wrong* than she knows about how to do it *right*: furthermore, if she *does* ride well, she usually says, 'Well, that doesn't really count, because it was only a few minutes.' She discounts her good experiences, whereas the skilful rider *grows* them. This is almost like putting a crystal in a super-saturated solution: like attracts like and very soon there is a much bigger crystal than the one you started with. Even a few moments of good sitting, or one good corner, can become fuel for future learning. Bad days, on the other hand, are discarded (whereas our club-level rider will go over and over them in her mind, torturing herself with her mistakes!). One very successful rider told me that she has a very clear memory of several particularly momentous rides, which she uses to cheer herself up when things are not going right. What is she doing? She is feeding her brain with the correct 'blueprint', so that it does not get entrenched in the wrong pattern. Nobody has taught her to do this: it came naturally to her – a lucky accident which serves her extremely well. As I said earlier, it is very unfortunate that the most sophisticated technology on earth does not come with a user's manual. If it did, little tricks like this would be everyday fare for all of us.

I was disappointed to discover that the top riders I interviewed were, I felt, somewhat restricted in their use of mental rehearsal. All of them related it almost solely to competition, and not to learning: they used it extensively before a dressage test or a jumping round, and they had tremendous detail in the feelings and the pictures that they created – but it was rarely a part of their behind-the-scenes work at home. Some of the jumping riders told me that the most important element in their mental rehearsal was the sound of the horse's hoof beat. The feels and the sights were both secondary to this sense of the rhythm, which was like the 'carrier frequency' for everything else. This was less strong in their rehearsals of flatwork, which were based more on feel.

One well-known dressage rider told me that whenever he was mentally rehearsing something which he expected to be difficult, he did it from the perspective of being inside his own body: he felt what he would feel and saw what he would see, with the horse's neck out in front of him, etc. But as soon as the content of what he was rehearsing was so straightforward that he expected no problems, he saw himself from the perspective of an observer – as if someone had taken a video of his test. Whenever some movement within his mental rehearsal did not come out in the way he wanted, he automatically went over it again: this was like a video recorder going into rewind – the tape sped backwards, and then he rode the movement again, correctly this time. Sometimes, he told me, he spent a great deal of time going backwards!

Most of the riders I talked to seemed to use a mixture of mental rehearsals in which they were inside their own body and those where they were seeing themselves from the perspective of an observer. One told me that until the advent of video, she had never thought of imagining how she looked. Now, she made sure that she was videoed before any major competition, and seeing what her mistakes looked like motivated her to spend a good deal of time imagining the feel of the corrections she must make. Another always used to do it from this external perspective, but at one point she spontaneously discovered that she could base her mental rehearsals on feel rather than vision. She was convinced that this made them significantly more effective. However, she was in the habit of doing them in bed at night, and a few years ago she would always fall asleep before she got to the end of the Grand Prix test. Not surprisingly, she never rode the end as well as she rode the beginning!

Some of my pupils – particularly those who have been on dismounted workshop courses with me – have become extremely creative in their use of mental rehearsal. I was tremendously impressed by one woman, who had also had mounted lessons with me on her own horse. This was a typical 15.2-hand thoroughbred cross. On him, she had begun to recognise and create the right feelings, and he was working well. When she came on a residential course without him, I asked her to ride a big warmblood. This woman is a lightweight rider who is barely over five foot, and she had never ridden a horse of this type before. On the first day she struggled, and although she improved during the lesson, she did not 'complete the circuit', and she went away feeling disappointed. However, the next day, as I was teaching someone else, I became aware that she was warming up in the field beside the arena; out of the corner of my eye, I kept seeing this horse moving past me in extremely good carriage.

'What did you do?' I asked her at the beginning of her lesson.

'Well,' she said, 'I was so fed up with myself that I went away and used mental rehearsal on the feeling I had from him yesterday, and the feeling I had from myself too. Then I compared them with the feelings I get on my own horse. I soon realised what had gone wrong, so I corrected it within the mental rehearsal, and then I came out today and rode it . . .' This is a superb example of self-motivated learning. What is more, it did not cost her a penny.

Another pupil of mine has told me about riding her horse before work each morning. She then has to rush to her office, and during her working day there is little time to think about riding. But at home in the evening, she sits quietly and contemplates her session of the morning. She too recognises the correct feels, but does not manage to produce them all of the time: as she reviews what she did, she usually finds that a voice inside her head realises what the problem was, and tells her, 'You twit, you forgot to X!' So she puts the missing piece into her mental rehearsal and finds out what effect it has. Then she goes out the next day and rides it.

Often the answer is much more obvious away from the heat of the moment than it is when you are sweating hard, and many of my important breakthroughs have come in mental rehearsal. (This becomes progressively easier, of course, as you begin to put more of the major pieces into the jigsaw.) Only the other day, I was teaching someone, and musing to myself about the feeling I had had when I was riding her horse: then I came up with a completely new idea, which I thought would solve the problem I had been having. When I got on and tried it, it fitted exactly. Very soon, it will become part of how I teach; but if I had used mental rehearsal only in competitive situations, my progress as a rider and a teacher would have been very much slower – even if I had been competing as regularly as most of the people I interviewed.

The top riders varied enormously in how consistent they were, and in how satisfied they were with their own performance. One rider told me that he felt that about one in ten of his schooling sessions at home lived up to his expectations! Others felt that they rode well enough almost all of the time, and that they had two or three days per month which were outstanding. One event rider was particularly disturbed by his lack of consistency in competition: when there was no chance of winning, he rode his best. But as soon as there was a chance of winning, mistakes crept in. This particularly affected his show jumping. After jumping a number of jumps very well, he would almost always meet one of them on a wrong stride – his horse would stand off and hit it or make an extremely awkward jump. He felt that his mind did not trust his body, and he was uncertain what he should do about it.

On the one hand, he was tempted to work on his technique, and develop that trust through gaining a very detailed and conscious knowledge of what to do. On the other hand, he was tempted to go out and jump really big fences – so big that he put himself in the 'do or die' situation which always brought out the best in him across country. To make the situation more distressing for him, he had ridden a great deal as a teenager, when he had been a 'natural' rider who never thought about anything but did everything exceptionally well. Then, he gave up riding, and came back to it years later: to his chagrin, he felt that he had lost his touch. His body had lost its natural balance, he was not so fearless and his reactions were slow. So as an adult, he was always comparing himself with this idealised memory of how he rode in his youth, and of course he could never live up to it. Although he is highly ranked in the world ratings, he cannot satisfy himself – a painful situation.

His dilemma expresses a question I often ask myself: in performing at this level, will conscious thought help him or hinder him? The answer, I think, is that it depends what he is thinking about. If he finds the right key on which to focus, and discovers the difference which really makes the difference, this will enable his mind to trust his body even in these very testing situations. (In effect, this is what Nick Faldo has done.) If he goes out and jumps very big jumps, I suspect that even if he solves his problem over these, the answer will *not* automatically generalise to the smaller jumps – where the scope for hesitation or kamikaze bravery will still exist. (It does not, after all, generalise from cross-country, where he does not have this problem, into show jumping, where he does.) So which will win out in the end – 'automatic pilot' or conscious knowing?

Perhaps there is no right answer, for the riders I interviewed also varied enormously in the degree of conscious knowledge they have about *how* they do what they do. Some had obviously been through a learning process which had included an important phase of conscious competence – and they had access to conscious knowledge which they knew would get them out of a tricky situation. Others had not: they had stumbled upon unconscious competence very early in their learning, but in some cases they felt that when things did go wrong, they had nothing to 'hold on to'. I found the most extreme example of unconscious competence in a dressage rider, when I asked him, 'What do you pay attention to when you are riding?'

He thought for a few moments, and then answered, 'The horse's brain, and what he's thinking.'

So I asked him, 'Has there ever been a time when you did not do this, and when you had to think about yourself and what you were doing instead?'

He thought for even longer this time: 'I don't think so,' he said, 'but wait! Yes, there was. I remember. It was the first time I ever rode one-time changes!'

In his book *The Pursuit of Sporting Excellence*, David Hemery interviewed sixty-two top-level performers, Lester Piggott being amongst those he studied. In the chapter on 'Concentration and Control', he writes about Piggott's focus of concentration:

> Lester said that he sees things that are going to happen before they happen. His focus is on the other horses and jockeys around him. He said that he would be taking in how much space there was between the inside horse and the rail and between the other horses; he would be focussed on what the other horses and jockeys were going to do before they did it. He would be assessing how much each horse had left, and aware of a jockey getting ready to make a move, and he would attempt to cover the action before it happened. He would know the form of each horse from reading the form book before going to the start and he knew from past experience how the other jockeys raced. He said that he had a minor focus on his riding position and how much energy his own horse had left, but the main focus was anticipation and knowing his options. His racing record sets him apart. Where most would be holding on and trying to steer at 40 mph, Lester gives us a focus on racing genius.

He also makes an interesting contrast to my young friend with the pony tail, who – like so many of us – is searching for enough spare attention to look up whilst she is riding! But one of the things which separates dressage riders from jumping riders, polo enthusiasts or jockeys is their preference for an *internal* focus of attention. The external world is almost irrelevant to them: but these other performers must leave their body to function on 'automatic pilot' whilst they pay attention to the changing world around them.

The American sports psychologist Robert Nideffer differentiates between a narrow or broad *internal* focus of attention, and a narrow or broad *external* focus of attention. Dressage requires primarily a narrow internal focus of attention, in which there are actually very few variables. In polo and racing, in particular, there are rapidly changing external circumstances, whilst in jumping, there are a series of external targets. Our preference for dealing with these different situations determines what sphere of riding we will be drawn to, and where our talents lie. This is one of the challenges facing event riders, who commonly excel at jumping but not at dressage. One up-and-coming young competitor told a friend of mine about his different experiences in the dressage and cross-country phases. Riding the cross-country, he said, was like going down a tunnel: nothing else existed except himself, his horse and the track they were following. If someone exploded a bomb nearby, he would not notice. But in the dressage he was always worried about the judge, about the people watching, about the score he was going to get and about whether he was going to look stupid. He was distracted by every little noise, and he saw every little movement which took place around the sides of the arena. Needless to say, so did his horse. It may be true that his brain has a natural preference for an external focus of attention, but there is nothing like imminent physical danger to focus the mind, and nothing like fear of being judged to defocus it!

One of my friends has been doing a similar research project with the members of the British Sport Karate team. Their captain, who has the most impressive list of medals to his credit, rates the ability to deal with these kinds of distractions as one of his major strengths. He deletes the audience from his mind and pronounces them 'not relevant'. He also sometimes deletes his opponent's face; that too is 'not relevant'. Our young event rider effectively does the same thing across country (although with him it happens naturally, and he does not have to think about it). His dressage scores will improve enormously when he can do the same in this context – otherwise all these distractions steal his energy. I have suggested to some riders that they demote the judge from her position of authority by imagining her with a long nose like a carrot, or sitting on the lavatory. When she becomes laughable instead of terrifying, it becomes far easier not to be disturbed by her presence.

One rider I interviewed, who had jumped Grade A show jumpers and also ridden round Badminton, compared the quality of her concentration in each case. 'There is nothing like the one and a half minutes (say) of a timed jump-off. My concentration is fantastic, and I love the buzz that I get from it. But on a cross-country round it takes too long, and there's all that galloping between fences. One's concentration has to let up a bit at times, and it just doesn't give me the same feeling!'

Interestingly, in response to my question, 'What does it take to frighten you?' she answered, 'It frightens me when I am coming up to a big parallel riding a horse who is on his forehand, and who I cannot balance correctly.'

'Do the fences ever frighten you?' I asked.

'No,' she said. 'It's never the fences themselves, and I do not have any particular "bogey" fences that I dislike. What frightens me is a bad approach.' Another event rider told me that he, again, was not frightened of the fences but was frightened by the thought of the mistakes that he might make.

Few top-level riders are, I think, frightened of injury – they simply view it as a nuisance which they would hope to avoid, and which could put them out of action for some time. But they accept that they are competing in a high-risk sport and that they might one day have to take the consequences. Club-level riders are much more often frightened of injury, and of the fences themselves. This can induce hesitant, uncommitted riding: if you say, 'Oh no, I hate riding big parallels,' the brain has nowhere to go. The power lies in the fence and not with you, so it is easy to remain in a stuck, paralysed state. But if you say, 'Aha, this one is going to need really good riding,' you are immediately channelled in the right direction. You are motivated to set the horse up well for the fence and to improve your technique. This kind of fear is much more productive: it directs and focusses the mind instead of clouding it.

Undoubtedly, most top-level performers have the experience of having plenty of time, even when they are in competition. When time seems to speed up, it is a sign that the rider's concentration has become disturbed. This happens particularly in dressage arenas, where anxious riders find that the corners start coming at them much faster than they do at home! The jumping rider who heard her horse's hoof beat so clearly in her mental rehearsal told me that she controlled time by experiencing it through the medium of the horse's rhythm, and this never varied whether she was riding in competition or at home. One of our top dressage riders told me that he felt just as in charge of himself, his horse and time when competing in the top national competitions at Goodwood as he did when he was riding at home. But during his first competitions abroad, he estimated that he lost access to about 50 per cent of his ability in the first test he rode, and about 25 per cent in the next. If there had been a third, he thought that he would have been back to normal.

Some top competitors felt that they responded very much better to the challenge of riding in large competitions than they did to the challenge of riding in small ones. I know some people who perform their best under extreme pressure – they like 'do or die' situations – but for many others these signal disaster. In response to them, people either 'pull themselves together' or 'fall to pieces'. (As we have seen, cross-country riding where there is imminent physical danger tends to inspire tremendous concentration, whilst dressage, and in some cases show jumping, give the rider much more scope for paralysing nerves.) In an interview published in *Horse and Hound* after the Seoul Olympics, Karen Straker stated that the pressure of riding in the Olympics was no worse than the pressure she had felt the first time she ever took part in the Pony Club area round (which really makes me question the pressure to which we often subject our children)! Natural competitors are probably in the minority, and one or two that I know tend to set up their whole life as a 'do or die' situation, where they are always facing adversity. They then feel much more alive than they do in a more mundane situation.

One top dressage rider told me that she felt she could completely rely on herself to ride at her best in competition. If she ever let herself down, she said, she would be unbelievably angry with herself. (Many people, however, are *depressed* by their bad performances, and this is not half so motivating next time round.) She also felt that dressage was, for her, a 'do or die' situation, because she had always had such difficult horses to ride that she did not dare to make a mistake! She had had one experience of being paralysed with nerves: this was at a competition after one in which she had been completely out of her depth, and she was worried about giving a similarly bad performance. Her mouth dried up, her heart was pounding and she rode the test with very little sense of where she was and what she was doing. 'If I always felt like that about competing,' she said to me, 'I wouldn't do it! I can't understand anyone who does it if they feel like that!'

There is one strategy which I think all top-level performers share. Firstly, they have a sense of how they want the horse and their body to feel within any movement. This is an overall body/horse feeling (as opposed to a part-body feeling), and it is the feeling they have when everything is going well. As soon as the feeling they are getting from their body and the horse does not match up to this 'reference feel', they become aware that something is wrong. This is the signal that they must repair the damage: and to do this, they will almost certainly need to pay attention to smaller pieces of the jigsaw and to have a *part-body feeling* as they adjust their positioning, rebalance the horse or lighten their hand. When they have made this correction, and brought their overall feeling back into line with their 'reference feel', they stay with this until they get the next signal that something is wrong.

This implies several things. The first is that the rider knows what it should feel like. (This is the first stumbling block, and it stops many people from using this strategy well.) Secondly, the rider is always making comparisons. Again, many club-level riders do not do this: they simply accept what they are given. I had an interesting experience recently in my jumping, when I was not riding the fences to my satisfaction. I made a comparison with my riding on the flat (which is my main specialisation), and I asked myself, 'How would I approach the problems I am having if this were flatwork?' I immediately realised that I would be making a different set of comparisons, and would be working from a much more precise 'reference feel'.

It was clear that my expectations were not high enough, so I made interventions to improve the canter which I would not otherwise have made. (When I am teaching jumping, I sometimes inspire people to do the same by asking them, 'Would Ginny Leng ride into that fence in the way that you just did? What would she have done?') My horse's jump improved enormously and I felt that I learnt something of tremendous importance.

This experience proved that I was not using my brain efficiently, and very many riders are performing way below par because of just the same problem. I did not need to learn *new* skills, I simply needed to utilise skills that I already had, but had not applied stringently enough in this context. I have jumped many fewer horses than I have worked on the flat, and I do not jump all that often; under normal conditions, this means that it could take me years to gain so much information that I would more easily begin to make these comparisons. (Or perhaps time and experience are not the key factors, since many riders never do this at all.) But now, I can short-cut my learning process considerably and can even refine my new strategy by jumping hundreds of different horses in mental rehearsal, in theory at least coming out of this as a much more experienced rider!

The next implication of the strategy is that the rider can move easily between a holistic body/horse feeling and various different part-body feelings. People who have been through a long period of conscious competence are usually good at diagnosing exactly which small pieces of the puzzle are missing and can home in on them easily. This can be harder for people who function from a state of unconscious competence – although for them, it may be easier to maintain a more robust body/horse feeling, which by virtue of their natural ability is less easily eroded. Paul Dennison, my teacher in Educational Kinesiology, says that people who can move easily between the two have access to an 'integrated high and low gear'. Some people get stuck in 'high gear': firstly, they do not recognise when things go wrong, and secondly, they cannot take their skill apart into its small component pieces. This stops them from making the necessary adjustments. Many children who are hyperactive are, he believes, stuck in a 'high gear' state. If we, as a species, did not have access to 'low gear' states, there would be the danger that nobody would ever say, 'Hold on a minute! Things are going wrong here . . .', and we might all act like lemmings and follow each other over the edge of a cliff! Other people become stuck in 'low gear' states, where they perceive everything as a mass of small pieces which they cannot put together. This is the state of many children who are classified as 'learning disabled': in effect, they cannot see the wood for the trees. Having access to the high gear but not the low gear, or to the low gear but not the high gear, brings the same limitations that a car mechanic would have if he either did not know how to take engines apart or if he was familiar with all the small pieces but could not put them back together! The ability to utilise both gears so that they become 'integrated' is not to be taken for granted. It is something to be worked at and developed, for all but the very best performers are weak in one or other of these states.

In computer language, the strategy is known as the TOTE model, where the letters stand for Test, Operation, Test, Exit. The first test is the discovery that something is wrong; then comes the operation which puts it right; this is then ratified by the next test. If all is well, the rider exits from the strategy, only to enter it the next time that her overall feeling fails her test. The cycle becomes infinitely faster and more streamlined the more it is repeated; the rider notices when things have gone only slightly wrong, so her intervention is smaller, and the operation can be performed much more smoothly (the numbering exercise I used with Janet in Lesson 5 helps to develop this skill). The skilful rider has a wide variety of operations which she can perform – 'The Symphony of Aids'.

I asked all of the riders I interviewed, 'What do you know now that you wished you had known two, five or ten years ago?' When I have asked this of more novice riders, they have frequently said, 'I wish I had known to spend £20 a month on a good private lesson instead of £5 a week at the local riding school.' In their past, they had been in no position to judge the quality of the tuition they were receiving. (I mean no disrespect to riding schools in saying this. The vast majority of them do an extremely good job.) The more advanced riders almost all said that they had become much more subtle and less forceful in their riding. Some of the men, in particular, were aware that they had over-used their strength, and they had over the years become much more appreciative of how subtle the rider/horse interaction actually is. With this improvement in their technique, they also felt more confident and less easily hassled.

All of them, I felt, were fully engaged in the process of learning, and all of them rated their commitment to it as a ten out of ten. None of them acted as if they thought they had 'arrived' – even though the rest of the world might be tempted to perceive them that way. Whilst most riders go once round the cycle which leads to unconscious competence (and then stop there), these top performers were in a continual search for improvement, and they were good at learning – regardless of how much consciousness was involved in that process. In that sense, they share a great deal with the riders that I teach, who become good at learning not through their natural good fortune but through *learning how to learn*. (The major difference between top performers and most of my pupils is that the latter spend a disproportionate amount of time in 'low gear', fathoming out how the various small pieces of riding fit together.)

One unanswered question is, 'Will riders who have learnt in this way ever be able to compete against the world's most talented riders, who naturally function from "high gear"?' I think it may be ten or twenty years before we know the answer to this. But Nick Faldo is certainly a shining example of what the willingness to spend time in 'low gear' can achieve, and I believe that the best performers of the future will be naturally talented riders who have access to 'integrated high and low gear' states. In essence, riding only consists of walk, trot and canter. In that sense, there is very little to it, so it is inevitable that the rider has to go over and over the same ground, time and time again. This can be boring, or it can be transformative. In riding, we spend so much of our time 'getting there' that it has to be as delightful to travel as it is to arrive. One of the hallmarks of quality learning lies in the sudden revelations that I have had on many occasions, and which T. S. Eliot talks about beautifully in *The Four Quartets* when he says, 'We shall never cease from exploration, and at the end of all our exploring we come back to the place where we started and see it all as if for the first time.' In these revelations – when you see walk, trot, canter and the positioning of your right seat bone, or your horse's rib cage, 'as if for the first time' – I believe that you are having one of the most magical experiences available to mankind – as magical, perhaps, as the perfection for which we all strive.

Bibliography

Bandler, Richard, and Grinder, John, *Frogs into Princes* (Real People Press, 1979).

—, *Trance-formations* (Real People Press, 1981).

Barlow, Wilfred, *The Alexander Principle* (Arrow Books, 1975).

Bennett, Deb, PhD, *Principles of Conformation Analysis*, Volume 1 (Equus Stable Reference Guides, Fleet Street Publishing, 1988); Volume 2 (1989).

Blakeslee, Thomas R., *The Right Brain* (The Macmillan Press, 1980).

British Horse Society, *Equitation* (Country Life Books, 1982).

Burger, Udo, *The Way to Perfect Horsemanship* (J. A. Allen, 1986).

Cade, Maxwell, and Coxhead, Nina, *The Awakened Mind* (Wildwood House, 1979).

Chopra, Deepak, MD, *Quantum Healing* (Bantam Books, 1989).

Crossley, Anthony, *Training the Young Horse* (Stanley Paul, 1978).

Decarpentry, *Academic Equitation* (J. A. Allen, 1971).

Dennison, Dr Paul E., *Switching On* (Edu-Kinesthetics, 1981).

—, and Hargrove, Gail E., *Personalised Whole Brain Integration* (Edu-Kinesthetics, 1985).

Diagram Group, *The Brain: A User's Manual* (New English Library, 1984).

Edwards, Betty, *Drawing on the Right Side of the Brain* (Souvenir Press, 1979).

Eliot, T. S., *The Four Quartets* (Faber, 1944).

Feldenkrais, Moshe, *The Case of Nora* (Harper and Row, 1977).

Ffrench-Blake, Neil, *The World of Show Jumping* (Pelham Books, 1967).

Gallwey, W. Timothy, *The Inner Game of Tennis* (Random House, 1974).

—, *Inner Tennis* (Random House, 1976).

—, *The Inner Game of Golf* (Jonathan Cape, 1981).

—, and Kriegel, Bob, *Inner Skiing* (Random House, 1977).

Gelb, Michael, *Body Learning* (Aurum Press, 1981).

German National Equestrian Federation, *The Principles of Riding* (Threshold Books, 1985).

Goody, Peter C., BSc, PhD, *Horse Anatomy* (J. A. Allen, 1976; 1988).

Green, Carol, *Jumping Explained* (Midas Books, 1976).

Harris, Charles, *Fundamentals of Riding* (J. A. Allen, 1985).

Hemery, David, *The Pursuit of Sporting Excellence* (Willow Books, 1986).
Hendricks, Gay, and Carlson, Jon, *The Centered Athlete* (Prentice Hall, 1982).
Herbermann, Erik F., *The Dressage Formula* (J. A. Allen, 1980; 1989).
Herrigal, Eugen, *Zen in the Art of Archery* (Vintage Books, 1971).
Holgate, Virginia, *Ginny* (Stanley Paul, 1986).
Hyams, Joe, *Zen in the Martial Arts* (Bantam Books, 1982).
Jensen, Clayne, and Schultz, Gordon, *Applied Kinesiology* (McGraw Hill, 1977).
Kapit, Wynn, and Elson, Lawrence M., *The Anatomy Colouring Book* (Harper and Row, 1977).
Klimke, Reiner, *Cavaletti* (J. A. Allen, 1973).
—, *Basic Training of the Young Horse* (J. A. Allen, 1985).
Leonard, George, *The Ultimate Athlete* (Avon Books, 1974).
Lewis, David, *The Alpha Plan* (Methuen, 1986).
Mairinger, Franz, *Horses Are Made to be Horses* (Rigby International, 1983).
Maltz, Maxwell, *Psycho-cybernetics* (Prentice Hall, 1960).
Masters, Robert, and Houston, Jean, *Listening to the Body* (Delacorte Press, 1978).
McBane, Susan (ed.), *The Horse and the Bit* (Crowood Press, 1988).
McCluggage, Denise, *The Centred Skier* (Bantam Books, 1983).
Morehouse, Laurence, and Gross, Leonard, *Maximum Performance* (Mayflower Books, 1980).
Müseler, Wilhelm, *Riding Logic* (Methuen London, 1983).
Neideffer, Robert M., PhD, *The Inner Athlete* (Thomas Y. Crowell, 1976).
Pearce, Joseph Chilton, *Magical Child* (Bantam Books, 1977).
Podhajsky, Alois, *The Complete Training of Horse and Rider* (Harrap, 1973).
—, *The Riding Teacher* (Harrap, 1973).
Prior-Palmer, Lucinda, *Up, Up and Away* (Pelham Books, 1978).
—, *Four Square* (Pelham Books, 1980).
—, *Regal Realm* (Pelham Books, 1983).
Rees, Lucy, *The Horse's Mind* (Stanley Paul, 1984).
Ristad, Eloise, *A Soprano on her Head* (Real People Press, 1982).
Romaszkan, Gregor de, *Riding Problems* (Pelham Books, 1968).
Russell, Peter, *The Brain Book* (Routledge and Kegan Paul, 1979).
Seunig, Waldemar, *Horsemanship* (Doubleday, 1976).
Sivewright, Molly, *Thinking Riding*, Book 1 (J. A. Allen, 1979); Book 2 (1984).
Smythe, R. A., and Goody, P. C., *The Horse, Structure and Movement* (J. A. Allen, 1975).
Steinkraus, William, *Riding and Jumping* (Pelham Books, 1971).

Swift, Sally, *Centred Riding* (The Kingswood Press, 1985).

Syer, John, and Connolly, Christopher, *Sporting Body Sporting Mind* (Cambridge University Press, 1984).

Thei, John F., DC, *Touch For Health* (T. H. Enterprises, 1973; 1987).

Totko, Thomas, and Tosi, Umberto, *Sports Psyching* (J. P. Tarcher, 1976).

Van Schaik, Dr H. L. M., *Misconceptions and Simple Truths in Dressage* (J. A. Allen, 1986).

Index